SUPERDIVERSITY IN THE HEART OF EUROPE

HOW MIGRATION CHANGES OUR SOCIETY

Superdiversity in the heart of Europe

How migration changes our society

Dirk Geldof

Acco   Leuven / Den Haag

First print: 2016

Published by
Uitgeverij Acco, Blijde Inkomststraat 22, 3000 Leuven, België
E-mail: uitgeverij@acco.be – Website: www.uitgeverijacco.be

For The Netherlands:
Acco Nederland, Westvlietweg 67 F, 2495 AA De Haag, Nederland
E-mail: info@uitgeverijacco.nl – Website: www.uitgeverijacco.nl

Cover design: www.frisco-ontwerpbureau.be
Translated by Ian Connerty

© 2016 by Acco (Academische Coöperatieve Vennootschap cvba), Leuven (België)
No part of this book may be reproduced in any form, by mimeograph, film or any other means without permission in writing from the publisher.

D/2016/0543/47   NUR 740   ISBN 978-94-6292-428-4

Contents

On superdiversity   9
Preface by Jenny Phillimore

Introduction   15

Chapter 1   From migrant labour to superdiversity   21
A short history of migration in Belgium   22
Actively searching for migrant workers   23
The crisis years of the 1970s and the illusion of a migration stop   26
The 1990s: political asylum and the expansion of the EU   27
Migration in the 21st century   28
How Belgium became a migration country   30

Chapter 2   The superdiversity of the 21st century   33
The transition to superdiversity   34
Majority-minority cities   35
Diversity within diversity   38
Superdiversity as a process of differentiation   44
Reality is changing more quickly than our language   46
New words for a new reality   53

Chapter 3   Migration from top to bottom   55
Growing poverty among ethnic minorities   56
Urban poverty   58
Superdiversity in social assistance   59

Put poverty on the agenda	61
A growing middle class	65
Towards a more dynamic vision	69
Cities as emancipation machines	71

Chapter 4   The need for a more cosmopolitan vision — 77

Old ways of looking at new realities	78
Beyond methodological nationalism	79
Beck's cosmopolitan vision	81
From 'either...or' to 'and...and'	82
Transnationality and ambivalence	84
A new modernity	86
Our cities are becoming more cosmopolitan	87
The children colour our cities	91
Cosmopolitan apartheid?	93

Chapter 5   Transnational lives and families — 95

Living across borders	95
Transnational networks and worlds	97
'Having your cake and eating it, too'	100
Many different types of transnationality	100
Different forms of transnationality	101
Transnational spaces	104
Transmigration or multiple migrations	106
Transnational relationships and families	109
Relationships and migration	112
Maternal love from afar?	116
Towards a multiplicity of different family models?	118
Challenges for family policy	121

Chapter 6   The hidden city — 125

The official city versus the real city	125
The importance of regularization campaigns	128

Undocumented migrants in Antwerp 130
Without papers, but not without a job? 133
Hidden in plain sight 134
Arrival districts 137

Chapter 7 They should just learn how to integrate... 141
What exactly do we mean? 141
Integration: a term with many meanings 146
Integration as a controversial concept 149
Does integration actually exclude people? 149
Is integration policy becoming irrelevant? 152
Can integration work across borders? 155
Social cohesion in superdiversity 156
Integration in an age of multilingualism 158
From integration to emancipation and participation 165

Chapter 8 Multiculturalism 2.0 171
The multicultural drama? 173
The arguments of new realism 176
Which multiculturalism is bankrupt? 178
Multiculturalism 2.0 183
In search of a shared citizenship 187
Towards a scenario of hope and empowerment 189

Chapter 9 Dancing around culture 191
Between redistribution and recognition 192
Between structure and culture 197
The advancing tide of culturalization 199
Not culture but structure? 201
Dancing around culture 204
Dealing vigorously and effectively with culture 206
Structure and culture 208
Active pluralism as the basic approach 210

Chapter 10 How to deal with superdiversity?	**215**
Living at a turning point	217
From division and polarization...	219
... towards hope and solidarity	220
Coda	**225**
Notes	**231**
References	**245**

On superdiversity

Preface by Jenny Phillimore

Director of the Institute for Research into Superdiversity (IRiS, University of Birmingham)[1]

Steven Vertovec's introduction of the term "super-diversity" appeared first in relation to London with an accompanied suggestion that the phenomenon might be observed elsewhere in the UK. Subsequently it might be argued that the concept has been widely adopted in Europe, often quite uncritically, and frequently used to describe the arrival of more migrants from more places to more places. Vertovec considers such approach as a *'one-dimensional appreciation of contemporary diversity'*. Rather he suggests we focus on the *'transformative diversification of diversity'* connecting ideas about the origin of people with other variables (reason for migration, age, occupation, generation. …) which shape their lives and opportunities.[2]

Since its original invocation understandings of superdiversity have moved on and certainly the focus has evolved from describing the complexification of populations following wide-spread new migration to the proposition that superdiversity offers a new way of looking at society. Further it has been suggested that superdiversity does not mean that all the contexts that proceeded it are erased, but that new migration adds an additional layer of complexity as it interacts with existing and ongoing multicultural populations: those who arrived in large numbers and who have subsequently become an integral part of our societies, and existing populations who might be described as native or autochtoon (in Flemish) and who originate in the country.

There is much evidence enabling us to argue that superdiversity represents the emergence of a *new* demographic reality. Although some argue that it harks back to earlier times of movement and mixing such as the Edwardian era in Great Britain when lack of legal restrictions on movement meant that travel was easy,[3] innovations enabled trans-Atlantic exploration,[4] and cities such as Guanzhou and Dhaka were the loci of business and trade housing people of many different nationalities[5], the scale, speed and spread of superdiversification exceeds anything previously experience and is in evidence across much of the developed world.

In OECD countries net migration has become the main driver of population growth in the 21st Century. In Europe an acceleration in change is evident. The contribution of net migration to populations has shifted from around 100,000 persons per year pre 1985 to 600,000 between 1985 and 2000 and in the past decade around 1,000,000 per annum. The advent of the so-called migration crisis, wherein one million individuals are expected to arrive in Europe from the Levant region alone in 2015, indicates just how quickly superdiversification can occur. The scale of change varies by country. For example Korea experienced a quadrupling of population born overseas between 2007 and 2013 yet the scale of diversification remains low with migrants making up less than 2% of the population (350,200 permanent arrivals) whereas in the same period immigration to Germany increased by 2,045,000 permanent arrivals.[6]

While some cities have, as Ndhlovu points out[7], always been diverse, and high levels of mobility are not new, what is notable is the spread of diversity from urban arrival neighbourhoods to suburbs and rural areas as well as to countries like Korea with little previous immigration experience. The 2011 census in the UK showed that rural counties such as Herefordshire in the Midlands region received unprecedented numbers of arrivals with a 213% rise since 2001. In Australia and Europe Government policy of dispersing asylum seekers and refugees to rural areas and small towns has led to totally new encounters with diversity, while in Canada and Australia the secondary movement of migrants and minorities from arrival zones to suburbs has become the norm.[8]

Yet the arrival of more people to more places is, as Vertovec argues, just part of the dynamic of superdiversity. It contributes to increasing demographic complexity but there are other factors shaping the diversification of diversity that are harder to trace in national data sets. Fran Meissner & Steven Vertovec illustrate that the diversification of migrants' origins is augmented by changing migration channels.[9] In just ten years from 2001 to 2010 migration channels vary enormously between temporary migrants, labour migrants, family migrants, humanitarian migrants, students, seasonal workers and others. For example Sweden experienced a shift from 55% work-related migrants in 2001 to just 5% in 2010 while the category of humanitarian migrants increases from around 25% to 39%. Such shifts are observed in many EU countries which are clearly experiencing major demographic changes and associated increase in complexity. Some diversification is driven by Government immigration and integration policy. Increasingly individuals' rights and entitlements to welfare and citizenship are conditional on their immigration status or length of residence rather than ethnicity or country of origin and these conditions shape the ways that individuals are able to live, their opportunities for inclusion and social mobility and their sense of belonging. Onward and return migration add further complications around for example the portability of welfare which influence individuals' decisions about if, when and where to migrate, at least for those who are not forced migrants.[10] Within Europe free movement and differential rights and entitlements accelerate mobility as individuals gain citizenship in one country and then move to another to benefit from more relaxed rules around enterprise or family reunion.

Superdiversity then is without doubt a new demographic phenomenon which extends way beyond London. Yet it is argued that the term offers great potential beyond describing a demographic state. Fran Meissner and Steven Vertovec[11] highlight the original intention to '*recognise the multi-dimensional shifts in migration patterns*' in three ways: descriptive to encapsulate changing demographic configurations (with the emphasis on change), as methodological bringing a new lens moving theory and method away from the ethno-nationalist approaches much critiqued by Wimmer and Glick Schiller[12] and as a focus of policy again moving beyond the ethno-focal to include/exclude other characteristics such as legal status and length of residence. Vertovec outlines some of the many ways in which superdiversity is being used by academics in their work which include moving beyond ethnicity as the sole focus of research, to argue for a methodological reassessment of different fields of enquiry, and to focus upon increasingly blurred distinctions around social trajectories.[13]

Perhaps the most attention focused on superdiversity has been upon the idea that superdiversity offers a new way of interacting with much attention placed on observing mixing in superdiverse micro-space. Scholars such as Susanne Wessendorf, Eric Laurier and Chris Philo and Sarah Neal and colleagues have observed interactions in parks, book clubs, coffee shops and fast food restaurants.[14] Suzie Hall looks at street level exploring how superdiversity emerges along Rye Street in London both spatially and over time.[15] In some respects her work focus echoes that of Jan Blommaert who uses linguistic landscaping to understand the ever changing nature of diversity in his home street in Antwerp-Berchem.[16]

Little attention has been paid to private and institutional spaces (workplaces, schools, hospitals) yet these are where people live, work and access resources interacting for specific purposes rather than simply because of co-presence. Wessendorf highlights the need to bring power relations, structural hierarchies and prejudices into analyses of interactions which to date have offered little insight into the ways that "everyday cosmopolitanism" shape attitudes to the solidarity that is needed to ensure social cohesion and acceptance of deservingness.[17]

Indeed superdiversity has been much criticised for romanticising difference and creating an illusion that difference has been de-politicised.[18] Some have observed that the term is conceptually vague offering little insight to the ways in which a superdiverse social context might be defined.[19] Others argue that incorporation of the term diversity brings with it a set of concerns around the downplaying of processes that underpin inequality,[20] failing to engage with processes of exclusion[21] and eschewing the structural by over-emphasising cultural or local differences.[22] These failings can be overcome. In recent papers I use a superdiversity approach to over-turn long held assumptions that culture was responsible for migrants' poor access to ante-natal care and associated above average mortality rates and argue that superdiversity provides us with a new way of looking at such inequalities that can disrupt the status quo.[23]

This book clearly demonstrates superdiversity as a demographic condition is evident in Belgium and the Netherlands providing the first detailed account of superdiversity as a national context which will aid our understanding of how superdiversity is developing and the nature of associated challenges and opportunities. The book moves beyond a simple focus on ethnicity or country of origin to identify multiple differences including migration status, class, language and transnational networks. *Superdiversity* tries to understand the transition from multiculturalism to superdiversity in Belgium using Steven Vertovec's superdiversity as an emerging theory, in combination with the work of Ulrich Beck and a variety of scholars.

The book begins to address some of the criticisms set out above with its focus upon poverty and inequality and their structural underpinnings providing an exemplar of how future analyses of superdiversity might proceed in other countries and opening up opportunities for comparative analysis. As such the book is of value to those researching superdiversity elsewhere in Europe and in those countries, which I demonstrate above, that are beginning to experience the arrival of more people from more places and complexification of their populations. Ultimately the book helps us to formulate some of the questions we need to ask, as superdiversification proceeds across the industrialised world, such as how can we take account of structure and de-essentialise our focus on culture? How can we think about living together without romanticising and over-simplifying interactions? How can integration proceed when individuals have multiple transnational connections? What policies do we need to develop to support the development of a new solidarity and increase the chances of inclusion and equality for all?

Introduction

'Diversity is not in the first instance a normative ideal, but rather an existing condition of the inhabitants of cities and the places where they live.'
Ruth Soenen, 2006. *Het kleine ontmoeten.Over het sociale karakter van de stad* (Brief encounters: the social character of the city), p. 45.

If the 20th century was the age of migration, the 21st century will be the age of superdiversity. The research projects, publications and debates of recent years show that superdiversity is growing faster than ever before. Flanders, Belgium, the Netherlands and other neighbouring countries are searching for new ways to respond to the reality, complexity and diversity of contemporary society. *Superdiversity. How migration changes our society* shifts the debate away from gridlocked ideological discussion about the desirability or otherwise of a multicultural society. In the 21st century, it is no longer a question of whether or not we want such a society, but rather a question of how we can best deal with the superdiversity that already undoubtedly exists. How can we avoid further polarization and how can we make it possible for the social capital of all the inhabitants of our cities to blossom and flourish? The book provides a synthesis of contemporary research into diversity, but is also an eye-opener and (hopefully) a step in the right direction towards the normalization of superdiversity and interculturality, a normalization that we so desperately need.

Society is changing more rapidly than our ways of thinking. This is particularly true for the way we react to increasing diversity. In Brussels, Amsterdam or Rotterdam the number of inhabitants with their roots in migration now form the majority of the population. Within the next decade this will also become the new reality in Antwerp and in many other European cities.

The 21st century will be the age of superdiversity. Ethnic-cultural diversity will unquestionably continue to grow within European society in the years ahead, even though almost every government will continue to cling to short-sighted attempts to limit further migration. The rapid pace of social change and growing diversity are sensitive issues for many people, issues that not only raise difficult questions, but also provoke insecurity and resistance. The more diversity becomes an inevitable part of all our lives, the more people in Europe seem to fall back on outdated nationalist frames of reference.

For anyone who takes the trouble to examine the demographic developments of recent decades in detail, the further growth of diversity will come as no surprise. The fact that it still surprises so many people, with our policy-makers leading the way, says much about our society and the way we have closed our eyes to the events that were taking place right in front of our very eyes. During the past half century most of the countries in Western Europe have evolved into immigration societies, yet we still find it hard to come to terms with the migration and the diversity inherent in this evolution. Our migration history is about a past whose passing we fail to accept and a present whose reality we refuse to recognize.

Is this perhaps the reason why researchers, officials and policy-makers in recent decades have so incorrectly assessed the speed of change and demographic transition?[1] During the final decade of the 20th century, most demographers were still predicting a relatively stable and slow rate of growth for the population in the Low Countries.

Occasionally, there were even warnings that too few children were being born to maintain the population at its existing levels, which would have negative consequences for the future funding of the care that would be necessary for the growing number of people who were living longer and longer. It was only after the turn of the century that there was a sudden awakening to the need to drastically revise the existing population prognoses. The number of inhabitants in Flanders is increasing quickly, certainly in our cities. And with this increase in numbers has come a corresponding further increase in ethnic diversity.

In this age of superdiversity, the debate often remains frozen in largely superfluous discussions about symbolic issues and rearguard actions. For example, in Flanders during the past ten years there has been an increasingly polarized debate about the wearing of headscarves by public officials and pupils at school. Debates of this kind serve only to conceal the realities of diversity and the inequality that exists in our cities. The difficulty that some people have in accepting the visible symbol of diversity in classrooms or behind the counter at local town halls is just one of the many processes of adjustment that society must undergo in its efforts to come to terms with a new and superdiverse context. In much the same way, the sporadic discussions about whether or not it is 'correct' to return well-integrated migrants whose requests for formal asylum have been turned down back to their country of origin also camouflages the reasons behind structural patterns of migration, which result, in part at least, from marked levels of inequality throughout the world.

Few subjects polarize society like the question of migration. This polarization confirms and strengthens the typical 'us-and-them' thinking of the past. Nevertheless, a new hybrid reality continues to develop, which now places many different people in our cities in a position somewhere between 'us' and 'them'. In this age of superdiversity, it will no longer be possible to use this artificial division. Who is 'us' and what does it say about 'us' if we want to use this term to set ourselves apart from 'them'?[2] The opposite also applies: how long will the people we label as 'them' remain set apart? At what point do 'they' become one of 'us'? The more we continue to push each other into polarized 'us-and-them' positions, the more difficult it will become to construct the dialogue that is necessary to enhance the process of cultural integration and do full justice to the complexities of our modern society.

Does the subtitle of this book – *How migration changes our society* – reflect the position of the 'host' community within an 'us-and-them' perspective? Is the book about 'autochtoon' or 'native' Belgians who are seeing 'their' society change? The Belgian journalist Tom Naegels has correctly stated that part of the problem is that some people are still unable to accept that 'allochtonen' or Muslims can also belong to the 'us' group, just like people who have lived here for generations.[3] This book looks at the problem from a different perspective. For me, 'our' society is the society of all the people who live here, whatever their origins. It is this society, our society, which is changing at lightning speed. I want to move beyond the stubborn but now largely superseded 'us-and-them' stalemate. I want to bring contemporary superdiversity into the daylight and examine it with an open mind. I want to describe this transition as it really is, with all the opportunities and conflicts that are always inherent in major social change. How can we develop a powerful response to this transition? How can we develop a language to conduct a meaningful dialogue about our common future? And what do these developments mean for those who work in the front-line of superdiversity; in childcare, education, social work, medical care or as policemen or officials in town halls?

In short, the book explores the transition to superdiversity in all its many aspects. It underlines the importance of a cosmopolitan vision. It questions the frames of reference we use to approach the subject of change. Perhaps above all, it goes in search of ways to allow the potential inherent in our superdiversity to come to full fruition and it highlights the pitfalls that we may encounter along the way. During the endless debates about the desirability of increasing diversity we have often lost sight of the need to maximize the possibilities that it offers for us all. This is the only sensible option for responding to superdiversity in a sustainable and forward-looking manner. We need to conduct an open and active debate, with pluralism as our starting point. This will demand transparency and mutual respect from all concerned. It will also require mutual commitment to dialogue and the desire to find solutions acceptable to everyone. Only then will it be possible to make a new and better future, based on the strength of all those who live in our cities.

Dirk Geldof

Chapter 1

From migrant labour to superdiversity

'Could it be that if cosmopolitan societies hold together, they do so around plural publics and as a result of active work by collective institutions, integrating technologies, and constructed narratives and feelings of togetherness, rather than around givens of historic community?'
Ash Amin, 2012. *Land of strangers*, p. 1[1]

The 21st century will be the age of superdiversity. Whoever is growing up today in cities like Brussels or Antwerp, Rotterdam or Amsterdam, Paris or Marseille, London or Berlin can scarcely imagine how little ethnic-cultural diversity there was just half a century ago. At the opposite end of the spectrum, many people still live in communities or districts where they hardly notice the rapid pace at which superdiversity is increasing in society as a whole.

Contemporary superdiversity may have developed relatively quickly, but it was not unexpected. The present-day population of Western Europe is the result of the migrations and migration policies of the last 50 years, in the period after the Second World War. To understand modern superdiversity, we need to understand the history of these migrations. It is also the history of the Belgian and Dutch people who saw their street, their estate or their district slowly change. At the same time, it is likewise the story of many families that migrated and whose migration story is now an integral part of our society.

A short history of migration in Belgium

In the debates about diversity, you often hear it said that it is a phenomenon of all times and all places. Migration was already known in the time of the Ancient Egyptians. It was also practiced by the Greeks and the Romans, sometimes voluntarily, sometimes with compulsion, if a region was conquered by force and its people turned into slaves. The current inhabitants of the United States and Australia are nearly all migrants, who pushed out the original Indian or Aboriginals populations. The entire history of European colonization is likewise a story of migration, with European settlers migrating to the countries of the South. This colonization was often characterized by huge differences in power, by exploitation and by the plundering of the natural riches of the colonized lands.

Of course, it is perfectly true that migration is indeed of all times and all places. But this historical qualification, which is sometimes used to put the superdiversity debate 'into its proper perspective', does little to help us comprehend the impact of the rapid social change being experienced by our societies today. To understand how countries like Belgium and the Netherlands have become immigration countries, we need to examine the migration history of the past half century.[2]

The impact of migration on Western society at the start of the 20th century was very limited. Before the First World War, only 3.5% of the inhabitants of Belgium had a different nationality, and the majority of these came from neighbouring European countries. During the inter-war period, Belgium began to attract first Italians, Poles and Czechs in relatively limited numbers to work in the coal mines of Limburg and Wallonia.

Our migration history was largely written in the second half of the 20th century.[3] Immediately after the Second World War, Belgium needed labour for the reconstruction process. The Belgian Government made arrangements with the Italian and Polish authorities to encourage organized migration. In this way, Belgium attracted some 77,000 South Italians and 20,000 Poles to come and work in the heavy mining and steel industries. As a result, the number of 'non-Belgians' living in the Belgium had risen slightly to 4.3% by 1947.

After the post-war reconstruction had been successfully completed, Europe enjoyed a period of unparalleled economic prosperity. In France, they still speak of *'Les trente glorieuses'*: the thirty glorious years between 1945 and the first oil crisis in 1973. This boom in economic growth went hand in hand with an equally dramatic surge in technological development. There was a strong and optimistic belief in progress, tempered only by the threat of the Cold War. Both industry and the rapidly increasing service sector needed new labour, but the economic boom meant that this labour was no longer available on the domestic market. As a result, from 1950 onwards Belgium tried to attract workers from Southern Europe, so that further waves of Italian, Greek, Spanish and Portuguese migrants began to arrive.

Actively searching for migrant workers

The golden years of the 1960s, when the economy continued to thrive, stimulated a further increase in the pace of immigration. The demand for new labour remained high. The (re-)introduction of women into the labour market was a first solution to this problem. Economic need went hand in hand with the rise in feminism, which saw a growing number of women who wanted an income of their own and an equal place in the economic and social life of the nation. At the same time, the first appearance of what letter became known as 'the consumer society' and the previously unseen increase in the purchase of consumable goods meant that for many families a second income now became a matter of necessity, if they wanted to 'keep up with the Joneses'. This combination of factors set in motion an evolution that moved away from the traditional pattern of families with the man as the breadwinner and towards a new pattern of two-income families.

Yet notwithstanding these developments, the labour market remained tight throughout the 1960s. In particular, it was difficult to find people willing to do heavy or low-paid work. For this reason, the Belgian Government, at the request of the business community, once again went in active search of migrant labourers from abroad. This time, the lands of origin were different and the rate of the migrants' arrival in Belgium was much faster than in the 1950s. Turkey and Morocco were now the main 'targets' for this new recruitment drive. In 1964, Belgium signed agreements with both countries (Morocco on 17 February and Turkey on 16 July) for the more systematic organization of economic migration and the reuniting of families previously split by such migration. The majority of this new wave of migrants were poorly educated labourers from the countryside or the mountains. For many of them, this meant that they underwent what was effectively a double migration process: first from the countryside and the mountains to an urban environment, and then from their homeland to a strange new country in the West. This double migration continues to play a role in the follow-up or chain migration that we are experiencing today.

In addition to mining and heavy industry, many of the new migrant workers were employed in the building sector for the construction of major infrastructure projects, such as tunnels, underground railway stations, motorways or harbour extensions. This was 'desirable' migration, partially spontaneous, but also partly organized by the state, in response to the demands of the business world and with the agreement of the unions.

This was not a phenomenon peculiar to Belgium. Neighbouring countries experienced a similar shortage of labour and a comparable increase in immigration during the 'glorious 30 years' after 1945. However, there were considerable differences in the lands of origin from which the different European countries sought their migrant labour. In many cases, colonial history and the process of decolonization played an important role, resulting in a strong influx of new workers from former colonial possessions. In France, for example, many of the migrants were from Algeria; in the Netherlands they came from Surinam and the Antilles; in the United Kingdom, they came from the countries of what is now the Commonwealth. Belgium was forced to adopt a different policy. After the granting of independence to the Belgian colony of Congo in 1960, many of the Belgians who had lived and worked there returned to their homeland, but very few of the indigenous Congolese population followed them.

The active recruitment of migrant workers in the 1960s led to a doubling of the number of 'foreigners' living in Belgium, in comparison with the situation at the end of the Second World War. In 1970, the country hosted 696,300 non-Belgian residents, or some 7.2% of the population.

The government regarded these migrant workers as a kind of temporary workforce, who would return to their country of origin after a number of years. This is also how many of the migrant workers themselves saw the situation. The spirit of the time is captured in the Canvas TV-report *Triq Salama* (Travel in Peace). In this report, Mohamed Abdeslam testified how his personal journey took him from Morocco to Belgium via Germany, and how he has built a life here for himself and his family during the past half century. As with many others, his migration began as something he regarded as short-term: '*We came here to work and to save, so that we could go back as quickly as possible. Some wanted to go home to get married, others to start a business... That was the idea.*'[4]

Today, we are paying the price for this idea of migration as something essentially transient: neither the government nor the migrant labourers themselves invested sufficient time, effort and money during these crucial early years in integration and the teaching of language skills. As time passed, the temporary migrant labourers gradually became permanent immigrants, especially if their families came from their homeland to join them. Unfortunately, it took many years for all involved to recognize the realities of this new situation.

The crisis years of the 1970s and the illusion of a migration stop

The truth finally began to dawn with the arrival of the first oil crisis in 1973. The explosive political situation in the Middle East led to dearer oil prices and a number of symbolic 'car-free' Sundays. This marked the end of the golden post-war period. Belief in progress gave way to economic pessimism in the face of a series of crises that have persisted (with brief intervals of respite) until the present day.

The oil crisis changed the situation on the labour market. As economic production fell, the demand for labour declined and unemployment slowly began to increase. In 1974, the Belgian Government decided to end its programme of organized labour migration, with what became known as 'the migration stop'. This resulted in the strict limitation of the number of new foreign workers entering the country. The term 'migration stop' created in the minds of many people (and still does) the illusion that the government had stopped or wanted to stop all migration into Belgium. But this was far from the truth. The migration stop did not mean that it was no longer possible for people from abroad to come to Belgium. Immigration certainly fell, but there was no question of stopping it. The limitations imposed on labour migration simply forced people to look for alternative migration channels, such as family reunion and political asylum.

Most of the migrant labourers had initially left their wives and children at home in their land of origin – primarily because this is where the majority of them intended to return. However, as the length of time the men spent in Belgium gradually increased, so their desire to have their families join them also increased. Family reunion logically ensured a secondary wave of chain migration. In addition, unmarried migrant labourers nearly always married partners from their land of origin, so that these partners also had right of abode in Belgium.

Alongside family reunification, requests for political asylum and the free migration of labour within the European Union were the most common legal channels of migration that brought people to Belgium during the late 1970s and 1980s. As the years passed, the gradual expansion of the EU and the principle of a free and common labour market made further migration possible within mainland Europe. This all resulted in a further increase in the number and share of non-Belgian residents living in the country. In 1991, there were 904,500 non-Belgians, or 9% of the population.

The 1990s: political asylum and the expansion of the EU

The 1990s mark an important turning point in the process that led to superdiversity. The migration of the 1980s continued, with the further reunification of families from countries such as Morocco and Turkey, but was now supplemented by three new developments of crucial importance. These developments not only led to a new increase in immigration in Belgium, but also led to a much wider diversity in the countries of origin.

The first of these factors was globalization. Migration inevitably followed in the wake of growing international trade, including an increase in the number of economic refugees seeking asylum. The second factor was the increasing number of regional wars that forced people to flee their own countries. These included the Gulf War of 1990-91, when Iraq invaded Kuwait but was later invaded itself by a United States-led international coalition, and also the disintegration of Yugoslavia and the Bosnian civil war of 1992-95, which resulted in a significant increase in the flow of asylum-seekers throughout Europe.

But the biggest impact resulted from the third factor: the fall of the Berlin Wall in 1989 and the subsequent expansion of the European Union. In the post-war period, the so-called Iron Curtain between East and West had prevented migration from Eastern Europe for more than four decades. The fall of the wall, the reunification of Germany and the systematic admission of countries from the former Communist Bloc to the European Union opened the doors to a new wave of migration from Central and Eastern Europe during the 1990s and beyond.

The combination of these factors meant that a new immigration peak was reached in the years 1998-2001, underlining the importance of the 1990s as the turning-point decade that forced the breakthrough leading to the superdiversity of today (see chapter2).

Migration in the 21st century

During the early years of the 21st century, the trends of the 1990s were continued and intensified, with a further increase in migration. The number of people with a migration background increased in most Western societies, including Belgium, as did the number and diversity of their countries of origin.[5]

On the basis of migration figures from 2012, we can see that two-thirds of all migrants in Belgium come from other European Union countries, making use of the fundamental European principle of the free movement of labour. The largest group amongst these EU migrants comes from neighbouring countries or from other member states of the EU15. But the most important new stream of migrants comes from Eastern Europe. The expansion of the Union in 2004 saw the accession of countries like Poland, and many Polish citizens took the opportunity to seek a better standard of living in the richer West. The entry of Romania and Bulgaria in 2007 was similarly followed by a rapid rise in immigration from both countries. Nearly all these cases are characterized by both a high outflow from and high inflow back to the countries in question, which is a typical feature of the pattern of 21st century labour migration, which is sometimes known as circular migration. Even so, there is still a positive overall migration balance from East to West.[6]

After Europe, Africa is the second most important continent from which new migrants originate. Roughly half of these come from Sub-Saharan Africa, with the other half coming from North African countries, with Morocco still as the largest contributor as far as Belgium is concerned. Each year migrants from Morocco account for 7-8% of the annual total of all immigrants in Belgium, which is equivalent to one in five of the immigrants from non-European lands. This means that roughly 8,000-10,000 Moroccans arrive in Belgium each year, continuing the trend of the past 40 years, which has consistently seen Morocco as the origin of the most important migration stream. Family reunification is still one of the key motives for this migration, in part because many Belgians of Moroccan origin remain attached to the marriage tradition that encourages them to seek marital partners back in Morocco.

As far as migration from Sub-Saharan Africa is concerned, the Democratic Republic of Congo is the most important land of origin for migrants arriving in Belgium, followed by Cameroon and Guinea. Another recent development has seen increasing numbers of migrants making their way to Europe from Asian countries, such as India,

China and Japan, but also from the more politically troubled regions of Iraq, Afghanistan and Armenia. Last but not least, the civil war in Syria had also increased the flow of migrants across the Mediterranean Sea, which has tragically become the most deadly of all the migration routes to Europe.

How Belgium became a migration country

Since 2000, the level of migration into Belgium has increased strongly. Today, Belgium has become an immigration country. Even so, the year 2012 also saw the first significant drop in the levels of immigration since the start of the 21st century, largely as a result of the legislation passed in 2011 to impose stricter conditions for family reunification. Nevertheless, this same year – 2012 – saw a total of 124,717 new migrants arrive in the country legally. At the same time, it should be remembered that the emigration flow has also increased by comparable proportions. In 2012, some 69,346 foreign residents left the country. This increase in (r)emigration points to a new trend in modern migration: more and more migrants are only staying temporarily in their host country, usually within the framework of the free movement of labour within the European Union. This is the phenomenon of transmigration (see chapter 5).

In other words, there is an increase in the totals for both immigration to and emigration from Belgium by citizens of foreign origin. Nevertheless, there is still a positive immigration balance, since the level of increase for immigrants continues to be greater than the level of increase for emigrants.[7] If the number of emigrating foreign nationals is deducted from the number of incomers, the result shows that there was still a net-inflow of migrants into Belgium of 55,371 in 2012. This inflow is equivalent to the population of cities like Ostend, Hasselt, Sint-Niklaas or Genk in Flanders, or Doornik or Seraing in Wallonia.

In this way, countries such as Belgium and the Netherlands have developed during the past half century from relatively homogenous societies containing a small number of people of foreign nationality into societies where people with a migration background form an increasingly large proportion of the population. Today, Belgium and the Netherlands – like most other West European nations – have become de facto immigration countries.

The combination of the demographic impact of the migration flows of the past 50 years and the likely further migration of the years ahead means that we must all prepare ourselves for a continuing growth in the cultural and ethnic diversity of our local communities. While it is possible to control (in part, at least) migration flows through adjustments in migration policy, it is far harder, if not impossible, to control demographic evolutions. While we have spent the past three decades discussing the desirability or otherwise of a multicultural society, a radical demographic transition has been taking place right in front of our very eyes. The result of a succession of migration waves has been a clear increase in the number of residents in Belgium with their roots in the migratory process.

According to the official population statistics, in Belgium there are now 1.2 million 'foreigners' – the official term for residents without a Belgian passport. This represents 11% of the total population. However, the figures based on nationalities alone tell us increasingly less and less about the ethnic and cultural diversity of this population. According to the UCL, at least one in five of Belgium's 11 million inhabitants in 2013 were born as a foreigner. The official figures for 2013 show that 1,195,122 people were registered as foreign nationals (the 11% referred to above), but 918,503 people – a further 8% of the population – are recorded as naturalized Belgians.[8] Yet even this still underestimates the level of ethnic and cultural diversity within the country, since many third generation children of migrant families were born as Belgian citizens.

Moreover, the figures for the country as a whole tell us little about the regional spread and the unequal distribution of residents with a migration background. In some communities there is little or no evidence of migration. For example, in the rural province of West-Flanders there are several municipalities were less than 1% of the population do not have a Belgian passport. In contrast, other regions have a much longer tradition of migration, such as the old coal mining districts of the Limburg or the steel-making areas of Wallonia.

In recent decades, it was above all the cities that became poles of attraction for migrant populations. As globalization increases, so the major cities are becoming more than ever the centres of important international networks. Brussels and Antwerp, but also Ghent and the Walloon cities of Charleroi and Liege, are now the main points of entry for migrant arrivals in Belgium.[9] The level of diversity in these cities is much greater than the national average. In Brussels, almost two out of every three residents have their roots in migration, while the figure for Antwerp is 46%. This trend is reflected in the Netherlands, where the largest concentrations of migrants are also to be found in the big cities. In this sense, living with diversity is likely to be one of the defining characteristics of urban life in Western Europe during the 21st century.

Chapter 2

The superdiversity of the 21st century

'It's very busy, as you can see. Not only for all the people making New Year greetings but also for a lot of people calling home for the Eid. 'He gestured to the computer monitor behind him, and on it was a log of the calls ongoing in all twelve booths: Columbia, Egypt, Senegal, Brazil, France, Germany. It looked like fiction, that such a small group of people really could be making calls to such a wide spectrum of places. It's been like this for the past two days, Farouq said, and this is one of the things I enjoy about working here. It's a test case of what I believe': people can live together but still keep their own values intact.'
Teju Cole, 2011. *Open City*, p. 112.

'I get on my bike each morning, and then I'm off to Nepal, China, Morocco, Turkey and Germany, before returning home via the Netherlands, says a regional nurse for the 'Kind en Gezin' (Child and Family) organization in Antwerp city centre. She visits the parents of new-born children in their home. 'I know their names and their addresses, and I usually know if the child is a boy or a girl. But for the rest, I have no idea which part of the world I am going to find behind their front door.'[1] As a result of the different waves of migration that have taken place during the past 50 years, Europe has developed from a society that was relatively homogenous in terms of ethnic-cultural origin to a society that is very diverse, with people from many different ethnic-cultural backgrounds now sharing the same cities.

In the last decades of the 20th century, there was much talk about the existence of multicultural societies. 'Multicultural' in this sense was more than a neutral descriptive term. It also referred to the forms of policy that tried to organize social integration between the original inhabitants of a place and the migrants who had come to live there. In general, this policy sought to promote tolerance and respect for other cultures or collective identities.

Much ink has been spilt and many words wasted in the spurious debate that has raged in recent years about the multicultural society and the supposed bankruptcy of multiculturalism (see chapter 8). However, the real question we should be asking is whether or not shifting patterns of migration have changed and are still changing our societies so completely that the term 'multicultural' is no longer adequate to understand and explain the rapid transformations of the past two decades.

The transition to superdiversity

Today's society and its diversity differ fundamentally from the situation that prevailed in the 1970s and the early 1980s. It was to describe the transition that has taken place during the past quarter of a century that Steven Vertovec first coined the term 'superdiversity' in 2005. With this concept, he sought to chart the changing migration patterns and their impact on London and on wider British society as a whole.[2]

Superdiversity is not just about the increase in diversity, but also – and primarily – about a growing diversity within that diversity. This means that ethnicity is just one of the elements that can be used to categorize and investigate today's abundance of diversity.

Since it was initially coined, the concept has been increasingly used in analyses. Jan Blommaert was one of the first in Flanders to apply the term to the changing situation in cities such as Brussels and Antwerp.[3] But what exactly do we mean when we talk about superdiversity and why does the term help us to better understand the changing realities of modern society?

To describe the changes that led to superdiversity as we know it today, I make a distinction between qualitative and quantitative changes. Whoever examines the migration statistics and the patterns of demographic evolution for the last two or three decades will notice a strong quantitative increase in the total number of people with a migration background, ranging from 'newcomers' to second and third generation children. This growing ethnic-cultural diversity has had, above all, a strong impact on the larger cities. At the same time, there has also been a qualitative transition, with widespread diversification within the diversity. Migration in the 21st century is characterized by a much wider range of countries of origin. Combined with differences in language, age, length of stay, social-economic position, civil and legal status, etc., this means that there are now many more different contrasts and levels within the migrant communities, as well as within society as a whole. Taken together, both these dimension have helped to create a new superdiverse reality, which is characterized by a greater complexity in the composition of local populations and an equally greater complexity and ambiguity in the interaction between the different elements of those populations. This growing differentiation means that a multidimensional perspective on diversity is essential.[4] With this in mind, we will now look at both dimensions in more detail.

Majority-minority cities

Ethnic-cultural diversity is increasing in all West European countries. The number of people in Belgium and the Netherlands with migratory roots continues to grow, not only in the major cities, but also in the smallest of municipalities. Having said this, regional differences are still considerable. In Belgium and the Netherlands, the impact of changing patterns of migration has been most noticeably felt in the big cities. In these cities, a fundamental change has taken (and is still taking) place towards a new superdiverse reality.

In an growing number of European cities people with a migration background now form the majority of the population. World cities such as New York, Sao Paolo, Toronto or Sydney have already been 'majority-minority' cities for several years: in other words, cities where the majority is made up from a varied range of different minority groups. This phenomenon is also starting to manifest itself in the heart of Europe, in countries like Belgium and the Netherlands. In cities such as Brussels, Rotterdam and Amsterdam, the inhabitants of Belgian and Dutch origin now represent less than 50% of the total population. Other cities in Europe – Birmingham, Malmö, Marseille and Stuttgart, for example – are likely to find themselves in the same position in the years ahead.[5] By the end of the current decade, the Belgian city of Antwerp will also have a local population where the majority of its citizens are made up from a number of different minorities.

This effect is not solely the result of present-day migration trends, but is also related to the age profile of the populations in many European cities. There is often only limited ethnic-cultural diversity among the older generations of urban dwellers, since organized labour migration in Western Europe only really started in earnest after the Second World War. But if we look at the opposite end of the age spectrum, we can see that children and youngsters are almost a mirror image of the older generations. In more and more Belgian, Dutch and other West European cities, a majority of the children now have a migration background. These children are the teenagers of the next decade and they will become the young people who during the next 20 years will move on to higher education, before entering the labour market.

Moreover, this young generation with a migration background will also form during that same period the majority of urban inhabitants of a marriageable – and childbearing – age.

In other words, anyone who looks closely at the age and ethnicity structures of urban populations not only sees a snapshot of those populations as they are today, but can also see how those populations will develop in the years ahead. Even without further waves of migration, diversity will increase strongly amongst young people and in urban societies as a whole during the next quarter of a century. A new influx of migrants will further strengthen this trend, but it is primarily the demographic composition of the existing population in European cities that will be responsible for the rapid transition to majority-minority cities.

What's more, this is not a specifically West European phenomenon. The same demographic transitions can also be seen in the United Sates, where since 2011 more babies have been born in migrant communities than amongst the 'white' American population. This brand-new generation represents the first majority-minority birth cohort, according to the American demographer, William Frey. This evolution towards cities and states with no clear ethnic majority – already known as 'no majority communities' – is developing so rapidly, that by the middle of the 21st century the majority of Americans will be made up from a polyglot range of ethnic minorities.[6]

According to the Dutch sociologist, Maurice Crul, in the very near future every citizen in every major city in Europe will belong to an ethnic minority, as is currently the case, for example, in New York.[7] The children of the migrants of the past 20 years, now in the second and soon in the third generation, will 'inherit the cities', to use the term coined by Philip Kasinitz and John Mollenkopf.[8] The difference between a city like New York and the cities in Europe is that European cities are evolving from a situation where in the recent past there was a very clear ethnic majority group. Within the space of two generation this majority has found itself transformed into a minority. This means, again according to Crul, that we will need to radically alter our thinking about who is 'integrated' and who is 'not integrated' in the new majority-minority cities of the future (see chapter 7). Until now, we have been living in a society where one group formed a clear majority of the population and where it was expected that the incoming migrant minorities should adjust to the customs, opinions and usages of that majority. In the new situation, in which there will no longer be a majority ethnic grouping, we will be moving towards a situation where everyone will need to adjust to everyone else. In other words, diversity will become the new norm. This conversion will unquestionably be one of the most challenging psychological process of our time.[9] Brussels, as the capital of Belgium and a European capital in its own right, is already a good example of this new kind of superdiverse city of the future, which already offers a number of possible answers to the question: 'what is the majority culture?'

Diversity within diversity

This all makes clear that superdiversity is more than just a quantitative transition. The nature of migration and its impact on societies within the host countries has changed and will continue to change. In addition to the overall increase in ethnic-cultural diversity, the chief characteristic of superdiversity is the diversification of diversity or, to express it in slightly different terms, a growing diversity within diversity. Our modern cities are typified by populations with a multiplicity of countries of origin, languages, cultures, religions, statutes and social positions. This results in diversity *between* groups and communities, as well as *among* those groups and communities. The 'complexity axis' and the interactions between all these different factors form the core of superdiversity.

Its basis, however, is a crucial change that has taken place in the fundamental pattern of migration. Half a century ago, Europe had to contend with only a relatively low migration stream from a relatively limited number of countries of origin to a relatively limited number of host countries. The present-day reality is that 21st century migration involves large numbers of people moving from many different countries of origin to many different host countries.[10] In post-1945 Europe, migration went hand in hand first with the demand for labour to rebuild the urban infrastructure destroyed during the Second World War and then later in conjunction with the process of decolonization and the need for organized migrant labour to support the economic boom of the 1960s. This resulted in a pattern of migration in most European countries as described above: comparatively few immigrants from comparatively few countries of origin. Within this pattern, each country had its own dominant immigrant group from a dominant country of origin, depending on the host country's migration and decolonization policies. In this way, for example, the Netherlands mainly received migrants from Surinam and the Dutch Antilles, but also to a lesser extent from Morocco and Turkey. In France, the majority of the migrants came from the former colony of Algeria. Similarly, Great Britain recruited its migrant workforce from the nations of the Commonwealth. Belgium concluded agreements with Italy and Poland to provide labour for the country's post-war reconstruction and later went in search of additional manpower in Southern Europe (Spain and Greece), before concentrating on workers of Moroccan or Turkish origin during the 1960.

The superdiversity we are experiencing today has developed from subsequent changes in these basic patterns of migration. The new migrations of the last two decades have been more widespread, involving numerous countries from all around the world. Globalization, the fall of the Iron Curtain, the resulting expansion of the European Union and the stream of economic and political refugees (primarily from Asia and Africa) has led to an exponential increase in the number of countries of origin. As the same time, these countries are experiencing a more diverse outflow of their home populations, with people now migrating to a greater number of different host countries.

These trends are reflected in Belgian migration patterns. Today, there is a significantly larger number of countries of origin than in the past. In 2012, two out of every three officially registered migrants came from another member state of the European Union. The other one in three came from countries spread all around the world. Even so, the migration streams of the past continue to make their influence felt, through a continuing flow of chain migration. In this respect, Morocco and Turkey are still the most important non-EU countries of origin for Belgian immigration, although the numbers of migrants expressed in percentage terms (for 2012) is quite small: just 6% for Morocco and 2% for Turkey.[11]

The consequence of this more diverse pattern of migration has been an increasing fragmentation in the background of migrants in ethnic, linguistic, legal, cultural, religious and economic terms. This fragmentation (or increased complexity) is one of the basic characteristics of superdiversity.[12] In the 1960s and 1970s, when the large majority of migrants to Belgium came from either Morocco or Turkey, it was still possible for people in the host country, if they were so inclined, to discover and understand the ethnic, linguistic, cultural and/or religious backgrounds of the people in the migrant communities. Today, this is no longer feasible, when migrants now come from dozens of different countries around the world. The answer to the question 'who are these migrants' is becoming ever more complex – and this is just one of the ways in which diversity within diversity is making itself felt.

There is, for example, a clear increase in the number of nationalities within the cities. Vertovec speaks of people from 179 different lands among the population of London. It no different elsewhere in Europe:

cities like Brussels, Amsterdam and Rotterdam also have around 170 different nationalities amongst their citizens – and this is before we even begin to explore the ethnic and cultural differences between people of the same nationality. This diversity in nationalities and ethnic-cultural backgrounds has also led to an explosion in the number of languages spoken in Europe's major cities. Vertovec estimates the number in London at some 300. Superdiverse cities are automatically multilingual cities (see chapter 7).

Religious diversity is also increasing. Islam is now a factor of considerable importance in Western societies, with a number of different tendencies coming to the fore and a growing number of mosques in many major cities.[13] Religion plays an equally significant role in many other ethnic-cultural communities. In Belgium, this can range from Polish Catholic masses in existing churches or sacred rites in the prestigious Hindu temple in the Antwerp district of Wilrijk, through to the growing number of 'shop churches' in the African and Hispanic communities. In the superdiverse Oud-Berchem district of Antwerp, Jan Blommaert has identified a basic religious infrastructure consisting of no fewer than 16 different places of worship or shop churches.[14]

In a parallel development, the number and diversity of migration motives is increasing as well, not only between communities, but also within them. There are still people who migrate to find work or to reunify their families, but there are others who now flee their homelands for political reasons, economic reasons or simply to find a better way of life. Some of these moves are permanent; others are intended to be temporary, such as students who often only intend to stay for the duration of their studies.

This diversity of motives is also reflected in the growing diversity of migration statuses. In Belgium, some people with a migration background are born as Belgian citizens or are naturalized as such.

Many others are seeking political asylum or have been recognized as political refugees, while a less fortunate group are still awaiting the outcome of the appeal procedure. EU citizens also stay in Belgium for a variety of reasons. Some are here as tourists; others are here to work, taking advantage of the free movement of labour within the Union, while yet others hope to settle here and perhaps even start their own businesses. A further group of non-EU citizens are allowed into the country for humanitarian or medical reasons, sometimes permanently, sometimes (with increasing frequency) temporarily. There are also people with dual nationality and others with no nationality (the so-called stateless persons). Last but not least, the cities of Belgium (and many other countries) also provide refuge to an important group of people whose stay has no proper legal basis (although many of them have applied to the authorities to have their situation regularized – see chapter 6). Nor should it be overlooked that many people have more than one migration status or evolve through a number of different statuses, each linked to a different set of (social) rights and obligations. A good knowledge of the frequently changing immigration legislation has become indispensible for today's social workers and many other professionals.

When considering superdiversity, it is also important to take account of growing differences in social-economic position. It is possible to find people with a migration background on just about every different rung of the social ladder, although perhaps not in the same proportions as non-migrants. Yet notwithstanding the greater risk of poverty amongst migrant communities, a growing middle class is nevertheless starting to emerge in most of those communities (see chapter 3). This middle class is made up from people who earn sufficient income from their own labour, their own businesses and/or their own property. They are often the owners of their own homes, but frequently sub-let part of the premises to others. This leads – often quite literally – to a form of social layering in superdiverse districts. Or as Jan Blommaert has observed in Antwerp: a Turkish shop on the ground floor, a Russian couple in the flat on the first floor, and a Polish building worker, an African preacher and a new arrival from Mongolia (employed as a waiter in a Chinese restaurant) in the small studios on the second floor.[15]

Diversity in diversity is not only growing within ethnic-cultural groups, but also between different groups. The position of the recent flood of refugees from Afghanistan, Iraq and Syria is very different from the position of the boat refugees from Vietnam in the 1970s or the first generation of migratory labourers from Morocco or Turkey. The differences within migrant communities is also increasing to a significant degree, depending on length of stay, legal status (and associated rights), knowledge of the local language, social-economic position, etc.

A last crucial characteristic of superdiversity is the growing importance of transnationalism or the extent to which migrants remain in contact with their network of family, friends and other acquaintances across national borders. This can mean contact with their family in their country of origin, but also in other European countries. The rapid development of communication options made possible by the mobile phone and the internet make it relatively easy for today's migrants to stay in more or less permanent contact with their 'significant others' in their home country or anywhere else in the world. In one sense, this also means that it is possible to live here but also to 'live' somewhere else at the same time (see chapter 5). Increasing levels of transnationalism and circular migration (where people do not intend to remain permanently in the host country) both serve to strengthen superdiversity.[16]

Superdiversity as a process of differentiation

Superdiversity is therefore more than just a synonym for what in recent decades has been referred to as the multi-cultural or diverse society. It is a new concept – perhaps even a new paradigm in the making – designed to help us come to terms with a rapidly changing reality. Growing ethnic-cultural diversity and the evolution towards majority-minority cities go hand in hand with the growing diversity in diversity. These transitions mean that we need new ways to look at these new dynamics, so that we can identify, recognize and understand them. The classic 'us-and-them' way of thinking (see chapter 4) is no longer appropriate in a society where the differences within groups can sometimes be greater than the differences between groups.

Superdiversity is about making the transition towards a society in which diversity is no longer something that exclusively affects the minorities in a community that is relatively homogeneous in ethnic terms. Superdiversity reflects the normalization of diversity, which thus becomes the rule rather than the exception for 21st century societies. Superdiversity wishes to give new insights into and a new language for the processes of diversification, which are not only the result of migration, but just as much of increasing individualization and the development of life styles and personal identities.[17]

When diversity within diversity grows, ethnic origin is no longer the only (and often not even the most relevant) characteristic to assess and regulate differences and interactions between different people and different groups in society. On some occasions, gender differences will be more relevant; on other occasions, differences in education and/or income, or differences in religious beliefs, or differences between those who live in the city and those who live around its fringes. These factors may also be related in some way to ethnic origin, but not necessarily so. But above all else, superdiversity is about the cohesion, combination and interaction of all these different forms of diversity. A focus on ethnicity can still be relevant as part of this process, but so too can differences in the country of origin, the length of stay in the host country, the mother tongue and religious beliefs. In other words, ethnicity is not the only way to approach and understand superdiversity. Being aware of the diversity within diversity means taking account of and actively involving these other forms of diversity.[18]

Consequently, superdiversity as a concept can help us to understand the growing diversity of Western societies and therefore allow us to better come to terms with this new reality of the 21st century. According to Frans Meissner and Steven Vertovec, the concept has descriptive, methodological and practical applications. In terms of description, it helps to identify and give form to changing demographic patterns, processes of differentiation and the increased complexities of social interaction. In terms of methodology, it encourages us to view the processes of diversification no longer from an exclusively ethnic perspective, but instead to develop a multiple and multidimensional perspective. In terms of actual practice, it can make a positive contribution towards the policy discussions and adjustments that many organizations will need to make in response to the new context, where (once again) it will be important to avoid a purely ethnicity-based approach.[19]

By trying to understand our societies as superdiverse societies, it may also be possible to transcend the polarized debate between those who are either 'for' or 'against' a multicultural society (see chapter 8), since superdiversity is not an ideological concept but rather a theoretical and empirical framework that can assist us in comprehending the complex and volatile nature of rapidly changing social realities.

Within the context of contemporary society, this invests superdiversity with new potential as an innovative frame of reference and analysis, which in time may well develop into a new paradigm for our age. Its multidimensionality unites different scientific and academic disciplines: sociologists, linguists, urban planners, social geographers, historians, pedagogists, etc. In addition to the theoretical development of the paradigm,[20] empirical research is also being conducted that focuses on the impact of the changes of recent years on cities in general and on day-to-day coexistence in superdiverse districts in particular.[21] This research is investigating a wide range of subjects: use of language and multilingualism,[22] education,[23] social care, health care and aid networks.[24] The common starting point for these projects is the challenges posed by superdiversity for each of these fields of expertise.

Reality is changing more quickly than our language

The speed with which our social realities are changing means that it is sometimes difficult to find the right terminology to express these changes. Real life is moving faster than the ability of our language to keep up with the ever increasing pace. Existing concepts are no longer adequate to describe an ever more complex situation. If we take 'ethnicity' as just one element of diversity, it soon becomes clear how we use a multiplicity of different terms drawn from a variety of different sources, often in a confusing or incorrect manner, to describe this element: migrants, foreigners, aliens, non-indigenous residents, migrant labourers, minorities, ethnic-cultural groups, asylum seekers, refugees, undocumented migrants, illegal immigrants, family unifiers, marriage migrants, second generation, third generation, etc. Moreover, not all of these terms are used in a neutral way. Some people like to lump together all the terms (and the people they are intended to describe), in their search to find a scapegoat for the manner in which society is being transformed. A similar kind of linguistic oversimplification and confusion characterizes the current debate about radicalization and the participation of young people from the West in the civil war in Syria.[25] But even those who have no intention to use language to stigmatize others are finding increasingly that they no longer have the right words to say what they mean or to explain what they want to explain.

In order to enter into a meaningful dialogue with each other and also to analyze our growing ethnic-cultural diversity in a constructive manner, it is crucial to first stop and reflect on the way we use specific words and terms relating to this subject. Diversity is not a pre-social category, but is a man-made concept, which has always been charged with the meanings that people have given to it. According to Thomas Faist,[26] it is a perceived and evaluated form of social difference, which has been constructed by social actors on the basis of clear dividing lines and classifications, in order to make clear who belongs to a society and who does not. Within this context, there is also a power struggle between different interpretations to achieve dominance. In this sense, language is not neutral, but colours our thoughts and the way we look at things.

In many day-to-day situations the ethnic background of a person is of no relevance. For example, it should make no difference to a bus driver if his passengers come from different countries and cultures. Nor should the passengers be concerned about the ethnicity of the driver: all they should be bothered about is whether or not he or she can drive the bus. But in other situations the residential status or ethnic-cultural origins of a person can be important. For a social worker it is vital to know whether or not the person he/she is trying to help is in the country legally and, if so, with what status, since people with Belgian and Dutch nationality will have access to a greater number of acquired rights than other EU citizens, applicants for political asylum or migrant workers without the right residence documents.

Having said this, a legal status or a passport does not say everything about the person in question. For instance, it does not necessarily tell you everything about their origins. On the other side of the coin, discrimination, prejudice and cultural differences do not disappear simply because someone has Belgian or Dutch nationality. In other words, it is sometimes necessary to look beyond nationality by taking account of a person's ethnic-cultural background. And sometimes, of course, it is not.

It is precisely in attempting to describe this kind of ethnic-cultural diversity that our language is often confronted with its own limitations and shortcomings. On the one hand, our existing vocabulary and concepts only cover a part of the reality they wish to convey. On the other hand, there is sometimes a huge gulf between the actual meaning of words in everyday language and the way those same words are used in the public debate about diversity. As a result, the reality of the debate is frequently distorted.

Consider, by way of example, the word 'migrant'. In its literal sense, the word means someone who migrates from one country to another with the intention of remaining there for a lengthy period of time. But in everyday language it is used in different ways: one 'migrant' is not necessarily the same as another. Depending on the circumstances, we either narrow or broaden the term. In Flanders, for example, the word is most frequently used to refer to people of non-European origin, particularly the Turks and the Moroccans. Dutch, German, French or American residents are seldom referred to as 'migrants', even though this is clearly what they are. In contrast to this 'narrowing' effect, the term is sometime broadened to include people who are just as clearly no longer migrants. For example, the children or even the grandchildren of migrants, many of whom were born here in Belgium and have never migrated anywhere in the true sense of the word, are still often described as being 'migrants'. 'Where do you come from?' is still a question frequently asked of many of these young people with a non-European ethnic origin who have lived in Belgium all their lives. Viewed in these terms, how many generations need to pass before these people are no longer regarded as 'migrants'? But the reverse is also true: how many generations need to pass before these people themselves no longer feel that they are still migrants?

We are equally subjective in the way we use the term 'foreigner'. In population statistics it is used as a neutral term to describe people with a nationality other than the nationality of the country where they are living. But things are not always as simple as that. From ancient times (and even in today's contemporary philosophical and ethical circles), the question of the foreigner's place in society and how they should be treated has always been a source of discussion and debate. For example, the French philosopher Jacques Derrida linked the concept of 'foreigner' with the reciprocal concept of 'hospitality', but also with the necessity of defining the concept in law.[27]

In daily use, the term 'foreigner' has acquired a negative or pejorative undertone, certainly when used in the plural and preceded by the emphasizing article 'the'. As with 'migrant', we seldom apply the word 'foreigner' to people with, say, a French or German passport. Conversely, children who are born into families where both the parents are Belgian or Dutch, but who originally came from a different ethnic background, continue to be addressed and treated as foreigners. According to the Brussels sociologist, Mark Elchardus, this 'foreignness' is in no way natural or innate; on the contrary, it is a man-made social construction. A part of the population in Belgium is regarded as being foreign by another part of that same population. What's more, they invest that 'being foreign' with a sense of fear. In particular, Europe in recent years has witnessed the very clear 'islamization' of the foreigner.[28]

Just how much society and language have changed in recent years is well illustrated by our use of the term 'migrant labourer'. In the 1960s and 1970s, most foreigners in Belgium were referred to by this term, meaning cheap foreign manual workers, mostly from Southern Europe, Turkey and Morocco. However, the term has become outdated and is now seldom used, because the migrant labourers of yesterday have become the non-indigenous residents and immigrants of today. The current forms of migrant labour, where people 'commute' on a temporary basis between the Benelux and countries like Poland and Bulgaria, are now referred to by terms such as 'intra-EU migration' or 'the free movement of labour'.

Another subject of fierce social debate in Belgium in recent years has been the use of the terms 'autochtoon/allochtoon'. The terms broadly mean 'indigenous/non-indigenous' or 'native/non-native'. In September 2012, the Flemish *De Morgen* newspaper decided that it would no longer use the terms, because they imposed an artificial division on the Belgian population as a whole. In March 2013, the people of Ghent and their city council both literally and symbolically buried the use of 'allochtoon'. There has also been a similar debate in the Netherlands about the desirability or otherwise of the continued use of the term.

In view of the heated nature of this debate, it is strange to recall that the words 'autochtoon' and 'allochtoon' were actually introduced in the 1970s as neutral terminology in a report by sociologist Hilda Verwey-Jonker for the Dutch government. Viewed from a purely etymological perspective, 'autochtonen' are the original inhabitants of a land or region. In a similar manner, 'allochtoon' literally means 'from another land or region'. According to the authoritative Van Daele dictionary of the Dutch language, 'allochtoon' actually has two meanings, namely: (1) originating or transported from elsewhere, not indigenous, foreign; or (2) a non-native inhabitant (i.e., used as an indicative term for people with a non-white skin colour, who were born – or whose parents were born – abroad; e.g. migrant labourers). This latter definition is still often used by researchers to chart the full range of ethnic-cultural diversity, including people who have since acquired Belgian or Dutch nationality. By this definition, an 'allochtoon' is therefore a person who lives in Belgium or the Netherlands but was born elsewhere or at least one of whose parents was born elsewhere.

Yet again, there is a noticeable difference in the way the word is used in everyday language, where it is generally taken to mean a person of a different ethnic-cultural background than the predominantly white, Christian norm. For this reason, the French, German or Italian residents in Belgium will not usually be referred to as 'allochtonen' – unless the Frenchman in question has Algerian roots or the German has Turkish antecedents – in which case the term probably will be used.

In other words, although their origin was intended to be neutral, the use of both words today is anything but neutral. Belgians and Dutchmen of non-European origin frequently ask how long they and their families will remain 'allochtonen' for the European residents of their country, the country where they were born and have lived all their lives. Both terms are now so emotionally charged that their original meaning has almost been lost. As a result, they are no longer adequate to describe the complexity of our superdiverse society.

In a similar manner, the word 'refugee' also covers a multitude of meanings. Officially, a refugee is someone who flees their own country because the situation there has become unliveable for them. People can flee for many different reasons: political reasons (e.g. war), religious reasons (e.g. persecution) or even personal reasons (e.g. discrimination against their sexual orientation). Increasingly, people also leave their homelands for economic reasons, desperately trying to escape poverty and find a better life for themselves elsewhere. In the 21st century, the number of ecological refugees will also increase, as climate change leads to greater expanses of deserts and massive flooding in different parts of the world.

Having said this, not every refugee is recognized or accepted as such. In the West, we tend to reserve the term for political refugees: the people who were forced to flee their country though fear of physical harm or persecution. In 1951, at Geneva, an international treaty for the status of refugees defined a refugee as *'a person who owing to a well-founded fear of being persecuted for reasons of race, religion, nationality, membership of a particular social group or political opinion, is outside the country of his nationality and is unable or, owing to such fear, is unwilling to avail himself of the protection of that country; or who, not having a nationality and being outside the country of his former habitual residence as a result of such events, is unable or, owing to such fear, is unwilling to return to it.'* (art. 1 of the Convention, as amended by the 1967 Protocol). On the basis of this international treaty, countries are obliged to give asylum to refugees. The terms of the treaty also make clear that a refugee cannot be forced to return to the country from which he has fled. A person recognized as a refugee receives a special status as detailed in the Geneva Convention for Refugees, which offers him protection in the country where his request for asylum has been accepted.

However, many requests for asylum are even nowadays rejected. Many refugees are not political refugees, but are economic refugees. In the West (and also in Belgium), people who flee their countries for purely economic reasons are not regarded as refugees at all, but are considered to be (illegal) immigrants, even though in practice political and economic reasons are often closely intermixed. People whose request for asylum is rejected are then ordered to leave the country as soon as possible. From that moment on, they are regarded as being in the country illegally.

This latter term – 'illegal' – is also a source of much dispute. An 'illegal immigrant' or 'illegal alien' is a person who has no legal status to be in the country in which he is currently residing or who enters that country unlawfully. Most illegal persons in Belgium are people who have had their applications for political asylum rejected and have exhausted all the various appeal procedures. The term also covers people who have come to Belgium through their family contacts or by some other means, but without having the required papers. People who are in the country unlawfully do not have a right to Belgian state benefits, nor to assistance from a Public Centre for Social Welfare (PCSW). They are, however, entitled to receive urgent medical treatment through the PCSW. This treatment is given partly for humanitarian reasons, but also for reasons of self interest: no society wants people with contagious diseases moving unchecked in its midst. Under the terms of the international treaty for children's rights, the children of undocumented migrants do have the right to attend school.

In exceptional circumstances, some people who are in the country unlawfully may nevertheless be allowed to stay on the basis of what is known as an 'individual regularization'. This special dispensation can be granted for a number of reasons. Most frequently, these reasons are humanitarian (the person concerned has been in the country for a long time, his or her children are in the country legally, etc.) or medical (the person needs urgent medical care that is not available in his home country). Occasionally, a host country may decide to give undocumented migrants the opportunity to make themselves known to the authorities, so that they can benefit from a 'collective regularization'. This happened in Belgium in 2000 and 2009 (see chapter 6).

New words for a new reality

If we look at the scale, nature and impact of migration, we can see just how drastically the migration process has changed Western societies during the past half century. During the last two decades in particular, we have evolved into a society with an ever increasing ethnic-cultural diversity as one of its basic characteristics. In Europe, the 21st century will be the century of superdiversity, with growing diversity within our diversity.

Nevertheless, we continue to view this new reality through old spectacles and to describe it using concepts that have become outdated. Our existing terminology is often inadequate to reflect the increasing complexity of the situation. Belgian and Dutch nationality can now often conceal a multitude of different ethnic-cultural backgrounds.

The words that we use to describe these situations are never neutral. They sometimes pin a particular identity to a person, even when that is not the intention. Young people who are born here as the children of Belgian and Dutch parents often find it difficult when they continue to be labelled as migrants or non-natives. Just exactly how long do you remain a migrant or a non-native?

Words cannot change reality, but they can influence people's approach towards it. Changing social realities means that we need a new language to reflect new situations. The debates in the media and in cities such as Ghent about the continued use of the term 'allochtoon' are symptomatic of this need. We must find new methods of expression that allow us to describe our changing reality more accurately. In order to better understand our superdiversity and the growing diversity within diversity, we must find new ways of looking at things. This will be dealt with latter in the book. But first we need to pause and examine the strong relationship that exists between ethnic-cultural diversity and inequality.

Chapter 3

Migration from top to bottom

'The underclass is integrally a part of a larger economic process and, more importantly, it serves the living standard and the comfort of the more favored community. (...) The poor in our economy are needed to do the work that the more fortunate do not do and would find manifestly distasteful, even distressing. And a continuing supply and resupply of such workers is always needed.'
John Kenneth Galbraith, 1992. *The Culture of Contentment*, p. 31 & 33.

Superdiversity is reflected at (almost) every level of the social ladder. This diversity also increases the social differences within and between communities. Questions about the social position of people with a migration background can no longer be answered with the same degree of certainty as was once the case. The perspective of the viewer also plays a role: who is analyzing the social position and within the parameters of which framework? Most migrants came here (Western Europe, Belgium, the Netherlands, etc.) to find a better life for themselves and their families. In comparison with the conditions in their countries of origin, most migrants have successfully achieved this objective. If we really want to understand the reasons that persuade people to leave behind everyone and everything they ever knew in their home country, we need to look at this situation not simply from the perspective of life in Belgium and the Netherlands, but also from the perspective of life in the different countries of origin.

Unfortunately, classic poverty research usually still operates on the basis of a different perspective: it analyzes poverty within national boundaries. Although many migrants are 'better off' in Western Europe than in their country of origin, their standard of living in comparison with the norm in Western Europe is often anything but good. The poverty statistics for people with a different ethnic origin are alarmingly high. 'Coloured poverty' is growing – and growing fast. Having said this, we need to be careful to avoid generalizations, since even in this area there is growing diversity within diversity: alongside a large group of people with a migration background who are living below the poverty line, there is also a growing middle class, both in terms of financial position and social position within the wider community.

Growing poverty among ethnic minorities

Even so, it is impossible to avoid the basic conclusion that, notwithstanding the emergence of a middle class, the majority of people with a migration background are to be found on the lowest rungs of the social ladder in Belgium. Poverty is increasingly becoming the poverty of ethnic minorities, certainly in the cities.

In Belgium, it has taken until well into the 21st century before poverty research has devoted systematic attention to the position of ethnic-cultural minorities. It was not until 2007 that clear statistics were first published in the report *De kleur van de armoede. Armoede bij personen van buitenlandse herkomst* (The colour of poverty. Poverty amongst people of foreign origin). These statistics showed that the majority of people living in Belgium with a Moroccan (56%) or Turkish (59%) background were living below the official poverty line as defined by the European Union.[1]

More recent figures are available in the Yearbook for Poverty and Social Exclusion. But the story remains the essentially same: people from other ethnic backgrounds are still strongly over-represented in socially vulnerable positions. While the poverty risk for people of Belgian origin during the period 2007-2009 was just 12%, the comparable figure for people of non-European origin was 37% – three times as great. For people of Moroccan origin, this increased to more than four times as great: 54% of the Moroccan community in Belgium live below the European poverty line.[2]

But it is not only the poverty statistics that are so alarming. Other social indicators show the same vulnerability of ethnic-cultural minorities. For example, the rate of unemployment amongst 'non-native' Belgians is much higher than amongst 'native' Belgians – and the gap between the two is much greater than in many other European countries. The fact that many young people with a migration background grew up in socially vulnerable families and fell behind at school certainly plays a role in this situation, but it does not explain everything. There is a clear mismatch between supply and demand, with too many people holding qualifications that are insufficiently attractive for the labour market. In particular, many newcomers find it difficult to get their foreign diplomas accepted by local employers. In addition, discrimination within the labour market and cultural differences, such as the more traditional gender patterns in ethnic communities, also have a negative impact.[3]

In terms of education, it is again clear that many people with a migration background in Belgium have a relatively low level of schooling. This applies not only to the first generation of often poorly educated migrant labourers, but also (to a significant degree) to their children and grandchildren. They often struggle to keep up at school and more of them leave school without qualifications. The poor educational and vulnerable social-economic position of many migratory parents is something that they all too frequently pass on to the following generations.[4]

Ethnicity by itself can never be an explanation for poverty and inequality. But it is certainly an additional (and increasingly important) element in the existing processes of social exclusion. It operates alongside inequality based on class, education and gender. This means that rather than studying the effect of an ethnic background on inequality in isolation, it is better and more relevant to investigate how ethnic differences supplement and enhance existing patterns of inequality.[5] In that case, the question then becomes: to what extent does a different ethnic origin increase the inequality of educational opportunities in children who grow up in a poorly educated family.

Urban poverty

The majority of people with a migration background in Belgium and the Netherlands live in cities. At the same time, the poverty risk of people with a different ethnic background is far higher than the poverty risk of the native population. This means that the level of poverty in most cities is far higher than in the 'whiter' areas that surround them. It also means that most of the poverty in the cities is increasingly coloured poverty.

There are no city-by-city statistics to show how many people are living below the poverty line. However, one reasonably reliable indicator is the number of people who apply for means-tested benefit from the Public Centres for Social Welfare and who have a right to social integration (RSI). This effectively means an entitlement to a minimum level of benefit or employment in a social workplace, in accordance with article 60§ 7 of the PCSW legislation.

In the Flemish Region as a whole in 2013, there were 4.3 people with an RSI per thousand head of population. The figures for the larger cities were much higher, with Antwerp (10 per 1,000) and Ghent (15.5 per 1,000) at the top of the table. Poverty in general is at a much higher level in the Walloon Region, with 14.1 people with an RSI per thousand head of population. The statistics for the major cities are also significantly higher than in Flanders, with Charleroi (27.8), Verviers (30.3) and Liege (38.7) leading the way. But the situation is most problematical in the Brussels Capital City Region, with an average of 26.7 people with an RSI per thousand head of population in its 19 municipalities.[6]

Superdiversity in social assistance

Superdiversity in society means that there must also be superdiversity in social assistance. However, the increase in diversity among the client populations is increasing more rapidly than the diversity in the social machinery of the host countries, simply because of the greater social vulnerability of those populations. The ethnic-cultural diversity of those applying for social assistance has grown dramatically in recent decades and continues to rise.

The large majority of the people applying for social assistance from the PCSW in Brussels and Antwerp are people with a different ethnic origin. In Antwerp, 70% of the applicants have a migration background. In Ghent, six out of every ten beneficiaries of a minimum benefit in 2013 were born outside of Belgium. And the story is much the same in other urban centres in Flanders: in Leuven, Mechelen, Ostend, Lokeren, Sint-Niklaas and Genk the level of ethnic diversity among people in financial difficulties is on the increase.

According to Monica De Coninck, the former chairperson of the Antwerp Public Centre for Social Welfare, these centres in the major cities are gradually being transformed into integration agencies.[7] The legal obligation to give everyone the chance to live a life that corresponds with the basic norms of human dignity is now being combined with greater guidance towards and greater assessment of the integration efforts made (and the results achieved) by the people receiving assistance. In other words, the assistance provided by the OCMW no longer focuses exclusively on helping its beneficiaries to find work, but also on the need for them to integrate more fully into Belgian society. This is taking place within the framework of a 'quid pro quo' approach, which expects the beneficiaries to do something in return for the benefits they receive, an approach piloted by the former burgomaster of Antwerp, Patrick Janssens.[8]

This emphasis on the need to make integration efforts (including the learning of the local language) in combination with actions to find employment has had a significant impact on the application of the benefit entitlement legislation. Without any amendments to this legislation having been made, there is now a clear restrictive application in a negative sense, emanating in the first instance from the urban PCSWs, but supported in part at least by subsequent judgements from the labour courts and other tribunals. This means that the right to assistance and the right to a minimum level of human dignity as foreseen in the PCSW legislation is becoming increasingly conditional. Need is no longer the exclusive criterion for offering assistance, but is now being coupled to an increasing degree with the requirement for the applicant to make greater efforts to integrate into Belgian society. This is gradually leading to a situation where there are different degrees of human dignity, depending on the ethnic origins of the applicant and the assessment of the efforts they are making to integrate 'properly' into a different way of life.[9]

In similar fashion, the Centra voor Algemeen Welzijnswerk (Centres for General Welfare Work or CAWs) have also seen increasing diversity among the people applying for assistance. In Flanders, the number of applicants with a migration background has risen from 21% in 2005 to 29% in 2011. In the CAWs operating in the big cities, the majority of the applicants now come from ethnic-cultural minorities. This is the case, for example, in the CAWs in Brussels (57-77%), Antwerp(42-62%) and Ghent (51%). But the situation is becoming equally dramatic in the areas surrounding the major urban centres, such as in the CAW for the Central Coast Region (46%) or in Vilvoorde (45%). During the past decade the number of applicants of other ethnic origin has increased each year in almost every CAW in the country. This indicates that social work in the 21st century will more than ever mean working in and with diversity.[10] At the same time, a number of thresholds still remain that make it difficult for people with a migration background to find their way to the help they need. Lack of familiarity with the entitlements on offer, combined with the barriers imposed by a lack of the right papers, language difficulties or cultural differences, all play a role. In addition to the formal channels of social assistance, a number of self-help organizations are now being set up in minority communities to overcome these problems. Unfortunately, collaboration between these informal organizations and the official authorities is not always easy.[11]

Put poverty on the agenda

There is something remarkable – certainly in Flanders – about the way we deal with increasing levels of poverty among ethnic minorities. In the first instance, it took an awfully long time before this type of poverty was (more or less) systematically included in poverty research and reports. This means that it is only during the past decade that coloured poverty – the name that is given for ease of reference to poverty amongst people with a different ethnic background – has been documented to any significant degree.

The next remarkable thing is how little social debate or reaction this coloured poverty data has provoked. The harsh figures that are painful and unacceptable to those in the migrant community seem to generate an (equally unacceptable) low level of social engagement and solidarity in response. Even within the organizations that seek to combat poverty in Flanders, the attention devoted specifically to coloured poverty is limited. As a result, these organizations tend to primarily represent the poorest classes of native or 'white' Belgian society. The diversity that exists at the bottom of the social ladder is not reflected in the public that these organizations are trying to help – or so concluded 'Motief'.[12] Their report also said that a number of poverty organizations have a negative image of poor people with a Muslim background. It is only during the past few years that the first (almost reluctant) attempts have been made by poverty organizations to respond to the needs of the poorest elements of the migrant community. In this respect, the 'Armoede Gekleurd' (Coloured Poverty) project, a collaborative venture launched by the Minorities Forum and the Network Against Poverty, was an important milestone in the struggle to give ethnic minorities a place on the agenda of the existing poverty organizations. But there is still much work to be done – work that is as necessary today as it has ever been – to persuade such organizations to amend their vision, objectives and methods.[13]

But it is not only the poverty organizations. Many others in civil society, as well as key figures in the policy domains, seem reluctant to place 'coloured poverty' on their agendas. As far as policy is concerned, there seems to be a preference for a focus first and foremost on employment activation, followed by child poverty. The fact that child poverty, certainly in the major cities, largely affects children from a migrant background goes without saying – and so the policymakers don't say it. But it remains open to question how far these poor children can be helped out of poverty if the structural position of their parents is not improved. Sadly, this question is seldom asked.

This apparent fear to make a specific theme of the high poverty figures among people with a different ethnic background seems largely to be based on two strategic concerns. On the one, hand, there is a desire to avoid individual or cultural guilt models (see chapter 9). A survey by the research department of the Flemish Government revealed that no fewer than half of all Flemings think that migrants have come to Flanders to benefit from the social benefits system, while only a quarter believe that migrants contribute to the region's prosperity.[14] Prejudicial conclusions of this kind can only be enhanced if the poverty figures amongst people with a different ethnic origin are made a specific theme – or so the argument goes.

In addition, civil society is anxious to build a consensus of support for greater solidarity and a stronger policy for the more effective combating of poverty in general. In a meritocratic society like ours, where success and failure are individualized and where poverty is often rationalized by the use of individual guilt models, it is not easy to achieve the kind of consensus that the NGOs are hoping to create. If an increasing number of poor people are seen to be those who come from a migration background, this threatens to further reduce – rather than enhance – the need for solidarity and structural measures in a society that is struggling to come to terms with its own superdiversity.

Finally, it also needs to be noted that the high levels of poverty have not led to loud protests from the migrant community itself. In part, this is because they have too little power to get the issue placed on the social and political agenda. But in part, they also fear to raise their voice in case they strengthen still further the prejudices with which they are already confronted. With newcomers there is the additional factor that a position of poverty in Belgium still compares favourably with the situation they left behind in their country of origin – and so they stay silent.

In other words, there are many reasons why the high level of poverty among people with a different ethnic background is not a subject of burning public debate. However, the question is how long can we continue to turn a blind eye to the reality of the situation, by focusing instead on the related problems of child poverty and inner city poverty? Or are we indeed right to turn a blind eye in this manner? Is this actually the best way forward? In our present-day society, ethnicity is a risk factor for (and an element of) poverty – just like low schooling, illiteracy, gender, position in the labour market or family situation. Moreover, like gender, for example, ethnic origin is, in part at least, an innate characteristic. You are not able to choose your family background, any more than you can alter the reactions that this background provokes in others. But at the same time, ethnicity is also to some extent an 'optional' characteristic: people of a different ethnic origin are free to decide how they themselves respond to that origin. Some people consciously maintain or even emphasize their ethnic origin. Others are keen to play it down. Both responses are a way of trying to deal dynamically with personal ethnicity. If, however, as a society we really want to wage war on poverty and stimulate the struggle for emancipation amongst the ethnic-cultural communities, the only way to do this is by daring to call a spade a spade. It is desirable, crucial even, that we should identify the problems relating to the breach of fundamental social rights of people with a migration background in explicit terms. We must be prepared to give poverty among minorities a name. Only then will it be possible to do something about these problems.

This can work to the benefit of us all. One of the most remarkable aspects of the situation, write Leo and Jan Lucassen in respect of the Netherlands, is that so little use is made of the human capital contained in the migrant community. They conclude that there is a fear that the success-stories of migrants may attract new migrants. As a result, no effective policy has been developed to transform what many people see as something negative – namely, the arrival of a growing number of migrants – into something positive – namely, the use of the migrants undoubted capabilities for the benefit of society as a whole.[15] These same conclusions can also be applied to migration in Belgium – and not only for asylum migration, but also for chain migration.

A growing middle class

There is, however, an important caveat. By devoting more specific attention to the poverty of people with an ethnic background, we must be careful not to create the impression that *all* people with an ethnic background live in poverty. In addition to more openly discussing the social vulnerability of the migrant communities, we should also focus attention on the fact that more and more migrants are successfully starting to climb the social ladder. This double image – of an unacceptable number of people in poverty, unemployment and poor schooling, contrasted with a growing middle class – has also been confirmed by the most recent research into the position of Belgians of Moroccan and Turkish origin.[16] However, this growing middle class is seldom mentioned in the social debate about the economic position of the migrant community, according to Lucassen & Lucassen. When talking of 'migrants' in this context, we usually mean the large majority of the migrant community that cause 'problems'. As a result of this selective approach, we are sometimes too pessimistic about the concept of migration as a whole.[17] And it is indeed true that in visible top functions we do often tend to overlook the migration background of the incumbents, although former Belgian prime minister Elio di Rupo frequently refers to his origins as the son of an Italian migrant worker in the coal mines of Wallonia. Less visible are the many Indians who fill most of the top jobs in the diamond sector in Antwerp, while the presence of the European Union and numerous national embassies in

Brussels provides a top layer of international functionaries that is typical of capital cities around the world.

Migration is by definition layered and dynamic. For those arriving at the bottom of the social ladder, there are still a number of different paths that they can follow to secure a better social-economic position. For many, education is a crucial lever. There are still far too few children from an ethnic background moving on to higher education, even though the overall number is systematically increasing. More graduates with an ethnic background are also making a successful appearance in the ranks of the professions, such as doctors and lawyers, not all of whom focus specifically on the needs of their own communities.

It is noticeable how we are inclined to individualize the education debate. Viewed from our meritocratic perspective, success is seen as the result of individual effort. On the other side of the coin, this means that failure is the result of a lack of effort. At best, we take account of the social situation in which young people grow up and we recognize that the educational background and income of their parents also play a role. We also accept (since it is patently obvious) that children from migrant backgrounds need to make an extra effort if they want to succeed at school, and certainly if they want to move on to higher education. But are these matters sufficiently reflected in policy? And do we create adequate opportunities for those whose educational struggle is so much harder?[18]

One of the most interesting and confrontational research studies to be carried out in recent years was an international project that compared second generation children of Turkish origin in different countries.[19] The starting point was the same in all cases: children of poorly educated parents with a migration background. As might be expected, the differences in the results of the different countries was sometimes great, sometime even greater than the differences between the results of the 'native' and 'non-native' pupils within individual countries. Even so, it was still possible to identify a number of important factors for educational success, such as the individual effort of the young people and the role of their parents. However, the role of policy was also identified as being crucial, and in this respect it is disturbing that Flemish educational policy was to a significant extent responsible for producing levels of educational performance among the local Turkish community that are lower than in several other countries and regions.

Maurice Crul and his colleagues have concluded that this international study turned the prevailing ideas about the necessary preconditions for the successful integration of migrant youngsters on their head. The integration debate largely emphasizes the position and attitudes of the parents, but the new results show that this is only one of the contributory factors – and not necessarily the most important one for achieving success at school. The nature of the school system and the educational policy that this system reflects are equally important, if not more so. In particular, it is the specific characteristics of the schools that determine whether or not second generation Turkish youngsters will be successful. And in many respects, these characteristics are the same as those that can have a similar restricting effect on poor children from 'native' working class families.[20]

This means that we will need to invest in more appropriately adjusted forms of schooling, if we wish education to serve as a successful social lever. Crul points out that between half and two-thirds of all the young people who live in a major European city and are less than 18 years of age have a migration background. Cities that are capable of tapping into the huge potential of these young people by offering them appropriate education are investing in their own future. Urban prosperity in the 21st century will be closely linked to the social and economic improvement of children with a migrant background from the second and third generations.[21]

Entrepreneurship is a second pathway to upward mobility for members of the ethnic minorities. Many migrants have started their own businesses during the past decades. Often, these were local shops and restaurants providing 'ethnic' products, but others were successful in developing large-scale businesses in sectors as diverse as construction, foodstuffs, services or even international trade. Moreover, their numbers are increasing all the time.

Last but not least, the acquisition and exploitation of property is another important way to help people from ethnic communities to climb the social ladder. For some people, it is paradoxical that their upward social mobility coincides with what might be called a process of 'gentrification'. The upgrading and revaluation of many previously 'deprived' inner city areas resulted in a rapid increase in property prices, which led in turn to the social 'dislodgement' of those who could not afford to pay the new prices. But for those who owned the property – including migrants – this was a golden opportunity to better themselves. During the 1970s and 1980s, when nobody wanted to live in these deprived areas, some migrants were able – often as a matter of necessity rather than choice – to buy dilapidated properties at a knock-down price. Decades later, when these districts suddenly became fashionable, they were able to sell at a huge profit. A typical example is the district known as Antwerp South, which was once little more than a slum but is now one of the most sought-after addresses in the city. Moreover, with the profits that some of the migrants were able to make as a result of this gentrification process, they were able to buy a number of other properties in other areas that are still less fashionable, in the hope that the process will repeat itself. As a result of this phenomenon, which is often linked to the pooling of family capital, an increasingly large group of migrants are becoming the owners of their own property.

At the same time, the number of landlords with a migrant background is also on the rise. Depending on the state of the property in question, rooms can be hired either to other members of the same family or community, or else (if the condition of the property is poor) to new migrant incomers, who are in the most vulnerable social position. As a result, there are increasing problems in many major cities with so-called 'slum landlords' – landlords who rent out sub-standard premises at extortionately high prices, often with other members of the ethnic communities as their victims. This is a complex and often paradoxical situation. Notwithstanding the appalling living conditions and the exorbitant rents, this type of rented property is often the only chance for newcomers to establish a foothold on the housing ladder, simply because they have no hope of finding alternative accommodation through the more regular housing channels. At the same time, this highly dubious practice contributes to the further growth of an ethnic middle class in these areas, which, in itself, is a 'good' thing. The justified attempts to combat slum tenancies of this kind therefore requires the better and fairer regulation of the bottom end of the accommodation market, in order to provide an adequate supply of affordable premises as social (publicly owned) homes, whilst at the same time encouraging the development of the private housing market in a more acceptable manner, thereby continuing to stimulate the desirable growth of a middle class among the migrant community.

Towards a more dynamic vision

This phenomenon of upward social mobility amongst the ethnic communities also means that we need to take a new and different look at the so-called 'concentration' districts, the districts in the major urban centres where large groups of people with an ethnic background are concentrated. All too often, we look at these districts from a statical perspective. If you take a snapshot of one of the districts, what you actually see is a concentration of social exclusion. There are higher levels of poverty and unemployment, lower levels of academic qualifications and often very poor housing conditions.

Yet while these factors certainly exist, they threaten to hide the dynamic that also exists within these districts. It was this dynamic that the Canadian-British journalist Doug Saunders wanted to make visible in his book *Arrival Cities*.[22] He investigated twenty urban centres all around the world, where migrants have moved (and are still moving) from the countryside (or from abroad) to the city. In each of these cities there are 'zones of arrival', the places where newcomers first try to establish themselves. In the South, these zones are often illegal slums and favelas, which gradually grow to become part of the ever expanding city. In Europe, the zones are usually the poorest districts in the city, with plenty of sub-standard rented accommodation, furnished rooms and sub-letting.

In good functioning cities and arrival zones, it can be seen that the newcomers not only find a place to stay, but that they can also find opportunities to grow and move up the social ladder. This means that they can either move to a better district elsewhere in the city or that they remain where they are, so that the district 'improves' and another district takes over the role of arrival neighbourhood. If we want to be able to see this dynamic, it is important that we should not concentrate exclusively on poverty statistics, but should look instead at the different trajectories that people in poor districts follow (or do not follow).

At the invitation of a previous city council, Doug Saunders also investigated the area of the city known as Antwerp-North or 2060-Antwerp.[23] Once again, he went in search of the social dynamic behind the poverty. He found that the districts in question were characterized by both globalization and glocalization. In the Stuyvenberg district, almost a quarter of all the residents move each year. Of all the people who lived in Antwerp-North in 2004, only half were still living in the city in 2010. The others had moved away to other towns and cities, or else had returned to their homeland or travelled on to another European country. This type of intensive translocation is also evident in cities such as Rotterdam and Amsterdam. According to Hans Entzinger, both cities are not only destinations for newcomers, but are also becoming more and more a kind of transit zone. The processes of upward social mobility in ethnic communities are increasingly linked to geographical mobility, which means moving to the fringes of the city, where there is more room and greater opportunities for further development.[24] Until they are able to make this move, a temporary existence in the streets and squares of the inner city, with its furnished rooms and informal jobs, represents the first rung on the social ladder for the large majority of migrants.

Looking at the transit function of these arrival zones helps to broaden our view of the dynamic of upward social mobility within the ethnic communities. At the same time, we must be careful not to romanticize the poverty and the informal survival strategies in these zones, with their insecure jobs, slum tenancies, human trafficking and criminality. If we want to fight poverty, structural changes are still necessary. Yet at the same time, we must also remain aware of the need to create sufficient room to allow bottom-up social mobility, thereby stimulating a dynamic that works to the benefit of important groups amongst the newcomers.

Cities as emancipation machines

This requires us to look at things in a different light; a light that takes the inherent power of urbanism as its starting point. Cities need to work as 'emancipation machines' for everyone who lives there, providing each resident – even those who are only there temporarily – with the necessary opportunities to develop as human beings.[25] Cities need to give people the chance to grow and to climb a rung or two (and sometimes more) up the social ladder. Facilitating upward mobility is one of the key functions of the modern city. This will require strong structural policies at high levels in various fields, such as social insurance, education, housing and the labour market. Within the urban context, these policy lines must be properly integrated. This is the only way to create the 'emancipation machines'we need.

The city as an emancipation machine is a stimulating metaphor, certainly in this new age of superdiversity. It raises the bar much higher than the often non-committal 'equal opportunities' discourse that we so often hear; a discourse which, moreover, only covers 'official' residents and takes no account of the many thousands of 'unofficial' residents who are hidden away in all the world's major cities (see chapter 6). But it bears repeating: the only way to achieve this emancipation objective is through the introduction of a stronger and more structural social policy, which also allows sufficient room for the informal dynamic at the heart of urban life to thrive and prosper.

By thinking in terms of the city as a transit zone or an emancipation machine, we also add a new perspective to the situation, by creating the prospect of a progressive life pathway. This offers the hope that not everyone will stay at the bottom of the social ladder all their life. At the same time, we must ensure that at every step along this pathway, even the very first steps, everyone can find a safe and decent living environment. When people finally leave the city, it should not be because they are fleeing poor conditions, but rather because they are moving on to the next phase in their personal development or emancipation trajectory. For those who opt to stay, there should also be room within the urban context for further growth and social mobility. The city must offer increasing space and opportunities for newcomers, both from at home and abroad, even if these newcomers are not yet part of the middle class.

It remains, however, a moot point whether or not the districts we are talking about have sufficient social capacity to make this possible.

The classic response to this situation is the introduction of measures designed to create a social mix in these districts by attracting sufficient members of the middle class to the most socially vulnerable areas. However, this policy all too often leads to social displacement and gentrification. Urban development projects do indeed often attract people from the middle class, but this usually results in an increase in house prices and rents, which makes it harder and harder for the district's poorer residents to carry on living there. In other words, the invisible forces of the property market slowly but surely force them to move to another (often even poorer) district, so that the basic problem of poverty is relocated rather than solved.[26]

For this reason, the concept of upward social mobility seems to offer better prospects for the generation of lasting urban social renewal, both in the so-called arrival zones and for the city as a whole.[27] This social mobility perspective means that the dynamic of superdiversity in the arrival zones and the desire of the residents in those zones to better themselves can be taken as complementary starting points for a new and more sustainable policy of urban renewal. Current attempts to regenerate our inner cities take too little account of this all-important factor. These attempts are characterized by the physical upgrading of property and other initiatives focused on greater liveability and social cohesion. This is fine as far as it goes – but it overlooks the huge potential lying dormant in these communities. In this way, crucial social and economic chances are missed. Opting for this new perspective has two important implications. Firstly, upward social mobility must continue to be possible within the city itself. Progress is likely to be slow and gradual; it will not always be made with leaps and bounds. This means that we will need to add some extra rungs to the urban social ladder, in terms of accommodation, employment, education and even leisure opportunities. Once again, this requires a stronger and more coherent social policy. Attempts to make cuts and savings in this area effectively deprive the poorer urban districts and their residents of the chance to make social and economic progress. In other words, we must spend more money here, not less.

Secondly, the new perspective means that we need to recognize the importance of 'binding' the urban middle class to the urban districts where their presence is most needed. This middle class does not need to be 'imported' from outside. The potential already exists within the city; it only needs to be stimulated and developed. This potential is the city's social capital and its presence is necessary to allow others to become upwardly social mobile as well. In order to 'bind' these social climbers to the city, it is necessary to add extra qualities and facilities to the districts from which they sprung; qualities and facilities that better meet their new aspirations. Based on this new vision, the question then becomes 'how' (and not 'if') the city can function as a transformation machine and how any obstacles to this functioning can be overcome. The strengthening of the emancipation function goes hand in hand with the strengthening of the city. In this respect, it is remarkable that so little is currently known about the living patterns and the living needs of people with a migration background. For example, the notion of what actually constitutes a 'home' can differ significantly, not only between newcomers and people who have already been in the country for some time, but also between people who belong to the same ethnic grouping. But in spite of the importance of this aspect, research into the living cultures within superdiverse cities and regions has only been sporadically carried out, both here in the Low Countries and elsewhere.[28]

The policy we need must therefore strike the right balance between the creation of a housing market that is affordable for everyone and at the same time enhances urban districts in a manner that will prevent a middle-class 'flight' from the cities. This requires an approach that combines comprehensive social renewal with the provision of sufficient social housing, so that pressure on the housing market can be kept within bounds. This in turn implies the need for an adequate number of nursery and primary schools in these districts, with secondary schools also within easy reach. Measures will also need to be taken both to improve the quality of life and defuse any possible tensions that may arise. In short, we need a policy that strengthens 'social binding' at all levels, stimulates emancipation and encourages upward social mobility. It is above all this latter aspect that is currently so difficult to achieve in Flemish and Belgian cities, given the current degree of social discrimination faced by newcomers and migrant residents of longer standing. Only when we have made full use of the potential contained in superdiversity will it be possible for our cities to fulfil their role as emancipation machines – to the benefit of all the cities' inhabitants, whether they come from a migrant background or not.

Chapter 4

The need for a more cosmopolitan vision

'I occasionally experience myself as a cluster of flowing currents. I prefer this to the idea of a solid self, the identity to which so many attach so much significance.'
Edward W. Said, 1999. *Out of place. A memoir.* p. 295.

Our image of ethnic diversity in society is constantly running after the facts. It simply does not square with reality.[1] All too often, we view the constantly changing present through the spectacles of the past. As a result, we think in terms of outdated and stereotypical images. This means that contemporary debates of crucial importance are conducted in the language of yesterday rather than the language of today and tomorrow – a shortcoming of which both sides in the debate, native and non-native, are equally guilty.

In times of change and uncertainty, people look for familiar things that they can cling on to for comfort and security. In these circumstances, the feeling of belonging to a particular group can often bring that comfort and security, because it is within groups that people built up social contacts and social capital. Being part of a group makes the world seem more comprehensible: the group is the place where you find points of similarity; the outside world is the place where you find points of difference. This 'us-and-them' thinking is common in many aspects of life, not just in the debates relating to social integration and people of ethnic origin. You can just as easily find the same thinking in similar debates between the young and the old or between men and women, where the participants tend to identify most readily with 'their own kind'. At a more mundane level, the supporters of one football club have a lot in common with the supporters of every other club, but it is the identification with that one specific club that makes all the difference. Why? Because it offers an identity that can be strengthened still further by emphasizing the differences with the others. Thinking in terms of 'insiders' and 'outsiders' is something that has happened throughout history, as was already demonstrated by Norbert Elias in the 1960s.

Being part of a group provides a person with a network and further strengthens their social capital within the group. At the same time, this can make a network with outsiders more difficult. Much depends on the degree of emphasis we place on the differences between 'us' and 'them'. In other words, how open or closed are the boundaries of our group? The American politocologist Robert Putnam made a distinction between two forms of social capital: 'bonding' and 'bridging'.[2] With bonding social capital, a person's social capital and networking within the self-chosen group increases over time. This relates to bonding with people in more or less homogenous groupings or within the home community. Bridging social capital relates to a more heterogeneous kind of relations: namely, between people of different ages, genders, social positions and/or ethnic-cultural groups.

Old ways of looking at new realities

Thinking in terms of 'us-and-them' is therefore common to all times, all places and all areas of life. Not surprisingly, this means that this kind of narrow-minded thinking also affects the participants on both sides of the migration debate. We as 'natives' against the 'non-natives'. We as Muslims against the non-Muslims. We as Moroccans against the Turks. And vice versa.

However, in this new century of superdiversity, the 'us-and-them' thinking of the 20th century is becoming more and more problematical to apply within the context of the migration debate. In some political circles it is still seen as a useful instrument to exaggerate the differences between different communities, in order to create a hostile image of 'the other'. In particular, populist politicians, especially on the extreme right, still use the 'threat' posed by outsiders to underline what they claim is the failure of the multicultural society. On the reverse side of the coin, many progressives want to bridge the gap between 'us' and 'them' as quickly as possible – which also shows that they, too, are also still trapped in 'us-and-them' thinking.

Unfortunately, the problem goes much further than the political use or misuse of 'us-and-them' constructions. In a superdiverse society, blinkered interpretations of this kind prevent us from adequately recognizing the complexity of society, particularly in the cities, and also blind us to the benefits that this complexity can bring. It is true that some circumstances still lend themselves to the easy exploitation of ethnic loyalties and the 'us-and-them' ideology. At the same time, many other circumstances illustrate how exaggerated, outdated and largely untenable concepts such as 'ethnicity' and 'nationality' have become. They are increasingly inappropriate to describe the constantly changing reality of our modern world and are hopelessly inadequate as a basis for future policy. The new demands of 21st century society require us to develop new ways of looking at today's fluid situations, in which increasing numbers of people from different backgrounds need to live and work with each other.

Beyond methodological nationalism

One of the main sources of inspiration in this context is the work of the German sociologists Ulrich Beck and Elisabeth Beck-Gernsheim. In his inaugural lecture to the German Sociology Congress in Jena in 2008, Ulrich Beck challenged his sociological colleagues to adjust their frames of reference to reflect the realities of the modern world. Far too often, he argued, modern research in sociology is still based on 'methodological nationalism'.[3] If we want to properly understand social inequality in this new century of globalization, it is no longer possible to do this by looking exclusively at the problems of inequality within the boundaries of our own nation state or, even worse, the problems of inequality experienced solely by the holders of the nationality of that nation state.

It is characteristic of this era of globalization that on the one hand national borders continue to exist in geographical terms, while on the other hand we can see how they are gradually being eroded in economic, social and cultural terms, so that we increasingly need to redefine them in political terms. Viewed from a nationalist perspective, the nation state is the entity that controls and structures society within a given geographical boundary that the state itself sets. However, the state also indirectly sets other boundaries as well. In this way, it is often too easily assumed that national boundaries also equate to nationality, economic, social and cultural boundaries as well. During the 19th and 20th centuries this was largely the case, but the globalization and migration processes of recent years mean that we now need to look at the situation in a different light. Global inequality is now reflected to a significant degree within our own national borders, irrespective of the passport a person holds. In this new era of superdiversity more and more people are crossing national borders than ever before (see chapter 5). And their frames of reference and their experiences of inequality transcend the narrow confines of the nation state.

Just as Ulrich Beck placed his finger on the wound for the sociological study of social inequality, so we need to take account of the same criticism if we wish to gain deeper insights into the superdiversity within our cities. If we attempt to analyze the realities of city life from a purely nationalist perspective, many of its secrets will remain hidden from our view. Multilingualism and linguistic problems at school are no longer capable of analysis by simply looking at the nationality of the children concerned, but also requires a knowledge and understanding of their ethnic background, as well as their general level of schooling and the socio-economic position of their parents. Similarly, when the population statistics show that migration from the Netherlands to a city like Antwerp is increasing, it is important in these superdiverse times to know that a considerable number of these Dutch citizens are of Moroccan origin, and that they have moved to Belgium because the regulations relating to family reunification with a partner from the country of origin have been made stricter in the Netherlands by the imposition of language and income requirements.

Beck's cosmopolitan vision

In short, if we want to understand superdiversity, we need to develop a new way of looking at things that moves beyond the dominant national perspective and the methodological nationalism that has governed our thinking until now, both in the fields of research and policy. Beck calls this new way of thinking 'a cosmopolitan vision'.

Unfortunately, this is a term that can lead to confusion. In the West, there has long been a philosophical tradition that expounds the value of cosmopolitanism or world citizenship, in which people are (or should be) more closely linked in a normative sense with mankind as a whole than with people of the same nationality in an artificially constructed nation state or region. Beck and Beck-Gernsheim translate this theoretical concept of cosmopolitanism into a new superdiverse reality for the 21st century, not as a normative concept but primarily as a framework for analyzing change empirically. In other words, the Becks argue for a new kind of empirical-analytical cosmopolitanism.

The cosmopolitan vision is both the result of this change, as well as a precondition for observing the change in a new and more meaningful manner. According to Ulrich Beck, this kind of cosmopolitan vision is the only way to investigate and come to terms with the realities of life in our cities without being blinded by the narrow-minded, 'pigeon-hole' thinking of the past, with its outdated focus on nationalities and ethnicity.[4]

From 'either...or' to 'and...and'

Nowadays, many people live lives of ambivalence, far removed from the certainties of the black-and-white world of yesteryear. In order to make clear the complexities and realities of this changing situation, the cosmopolitan vision attempts to replace the dominant 'either... or' way of thinking with a more flexible 'and...and' logic. Classic sociology and most of our policy makers remain locked for the time being in the 'either...or' mode. We try to cordon off what is 'ours' and 'familiar' from what is 'theirs' and 'strange', usually by means of applying territorial 'either...or' criteria to the question of identity. This meta-theory of identity-society-politics alienates us still further from the reality of the world of 'and...and'. Having a cosmopolitan vision is one way (probably the only way) to move beyond the limitations of 'us' and 'them', allowing us to discover and understand the benefits of 'we together'. But what does this actually mean in concrete terms? An example may serve to clarify.

Viewed from the perspective of 'either...or' logic, people in Belgium are either Belgians or migrants. This reasoning is based on the migration patterns of the post-1945 era. In proportional terms, there were relatively few migrants, the large majority of them belonging to the first generation and coming from a relatively small number of countries of origin. In those days, the migrants did not have a Belgian passport or Belgian nationality. In other words, there was a fairly simple relationship between nationality and ethnic origin, both for the local population and for the migrants themselves. Moreover, this was a situation that applied in almost every other country in Western Europe.

However, it is no longer possible to explain and understand the complexities of superdiversity by using exclusive categories of this kind, which leave no room for ambivalence. A new reality has grown up between 'us' and 'them', a mixed reality of people who have acquired Belgian nationality but have their roots in migration, children who have been born here but also have a migration past, and people of other ethnic origins who have migrated here in recent times. In this sense, globalization is reflected locally in the superdiversity of our cities, and in the associated process of 'glocalization'. More and more of the people who live in 'our' country are people with a migration background, but it is difficult to pin them down to a single nationality or characteristic: they are from Borgerhout, Antwerp *and* Flanders, and they are both Belgian *and* Moroccan or Berber. Classic assimilation theory argues that a double ethnic identity is impossible: a person cannot be both quintessentially Belgian and Turkish. But in recent decades there has been a growing realization that many 'allochtonen' (non-natives), especially those in the second and third generations, have developed more complex patterns of identity, in which religious beliefs can play an important role. Complementary or double patterns of identity are therefore becoming more common.[5]

This transition from an exclusive 'either...or' to a more inclusive 'and...and' thinking is a crucial step in developing a cosmopolitan vision. Whoever tries to understand superdiversity from an 'and...and' perspective will be rewarded with deeper insights into the reality of a world in which it is no longer possible to pigeon-hole people of the basis of a single characteristic. Superdiverse societies are societies with multiple and layered identities.[6]

This multiplicity of identities is already a reality today. It is perfectly possible for a Dutch youngster of Moroccan parents to speak perfect Dutch (with a true Rotterdam accent) and to be a supporter of Feyenoord. Will he have a Dutch girlfriend (i.e. a white native) or will he have a Moroccan girlfriend, who was also born in Rotterdam? Or will his future bride come from his (grand) parents' country of origin, perhaps through the mediation (or even under pressure) from his family? And must this young Dutchman first move to Antwerp, in order to be able to bring his Moroccan bride to Europe more easily, since the migration laws in the Netherlands are stricter?

This same layered identity can just as easily be found amongst youngsters of Turkish origin in Belgium. Perhaps they live in Antwerp or Ghent, but also have family in Berlin and back in the mother country. They work in their father's business, and have trading contacts with Turkey, but also with members of the Turkish community in the Netherlands. Whenever there is a new earthquake in Turkey, they are amongst the first to launch aid campaigns and solidarity actions. Some of them also follow political developments in Ankara and they certainly follow the fortunes of Galatasaray and Fenerbahçe, and ride through their home district, tooting their car horns, if their favourite team wins. They will also support the Belgian national football team, but if Belgium has to play Turkey that can make things really difficult...

Transnationality and ambivalence

The cosmopolitan vision also takes account of this ambiguity and is therefore compatible with many other theories of intercultural communication and methodologies for dealing with diversity. The concept of multiple identities is recurring more and more as a common theme amongst all these theories.

If we truly want to move beyond 'us-and-them' thinking, then we must also take into account the concept of multiple citizenship. We must recognise that people can be both African and an Amsterdammer; simultaneously Moroccan, Antwerpenaar and Belgian or Turkish, Dutch and European; both a resident of their inner city district and a citizen of the world. But in addition to formal multiple citizenship, we must also be aware of the effects of more informal layered identities and roles, as well as the ambiguities that exist between these composite identities and roles. Identifying and coming to terms with this ambiguity or ambivalence is one of the key characteristics of the cosmopolitan vision.

Is someone 'one of us' because he has the same nationality? Or does he remain 'one of them' on the basis of his origins, appearance, beliefs or language? The cosmopolitan vision recognizes the 'otherness' of people and their multiple backgrounds. It is open to increasing nuance in matters of identity and accepts the gradual blurring of the dividing lines between 'us' and 'them'. It takes ambivalence as its starting point, instead of clinging to the artificial and rapidly disintegrating identities of the past. It also values this ambivalence as something positive, and therefore helps to prevent people from turning back through fear and anti-modernism to the old, constructed personas of the 20th century, which can only lead to increasing fundamentalism of both sides.

It is equally important to take account of growing transnationalism (see chapter 5). As a result of changes in patterns of migration, communication and mobility options, our superdiverse world is also increasingly becoming a transnational world. People might live here physically in Belgium, but a part of them also lives 'virtually' elsewhere, linked in their thoughts (and by Skype and the internet) to their homeland and to other countries where members of their family reside. Transnationalism and transmigration lead to multiple membership of different communities, with multiple relationships across nationalities and national borders as a result. The distinctions between citizens and non-citizens, inlanders and foreigners, human rights and national rights all become more blurred. This in turn makes it more difficult to distinguish between national and non-national inequalities. Consequently, this brings contradictions relating to international inequality and social justice into sharper focus within the boundaries of our nation states.

A new modernity

Migration is not only changing the world we live in, but also the way we think about reality. We in Western Europe are the product of the first age of modernity, which lasted throughout the 19th and 20th centuries. This age was dominated by 'either...or' thinking. The 'ideal' of ethnic and national homogeneity was derived from the nation states that were created during this period. But in world history as a whole, multiple ethnicity has generally been the rule, with national and ethnic homogeneity as the exception.

The continuing dominance of the national vision means that real society is being subordinated to (the rules of) the nation state. This methodological nationalism presupposes a number of existing societies that live alongside each other rather than with each other. Moreover, the world view of the social sciences is also heavily coloured by the contradistinction between national and international. As a result, we often fail to correctly interpret and understand the role of cultural plurality within our societies. We either expect a kind of universal homogenization (e.g Mc Donaldization) or else an incompatibility of different perspectives.

In contrast, cosmopolitanism means precisely the recognition and acceptance of the 'otherness' of others, ignoring (or rather transcending) the misunderstandings created by territoriality and the homogenization of culture. With the transition to a worldwide risk society and its inherent superdiversity, we are now experiencing what Beck calls the start of a new or second age of modernity, which is specific to our 21st century.

In this way, Beck's vision opens the door to the possibility of new intermediary forms of identity and ambivalence, but at the same time creates the risk of ignoring current identity and integration problems. If ambivalence is emphasized too strongly, it has a tendency to minimize or even bypass the structural discrimination that people with a migration background are currently experiencing. In short, the vision in this respect is too optimistic and too individualizing. It is not the case that all social frameworks will disappear overnight, so that people are free to choose their own identity and develop their lives as they best please, detached from all ties of family, country, nationality, history, upbringing and social class. It is true that there is indeed an increasing number of mixed forms of identity, but not every form of ambivalence offers the same opportunities for social improvement. Having said that, it is also true that the existing categories that help to determine people's choices and preferences are becoming increasingly complex and more ambivalent every day. In other words, it is important to be aware of both growing ambivalence and transnationality on the one hand, and the existing forms of group pressure that can strengthen social discrimination on the other hand.

Our cities are becoming more cosmopolitan

Whatever it minor shortcomings, the cosmopolitan view certainly helps us to understand superdiversity in society, particularly in our major urban centres. Superdiversity is slowly transforming cities like Amsterdam, Rotterdam, Brussels, Antwerp and Ghent into cosmopolitan cities. The top-down effect of globalization is being increasingly felt in the streets and squares of each of these cities. At the same time, the bottom-up effect of globalization is also being felt, with a new dynamic being clearly evident in the districts that are now occupied by peoples from all around the world. Moreover, an infrastructure is gradually being developed that reflects this superdiversity, with the arrival of special telephone and internet cafés, currency exchange and dispatch offices and an ethnic middle class of local businessmen and store holders. In the 'global city', the influence of globalization from both top and bottom merge to create a new and exciting environment, where the concept of identity is no longer the same as it once was.[7]

This leads to a curious situation where people are living close to each other, yet also separated from each other. The modern city is a place where many people meet and share a limited space, but it is also a place of avoidance, where people live alongside each other rather than together with each other. In short, modern cities not only contain a superdiverse dynamic, but also a contrasting dynamic characterized by tension and conflict, not only between 'natives' and 'non-natives', but also between many other diverse groups of inhabitants.[8]

If we look at the development of the populations in our major cities purely from a nationality perspective, it is possible to note a gradual increase in the number of nationalities present in each of them. Nevertheless, the official population statistics are giving an increasingly incomplete picture of the reality of the situation. If we want to identify and examine the true level of diversity in places like Brussels and Amsterdam, we need to look further than the bald nationality statistic recorded by the civil registration office. The classic 'national' vision based on individual nationalities has reached its limits. The truth is that our cities are much more diverse than the population statistics alone would suggest. The 'legal' city is telling us progressively less and less about the 'real' city.

If we want to go in search of real diversity in our cities from a cosmopolitan perspective, taking account of naturalizations is the first correction that we need to make to the official nationality statistics. When we think of Belgians or Dutchmen, we are all too easily inclined to think of 'autochtonen': the (white) natives. But it is not because a person holds a Belgian or Dutch passport that this person thinks of himself as a native or is treated as such by others. An increasing number of residents in both countries (and elsewhere in Western Europe) have a nationality that does not reflect their ethnicity. The simple nationality figures conceal a much larger group of residents with very different ethnic backgrounds: children of the third generation who were born here and therefore automatically receive either Belgian or Dutch nationality.

Another factor that is not taken into account by the official population statistics is the fact that many people are not formally registered in the cities where they live. Some are registered for fiscal reasons in the town where they have a second home, perhaps because the level of local tax is much lower there. Students living in temporary student accommodation in the major cities will usually continue to be registered in their home town, where their parents live. People with financial problems sometimes fail to register with the city authorities, so that their creditors cannot find them. But there is also a significant group of migrants who are not registered because they are in the process of seeking political asylum. In the 1990s, the Belgian government tried to spread asylum seekers more evenly across all the country's many municipalities. However, the majority of the asylum seekers gravitated to the major cities instead, often in search of fellow countrymen or affordable accommodation that was harder to find in the more residential areas of the smaller towns and cities. These smaller towns and cities were often glad to see them go, and some of the Public Centers for Social Welfare even offered to hire houses for them in the nearest larger city.

Although they are not included in the official population statistics, the presence of the asylum seekers in our major cities is well known. The same cannot be said for the growing number of undocumented migrants, who have never made an application for a residence permit or whose application for such a permit has been turned down, so that they must leave the country. Theoretically, their presence in the cities is 'illegal' and so they try to remain hidden from view. But in some districts there are now so many of these 'invisible ones' that they cannot help but become visible; at food distribution centres, at schools for their children or sometimes even on the streets. If they work at all, they try to do so outside the system, often as casual labourers in bars and restaurants, or in back street workshops or on building sites. Many come here searching for a better life, perhaps before returning home again, but that better life is often much harder to find than they imagined, so that their plans – and the length of their stay – frequently need to be revised (see chapter 6).

Finally, we must remember that many thousands of citizens from both old and new members of the European Union are now living in our major cities, often with a legal tourist visa or on detached duty from companies in their homeland. Others stay here illegally, working in the 'black' in low-paid jobs as cleaners, painters, handymen, etc. In many cities, the Poles are now becoming a visible group, with their own networks. They can be recognized by the many Polish number plates on our roads, from the packed 'commuter' buses that take them back and forth between Belgium and Poland, and the growing number of Polish shops, cafés and even churches in our cities. Their way of dressing is also different, as (of course) is their language. If you want to find them, they are hard to miss.

In short, anyone who looks at the diversity in our cities with a cosmopolitan view and without prejudice will see more of the superdiverse reality than the population statistics reveal, and will also learn more about the complexity of that reality. Our 'real' cities contain many thousands of residents who are not recorded in the official figures and their ethnic-cultural diversity goes far beyond a straightforward listing of different totals for different nationalities. Some cities are already majority-minority cities, and many others will become so in the near future, so that the majority of the citizens will be of a 'non-native' ethnic origin.[9]

The children colour our cities

The analysis that we have made so far only provides us with a photograph of superdiversity, a momentary image of the current situation. We can get a better picture of demographic and social change if we look at their evolution over time. This will give us a film, as it were, instead of a photo. Demography works in processes and waves, which are translated into age pyramids and cohorts, finally giving us the image of the cities we are looking for. All the major European cities are currently undergoing a period of far-reaching change. These changes are taking place faster than changes in the local political situation. The focus of most political parties on the white middle class precludes the possibility of an open debate and an open vision for diversity. As a result, the political world is not fully aware of many of the most crucial developments that are occurring. Consequently, we often see the policies of yesterday being applied to the superdiverse cities of tomorrow.

How should we imagine the situation in the real cities in twenty years' time? We can already get a glimpse of this future if we look at the nursery and primary schools of today. In most of the major cities in Flanders and the Netherlands, the majority of the children born in the big cities have at least one parent with a different ethnic background or whose mother tongue is not Dutch.

Diversity is therefore already a reality in every school in the Low Countries. Some schools have chosen to follow this path deliberately; other largely 'white' schools were forced into the decision, having no choice at the end of the 20th century but to open their doors to real world of diversity, if they wanted to survive. For this reason, it is today possible in all our schools to find (albeit in varying degrees) a wide range of different nationalities, a palette of different ethnic backgrounds and a multiplicity of different outlooks on life. The nursery and primary schools of today are a mirror image of the flow of people that will be entering the housing and labour markets in 15 to 20 years' time. If you look closely at the current populations in these city schools, you will see the diversity that will further colour those same cities in the years ahead. And the picture you will get will be much clearer than the one offered by the demographic statistics of the experts.

In Antwerp and Brussels, 70% of children under the age of 10 already come from an 'allochtoon' (non-native) background. In Antwerp, just over half of all the city's inhabitants under the age of 40 have a different ethnic background. Among the over-40s, this figure drops dramatically. In other words, the superdiversity of tomorrow will intensify even without further streams of migration. Its inevitability is guaranteed by the age structure of both the elder native population and the younger non-native population. The children and teenagers of today now colour our nurseries and schools. Tomorrow they will colour the labour and housing markets. Just as importantly, they will further colour our society as a whole – since once they reach marriageable age they will give birth to new generations of superdiverse children of their own. This demographic evolution, occurring over the next two decades, will ensure that the 21st century will truly be the century of superdiversity.

While many politicians are focussing narrowly on the further limitation of future migration (for example, by attaching stricter conditions to family reunification or asylum applications), an analysis of the current demographic situation makes clear that diversity will continue to increase, come what may. For this reason, it is more useful to enter into a dialogue about how we can best deal with superdiversity and how we can guide and shape the transitional changes that it will inevitably involve. Instead of trying to reduce the number of Moroccan or Turkish families reunited in Europe, politicians could better spend their time by trying to bring down levels of poverty among ethnic communities or by increasing appropriate educational opportunities for children with a migration background.

Cosmopolitan apartheid?

A cosmopolitan view is therefore a way of looking at and analyzing diversity, so that we can get a better picture of the real superdiversity in our cities. However, it is important to mention two key nuances, to prevent this picture becoming a distortion of the new reality.

In the first place, I use the term 'cosmopolitan' in extension of Ulrich Beck's usage; namely, as an empirical categorization that can help to better describe the new superdiverse reality in our cities, in which more and more people from different countries around the world are coming to live, while still maintaining transnational contacts with their countries of origin. In other words, it is not a normative concept that follows the Kantian tradition of universal citizenship and openness towards the world in general, or which sees the common good of all people, including 'the other', as the highest ideal. In cosmopolitan cities there are also many 'autochtoon' native residents, who are having major difficulties accepting the transition to a superdiverse society and who dream (either secretly or openly) of a return to a more familiar and less multicultural way of life.

Moreover, it is not the case that people with a migration background should automatically be seen as 'citizens of the world' or that we should attribute to them cosmopolitan and normative ideals that many of them do not possesses. In their search for something to hold onto in a strange and foreign land, many of them do indeed fall back on the familiar securities of their own community, religion or culture. Here, too, it is possible to find a small group that is against modernization. The Brussels politologist Bilal Benyaich has rightly pointed out that it is an illusion to think that 'cosmopolitan' Brussels will produce an endless stream of 'world citizens'.[10]

My second caveat follows on from this point. In superdiverse cities, even in cities were the majority of the population is made up by ethnic minorities, a large number of the inhabitants live alongside each other and not with each other. Even though ethnic-cultural diversity is increasing in many districts in our inner cities, the difference between districts with a lower number of people with a migration background and districts with a high number is immense. In these districts not only do people live separated from each other geographically, but they are also separated from each other in the labour market and even by their leisure pursuits. In other words, there are still many areas in our cosmopolitan cities where segregation or a kind of informal apartheid still takes place. These ethnic dividing lines coincide partially – but not entirely – with the socio-economic differences between the rich and the poor, and the well educated and the poorly educated.

In the novel *Open City* by the Nigerian-American author Teju Cole, the main character – Julius, a young psychiatrist with a Nigerian background – tells about his experience of a concert of classical music at Carnegie Hall in the heart of New York. *'Almost everyone, as almost always at such concerts, was white. It is something I can't help noticing: I notice it each time, and try to see past it. (...) I am used to it, but it never ceases to surprise me how easy it is to leave the hybrity of the city, and enter into all-white spaces, the homogeneity of which , as far as I can tell, causes no discomfort to the whites in them. The only thing odd, to some of them, is seeing me, young and black, in my seat or at the concession stand.'*[11]

Chapter 5

Transnational lives and families

'Wer Weltfamilien, deren Leben durch das Überschreiten von Grenzen, die Zugehörigkeit zu mehreren Staaten seine Prägung erhält, ausschließlich innerhalb eines Nationalstaates untersucht, der verfehlt die Wirklichkeit – Motive, Normen, Zwänge, Handlungschancen – von Frauen und Männern in Weltfamilien.'
Ulrich Beck & Elisabeth Beck-Gernsheim, 2011. *Fernliebe. Lebensformen im globalen Zeitalter*, p. 184-185.

More and more people are living across borders. Their lives and networks are not confined by national frontiers, but also involve contact with family and friends in their country of origin or in other countries in Europe and around the world. This growing transnationalism will become a basic characteristic of migration and superdiversity in the 21st century, according to Thomas Faist.[1] Having a cosmopolitan vision therefore also means being aware of this phenomenon. What does living across borders and in different worlds really mean? And how will it change our society?

Living across borders

Globalization has not only increased the international flow of goods, but has also increased the flow of people around the world. Tourism has already been one of the strongest international growth sectors for many years. But transnationalism is something very different from a single journey for your holidays. It means living in one land, whilst part of your life is also experienced in one or more other lands. This requires people to maintain intense personal contacts across national borders, combining different environments and cultures and travelling back and forth between different places, if not physically then at least in their minds. In this way, worldwide families can be created.[2]

These worldwide families are not only migrant families. Each year in Europe the number of families with a child studying abroad for several months as an Erasmus student is on the increase. Bringing home the washing each weekend is hardly an option in this case, but weekly contact with the home front by telephone, e-mail, internet or Skype is perfectly feasible. Facebook and other social media sites make it possible for young people to live in one place, but at the same time to maintain their networks at home with family, friends and other students. These young people are living abroad, but they are also living here, even if only for short periods at a time.

At the other end of the age spectrum, much the same is true of an increasing number of elderly people. The 'Benidorm Bastards' and all the other sixty-plussers who spend the winter in warmer climes have also developed a transnational lifestyle. During the summer months they live in Northern Europe, but once the winter approaches they head off south to the sunshine of Benidorm, Marbella and Alicante. Their pensions continue to be paid from their home countries, but for six months of the year are cashed and spent in Spain, Portugal and Italy. Their families continue to live here, with their circle of friends and acquaintances being split between here and there.

Managers with international functions in the business world, senior administrators in international organizations and top university academics are other examples of people who live transnational lives. They work abroad for a number of years, with the intention of returning home at the end of their posting, unless they decide to accept a new position overseas. Sometimes this can even lead to permanent migration. Their network of family and friends is often spread over several countries, so that a transnational approach is the only way to stay in touch.

For people with a migration background, transnational contacts are the cement that binds together their family networks across different national borders. This process of cosmopolitanization is an everyday reality for many migrant families. In some of these families, children of the second and third generation marry partners from the country of origin of their parents or grandparents. This often results in a new set of relatives in the old homeland, to add to the many other relatives and contacts who have migrated to different countries in Europe and elsewhere. A typical migrant family in Belgium might have relatives here, relatives in the land of origin and relatives in the Netherlands, France, Germany and other member states of the EU. Solidarity plays an important role in these extended family networks, a solidarity that stretches across both generations and national borders. Periods of serious economic crisis, such as are currently being experienced in Greece or Spain, give a further impulse to migration, with people from the worst affected countries travelling to join members of their family who live in countries that are better off. A good example of this is the so-called 'Spanish route': Moroccan migrants with Spanish nationality, faced with almost zero employment prospects in Spain, now regularly search out their (often distant) relatives in cities like Brussels and Antwerp, in the hope of finding work there.

Transnational networks and worlds

Within the context of diversity, we first need to look at transnationalism from the perspective of people with a migration background living here (in Belgium, the Netherlands, Northern Europe, etc.). As a result of the intensive migration process of recent decades, there are more people than ever before, certainly in the cities, who can no longer be defined by a single nationality or identity. They are part of 'transnational networks', worlds that are full of expectations, ambitions and contradictions. Transnationals are sometimes inlanders, and sometimes not, dependent on the perspective. They maintain links with their home country and with family and friends in other migration lands.

At first glance, this might seem like nothing new: most migrants have always maintained a form of contact with their country of origin. What is new, of course, is the intensity and the impact of this transnational contact in our modern world. More than a century ago, migration meant saying goodbye to your family forever. The majority of the more than two million passengers who travelled on the legendary Red Star Line from Antwerp to the United States between 1873 and 1934 were poor European migrants, hoping to find and live the American dream. At best, all they could manage was to send an occasional letter or postcard back home, which they often had to dictate to others, because they were illiterate. It usually took weeks or even months for these simple messages to arrive and just as long again before any reply was received. Even as late as the 1950s and 1960s, communication between Flemish tobacco workers in Ontario, Canada, and their families back in Belgium had scarcely improved.[3]

For the migrant labourers working in the Low Countries during this period, the distances between their host country and their homeland were much shorter, but communication was no more direct. They wrote or dictated letters, spoke messages into tape cassettes and sent them off by post. Once again, it was weeks before they got a reply. For urgent matters, it was possible to send a telegram for those living in the city, who were able to afford it. Later on, there was also the telephone.

The developments of the last half century in communications technology and mobility mean that the communication options open to migrants in the 21st century are fundamentally different from the past. Transnational contact is now within easy reach for almost everyone. Mobile telephones and telephone shops make direct conversation possible with even the remotest corners of the world. The wider availability of the internet adds the options of e-mails, social network sites and Skype. Satellite dishes and the internet also make it possible to follow the news and media in their home country, almost as if they had never left. Last but not least, the huge increase in affordable of mobility during the last 50 years, with the growth of low-budget air travel and the improvement of road and rail networks, means that it is now feasible for migrant families, even with relatively low incomes, to return regularly to their country of origin for important family events or even just for their holidays. It is also common for members of the same family to lend each other money to make these journeys possible.

But if many people with migratory roots only return sporadically to their country of origin in a physical sense, they are mentally 'commuting' backwards and forwards all the time. In this respect, there are two crucial differences between migration in the 20th and 21st centuries. Nearly all the migrants here in Belgium now have a sufficiently large network of family, friends and fellow countrymen living in relatively close proximity, so that they can experience the living environment of their country of origin in their own communities in Brussels, Antwerp or elsewhere. Moreover, regular and often intense direct contact with the homeland or with family members who have migrated to other countries, made possible by modern communications technology, is now available to even the poorest members of migrant society. As a result, transnationality has become one of the core characteristics of 21st century superdiversity.

'Having your cake and eating it, too'

The concept of transnationality stands in sharp contrast to other existing concepts in our social system. As a result, it often appears both politically and analytically provocative. It seems like the migrants are able to have their cake and eat it, too. They are 'over here', but at the same time a part of them is still 'over there'. In other words, they have found a third way between 'us' and 'them'. Or as Ulrich Beck puts it: which 'us' do we mean, when we talk about 'us'?[4] In this way, transnationalism is able to transcend methodological nationalism, which seeks to reduce multiple nationalities to the 'either...or' category. Instead, transnationalism focuses precisely on that multiplicity and the ambivalence that goes with it.

Failure to recognize multiplicity quickly leads to one-sided judgements. Migrants are often described as uprooted, un-integrated, homeless, stateless, neither one thing nor the other, etc. But this is just one side of the coin, viewed exclusively from the perspective of an outdated concept of nationality. In a superdiverse world, we should instead be seeking to recognize that the building of bridges between two or more different cultures is becoming a defining characteristic of our own society. Transnationalism is not only about difference and division, but is also about the possibility to give shape and form to your own life and your life in society within the framework of a cultural mix. In this way, Eric Corijn argues that Brussels is increasingly becoming an arrival city, where people often have a double affiliation, both to their place of origin and to their new place of arrival.[5]

Many different types of transnationality

People build their own transnational frameworks within the context of a cosmopolitan reality. In recent migration research, several reports have referred to this increasingly evident phenomenon: a series of processes through which migrants in different places forge and maintain social relations that link their host country with their country of origin. These processes are now known collectively as transnationalism, to emphasize the fact that nowadays many migrants build up social fields that cut across geographical, cultural and political boundaries.[6] It is important to realize that the bonds that tie the migrant to a nation state are not exclusive. Equally, the space in which the transnational activities of the migrant take place is not clearly divided between the 'old' country and the 'new' country. If members of the same family have migrated to different lands, we can be talking about a network that stretches across Europe.

Thomas Faist has described the development of transnational spaces, in which the key determining factor is not geographical mobility, but rather the intensity of migrant contacts across different borders. For this reason, he also refers to transnationalism as 'a way of life'. Transnational social spaces not only presuppose an attachment and interconnectedness between networks, organizations and communities across the borders of nation states, but also mean that a number of migrants effectively build and organize their lives across those borders. This might involve contacts with family or friends, business contacts, etc., but it can also involve cross-border political participation or cultural exchange. In this respect, the internet is playing an ever increasing role, allowing communities to develop that keep each other informed about various migration options and/or serve as a meeting forum once migration has taken place.[7]

Different forms of transnationality

A wide range of different cross-border contacts are concealed within the concept of transnationality. Many of these transnational contacts remain invisible for the outside world. Telephone calls are made and e-mails are sent often from the privacy of the migrant's own home. There is also a more widely available (but no less hidden) communication infrastructure that facilitates and supports transnational contacts. In superdiverse neighbourhoods the number of telephone shops and internet cafes, together with the prices they offer for their services to different countries, say much about the ethnic composition of the people living in that district, whether they are officially registered with the authorities or not. The offices of Western Union and MoneyGram provide a basic international service for cross-border financial transfers, which in money terms now exceed the level of national development aid to overseas countries.[8] Specialized travel bureaus provide cheap trips for family visits to Morocco and Turkey, for the Haj to Mecca and for other transnational visits. Equally specialized retail outlets provide products from the lands of origins or arrange for the export of products from here in the opposite direction. Last but not least, the many thousands of satellite dishes that dot the skylines of the migrant districts in cities like Antwerp and Amsterdam make clear that the migrants are not only following local media channels, but also the media channels in their homelands.

What types of contact are we talking about, exactly, and how frequently do they take place? All the relevant research is unanimous in underlining the importance of these contacts as a self-evident part of every migrant's life. Usually, the research makes a distinction between three different kinds of activity: social-cultural, political and economic. Figures for Flanders are available for the first two categories for the Moroccan and Turkish communities in Antwerp, Ghent and Genk.[9]

These figures show that the level of 'socio-cultural contacts' with family in the country of origin is still fairly intense in both communities. 57% of the people with Turkish origin who were questioned said that they still have contact with their family in Turkey at least once each week by phone or via the internet; for 9%, this contact is daily. The comparable figures for the Moroccan community are 47% and 6%. There is a similar correlation in the number of families visiting their country of ethnic origin at least once each year: 60% in the Turkish community and 54% in the Moroccan community. A massive 90% of people with a Turkish background living in Antwerp, Ghent and Genk watch Turkish language broadcasts at least once each week, with 77% of them doing this daily. The figures for those with a Moroccan background watching Moroccan programmes are 63% (weekly) and 45% (daily).[10]

For many families, one of the most frequent 'economic transnational activities' is the sending of money or goods back to family in the country of origin. However, in this case there are more significant differences between the Turkish and Moroccan communities in Flanders. 54% of people with a Turkish background say that they never send money back to Turkey and 71% say that they never send goods. One in five sends money back once each year, while just one in four do this more than once. The figures for the Moroccan community demonstrate a higher degree of transnational solidarity. Only 37% of people with a Moroccan background say that they never send money. 30% do this at least once per year and another one in three do it more than once. Almost half of the Moroccan families in Flanders also send goods back to their family in the home country at least once each year. There are also some indications that financial remittances are more common amongst first generation migrants and/or by people who migrate at a later age.[11]

The third dimension is 'political contacts', which means that migrants continue to be politically active in their country of origin from their new base in their host country. In this respect, the difference between the different ethnic communities in Flanders is considerable. Within the ranks of the political refugees, there is (as might be expected) a much greater desire to remain involved in the political life of their former homelands. In some cases, opposition to the ruling government is only possible from a safe haven abroad, where opposition groups often have quite extensive networks, particularly in Europe. Examples of this include the role played by the Zairian opposition in Belgium and the Kurdish networks in several European lands. In other cases, financial resources are gathered from within the local ethnic communities overseas to provide political and material support to opposition movements back in the country of origin. The internet and social media make cross-border participation in political activities much easier (and much safer) than it used to be. As a result, the political communities 'in exile' are becoming increasingly important. Stuart Hall contends that in future we will need to be increasingly aware of the importance of these transnational political connections. What, he rightly asks, constitutes effective membership of a political community in a world where transnational communities and relations are making it systematically more difficult to define this membership in terms of the boundaries of the nation state?[12] Another aspect of this transnationalization of political contacts is that conflicts elsewhere in the world can actually create tension between ethnic communities living here in Belgium and elsewhere in Europe, which can colour the way in which these communities are viewed.[13]

Transnational spaces

The continued existence of different forms of transnational contact has often generated a degree of mistrust within the host community. Critics see this as a lack of willingness on the part of the ethnic communities to integrate. However, Thomas Faist rightly points to the duality of the discourse about the impact of transnationalism on integration. In the case of well educated and well paid migrants, these transnational contacts are often interpreted as a facet of their upward social mobility. With poorly paid and poorly educated migrants, these same transnational contacts are seen as a sign of – and reason for – their lack of upward social mobility and their failure to integrate. Many members of the indigenous populations in Europe see a transnational orientation and transnational practices as clear evidence of the unwillingness of the migrant community to learn the language and culture of their new homeland, which they in turn regard as the primary cause for their deficient social, cultural and economic integration into the wider community as a whole.[14]

Notwithstanding this popular perception, some recent research reports indicate that transnational contacts are indeed compatible with integration and in some cases can even enhance it.[15] Research conducted among the Moroccan and Turkish communities in Antwerp, Ghent and Genk revealed that engaging in transnational activities does not necessarily exclude the possibility of successful integration. In other words, transnationalism and integration can be combined, although there is one factor in particular that continues to have a negative impact: watching television from the home country. The statistics show that the more people watch Moroccan and Turkish television, the more they feel Moroccan and Turkish and the less they feel Flemish and Belgian. In particular, homeland television acts as a block on learning the local language.[16]

In their research into the Moroccan, Turkish, Ghanaian and Chinese communities in Belgium, Nathalie Perrin and Marco Martiniello similarly found no indications that transnational practices act as a hindrance to the integration of these ethnic groups into Belgian society. On the contrary, people who are active in the transnational environment systematically increase their symbolic capital, which makes it easier for them to strengthen their position in the local community. If transnational practices have any effect on the integration process, this effect is directly the opposite of what the 'assimilationists' claim: it is not because a migrant engages in activities that are focused on his country of origin that he fails to invest time and energy in his new homeland. The experiences of those questioned as part of the project suggest that following the acquisition of a certain degree of status within their community and within wider Belgian society, people with a migration background gradually have more and more confidence in their new homeland and often reorient their activities accordingly.[17] Much of the existing research relating to transnationalism has become outdated. The rapid developments in communication technology have made transnational contacts an integral part of the way people live their lives today, with networks that stretch across borders, balancing between different societies in a world where the borders of time and space are changing and becoming ever vaguer all the time.[18]

Transmigration or multiple migrations

Transnational contacts are usually conducted within a classical pattern of single migration. The people in question have either emigrated from their homeland themselves or are the children and grandchildren of parents and grandparents who emigrated. As a result, the transnational contacts are made from a fairly stable place of residence in the host country.

However, in our superdiverse society, alongside the classic pattern of single migration, we are now increasingly witnessing more complex multiple patterns of migration, where people migrate more than once or even semi-continually. An increasingly important group of contemporary migrants come and goes, either returning to their homeland or moving on to their next destination, in a process of near continuous mobility. Often they do not know in advance how long they will stay in any one place, nor do they have much idea when their wanderings will finally come to an end, so that they can settle down more permanently at a particular location. Their available financial resources, their possession of the relevant documents, local employment opportunities and the existence of family networks are all factors that influence their choices. This type of transmigration take matters a step further than the simple preservation of transnational contacts: it is the active (rather than the virtual) living of a life that goes beyond the confines of national borders in a pattern of repeated migrations. At the same time, however, the existence of transnational contacts and networks makes this kind of flexible migration more feasible.[19]

These changing and more complex patterns of migration are part of the transition towards superdiversity. Glick-Schiller, Basch and Szanton-Blanc first introduced the term 'transmigrants' to describe a group of migrants whose day-to-day existence was characterized by multiple, simultaneous and continual associations across national borders. The public identity of this group of people is therefore created by their relationship with a number of different places and communities.[20]

This means that for transmigrants migration is not a question of a 'one-way ticket', a single act of migration following which the person or family concerned tries to establish a new life in a new land. In part of the classic migration literature, this was seen as a process that would usually take place over three generations, following which permanent rooting and integration in the host community was assumed to have been completed. This classic image, which was applicable to much of the migration to Europe during the 19th and 20th centuries, can no longer be validly used to describe migration in the globalized world of the 21st century, with its economic, societal, cultural and political interconnectivity and its social processes that transcend national frontiers. In this new context, migration for many people becomes a continual and complex process, as a result of which they remain connected to a number of different places. These people 'commute' between different countries, where they build and maintain new networks that take no account of the classic limitations set by the geographical borders of the nation states.[21]

Transmigrants cannot be defined in terms of the motives that made them leave their homeland or by their choice of their final destination, but instead by the experience they have acquired as a result of their continual crossing of borders, whether through accident, necessity or design.[22] Transmigration therefore relates to the strategies of part of the migration population that follows different trajectories and settles in different places across a number of national boundaries.

As a result, transmigrants are less oriented than other migrants on one specific country, but combine a number of ambiguous orientations that are simultaneously focused on their country of origin, the country where they are currently staying and the destination(s) to which they next plan to move. In contrast to migration strategies which aim at a long-term stay or perhaps even permanent settlement in a host country, transmigrants prefer a form of flexibility that better matches their life style, with networks and relationships at a variety of locations.

Transmigration also includes forms of circular migration (commuting between a land of origin and a temporary host country), intra-EU migration and people in transit situations. This last group usually wants to pursue a more classic linear migration trajectory, but circumstances often dictate that this is not possible, so that they need to make a number of temporary 'transit' stops, before they can ultimately reach their final destination. This, for example, is the situation of the many migrants, often without residence documents, who live in temporary camps outside the Channel ports of Flanders and Northern France, hoping one day to stow away on a lorry or train that will take them across to the 'promised land' of England.

Transmigration can also be the result of deliberate labour market choices, where people seek to take advantage of employment opportunities that require them to regularly move across national borders. This is clearly reflected in the increasing importance of intra-EU migration, certainly since the economic crisis of 2008. Many classic labour migrants in South European countries such as Spain and Italy, where they have lived and worked for many years, are now being 'obliged' to undertake a second migration to countries like Belgium, where they hope to find new jobs and a better way of life. For the majority, this is an unplanned migration: they would prefer to stay in Spain or Italy, but the economic downturn and resulting unemployment means that this is no longer possible. The crisis has turned these classic labour migrants into transmigrants and transformed their host countries into transit destinations. Other forms of trade, sometimes linked to the notorious VAT-carousel or money-laundering practices, can also contribute to transmigration.[23]

In other words, the term 'transmigration' covers a wide range of individuals and families, with an equally wide variance in the extent to which they are accepted in the countries where they stay. Dependent on their social class, economic status, gender and ethnicity, some transmigrants are treated on an equal footing with classic migrants in a number of areas of life, but are treated unequally – and therefore become vulnerable – in others.[24]

Transnational relationships and families

It is therefore clear how superdiversity in the 21st century has also globalized individual families, so that they live increasingly across different national borders. This can range from having partners, parents or children living abroad, to having whole networks of family members, friends and acquaintances spread over several different countries. Gradually, more and more research is being carried out into the nature of these transnational contacts and activities. But if we try to look at the reality behind the statistics, what does this all really mean for the families who live cross-border lives, either from necessity or choice? How have these families changed in this era of globalization and migration? How much distance can familial love actually cope with before it becomes diluted? How can new and border-transcending forms of love and meaningful family ties be developed in a world that is becoming more transnational every day? These are the core questions in the recent book *Fernliebe. Leben im Globalen Zeitalter* (Distant Love) by the German sociologists Ulrich Beck and Elisabeth Beck-Gernsheim.[25] These questions are relevant, both for the transnational families themselves, but also for the people who seek to help them during their travels through our increasingly globalized world, which forces them to confront the problems of dealing with family relationships across different national borders.

Distant Love focuses on the impact of globalization on both immediate and more distant family ties. A stock market transaction seems an unusual angle of approach to investigate family relationships, but the acquisition of Skype by Microsoft for an astronomical 5.9 billion euros in 2011 says much about the crucial significance to these relationships. Skype allows families to telephone each other free of charge via the internet, but also with a direct visual connection (using the camera in your computer or a webcam). At the time of the sale in 2011, Skype had 660 million registered users, for both professional and private conversations. The growing importance of Skype tells us much about the growth of what Beck and Beck-Gernsheim refer to as 'world families': relationships between families who live in different countries and even in different continents. It is within such families that the differences in our globalized world are reflected in concrete terms. We live increasingly in a world in which our nearest and dearest are often separated from us by considerable distances and where people who come from far away are frequently our nearest neighbours.[26]

As a result of this growth in the number of world families, new and different forms of interaction have been developed that take account of distance and proximity, or equality and inequality. The image of the 'normal' family, living within national borders – the classic Western 'nuclear' family – has now been supplemented with an alternative set of interpretations and expectations relating to family life, relationships and the bringing up of children. This has resulted in new forms of social interaction, distant or otherwise, which are regularly subject to turbulence and confrontation.

The majority of families still live in a single country with a single citizenship. The parents and the school-going children generally live in the same place and in the same house, and share a common origin and language. Nevertheless, a growing number of men, women, children and families no longer conform to this stereotypical picture. Whether by accident or design, they live and experience their familial solidarity at a distance and across various national frontiers. This does not mean that the classic national family is directly opposed to their transnational counterparts: they are merely the two different extremities of the same continuum. In other words, we are not talking about an 'either...or' situation, but rather about families that are either more or less globalized.

World families often incorporate with increasing frequency a number of global contrasts and contradictions. The key question is therefore what will happen if national borders, the international rule of law, migration legislation and the distinction between the first and third worlds all conspire to cut through transnational family ties. According to Beck and Beck-Gernsheim, for an increasing number of people the three most important existential connections – with the place where you live, with your country of origin and with your family – no longer automatically coincide as they once did.[27] In this sense, globalization is not only responsible for the growth of transnational companies, but also of transnational families.

Relationships and migration

In this globalized world, we are seeing a gradual increase in the number of cross-cultural marriages, through which people from different ethnic backgrounds seek to build a new life together. Beck and Beck-Gernsheim also regard this type of mixed relationship as a form of transnationalism, since couples often live across dividing lines of religion, culture and ethnicity within one and the same country. Transnationalism can therefore relate to families with the same cultural-ethnic background who live dispersed at more than one location around the world, but also to people with different cultural-ethnic backgrounds who currently live in one location, but with members of their families dispersed at other locations around the world. In both cases, the family is the place where the differences of our globalized world are most clearly reflected.

Beck and Beck-Gernsheim quite rightly warn us against falling into the ethnic-cultural trap: it is not because the partners come from different ethnic-cultural backgrounds that these backgrounds can automatically be used as an explanation for all their differences. Differences in relative power and ability also very often play a crucial role, particularly in terms of the relationship with the majority culture in a country. If you do not yet know the language or understand the laws of your host country, you will be more dependent on your partner who already has a better knowledge of these matters. Mixed couples are also frequently confronted with the prejudices of classic 'us-and-them' thinking.

Bicultural couples emphasize that their situation is not special, just different. They need to position themselves differently in relation to the majority culture and quickly need to become specialists in intercultural communication on a daily basis.[28] In their relationship with each other and with the outside world, they learn how to deal with cultural signals, expectations and norms. Mixed marriages are a continuous exercise in learning to live with differences. This process is not always an easy one and can sometimes be explosive, as can the reactions of both families.

At the same time, we can see that relationships and migration often go together. Family reunification as a result of marriage is for many people the easiest legal way to acquire right of residence in many European countries. Precisely because these countries try to discourage migration via asylum procedures and illegal migration of all kinds, the importance of marriage migration on the basis of family reunification is increasing in importance, also across ethnic-cultural dividing lines. In several countries, the marriage market is quite literally that: a market, with a growing level of commercialization. Relationship bureaus acts as intermediaries to find partners from the so-called 'bride-donor countries' – the Philippines, Russia, Eastern Europe, etc. – for Belgian and Dutch clients (usually men) who are eager to marry. In classic migration communities, local websites provide detailed information about how best to deal with the immigration authorities of the prospective host country. These sites are targeted at people from the same ethnic background (for example, a Belgian with a Moroccan background who opts to marry someone from his parents' or grandparents' country of origin), as well as people from different ethnic backgrounds (for example, a native Belgian who wants a young Filipino bride).

In this way, more and more world families are being created. Cultural conflicts, age differences and unequal power/abilities mean that these mixed (and often 'arranged') marriages are not always the most stable. Moreover, as the importance of marriage migration grows, so there is a tendency in the media and also in political circles to portray it negatively, almost to the point of criminalization (dixit Beck and Beck-Gernsheim).[29] As a result, there is now a twilight zone that ranges from marriages of convenience, through forced or arranged marriages, to human trafficking of the most disreputable kind. Even so, it is important to keep a proper sense of perspective. Not all mixed marriages are marriages of convenience (or worse). Many are based on genuine love and affection. An examination of the procedures applicable in Antwerp for mixed couples who want to marry in the city does indeed reveal its fair share of phony marriages, but it reveals just as many cases of honest young couples, who often feel humiliated by the interviews in which they are asked to reveal intimate details about their partners, just so they can 'prove' that they know each other sufficiently well to get married.[30]

But in such cases there is more at issue than the suspicion of a forced or fake marriage. A marriage of convenience that aims only to obtain a valid right of residence for one of the partners goes against the traditional Western idea of love and is therefore a cultural taboo. In some cases, however, these marriages are the result of an individualized group process, which we can only understand if we view it not only from the perspective of the host community, but also from the perspective of the society that the people in question are leaving behind and, in particular, the role that family networks play in that society. Marriage migration always involves the marriage of two different worlds. For many families in poorer countries marriage migration is a way to invest in the future. In our age of increasing globalization and migration, a new marriage criterion is now taking root in the lands of the second and third worlds: does the marriage of one of your children open up migration perspectives? Viewed in these terms, it is distance, not proximity, that is an attractive quality in a prospective marriage partner.[31]

In other words, if we examine the 'misuse' of marriage migration from the perspective of the country of origin, the situation immediately becomes more complex: the 'victims' of marriage migration are often also the 'perpetrators', although it might be more accurate to call them the 'actors'. These are men and women who – sometimes in discussion with their family, sometimes alone – have weighed up all the pros and cons, and have decided to exchange the certainty of a life in poverty in their homeland for the uncertainties of marriage migration and the chance of a better life in the West. They are prepared to take risks and make sacrifices in their relationship, at least until they have acquired their residence papers. It should become easier for us in the West to understand the logic behind this decision if we remember their alternative: remaining all their lives in the often miserable conditions of their country of origin. At the end of the day, these people are simply trying to better themselves – which is a basic human aspiration.

The contrast between the freely chosen romantic love of the West and the concept of the forced or convenient marriage in other parts of the world is gradually becoming more and more blurred, as a result of intermediate forms, different combinations and transitional periods. Even so, our current image of the world still takes as its starting point freedom of partner choice based on love, with equal freedom of choice regarding the procreation of children within that partner relationship. However, the increasing individualization of society in the West means that these partner relationships are often no longer for life and that a successive number of freely chosen relationships is now becoming much more common. This has resulted in the creation of a complex range of composite families. Western society has come to terms with these developments but seems to have more difficulty in adjusting to the very different views on personal relationships that exist in other parts of the world and are often reflected in migration communities. These different views often collide – as recent research into false marriages, divorce conflict and family counselling clearly shows. These are problems faced every day by local government officials, judges and social workers. And also, of course, by the people involved in the relationships themselves.

Maternal love from afar?

Transnational relationships are not just about partner relationships; they are also about the relationships between parents and their children. Meg Wilkes Karraker has analyzed the development of 'global care chains': personal networks of paid or unpaid family care workers operating across the borders of different nation states.[32] In their description of what they call 'the nanny industry', Beck and Beck-Gernsheim have shown how Filipino mothers and mothers from other migration countries leave behind their own children to look after the children of Western families as a nanny or nursemaid in Europe or the United States. The children who stay behind in the Philippines are then raised by other family and/or friends. The geographical distance that this kind of arrangement involves challenges our traditional Western image of the essential proximity of family relationships, just as the cultural distance involved challenges our image of love within those relationships.

With the feminization of migration in the 21st century and the growing need for (family) care workers in the West, women are occupying an increasingly important position within the flow of migrant labour. Nowadays, there are a growing number of 'non-native' female employees amongst the staff of Europe's retirement homes and hospitals, but also in the home care sector, where many migrant women now work as cleaners, cooks or general carers. Some of this work is 'official' – for example, through the social service voucher system in Belgium; some of it is undeclared. Families with two incomes and single-parent families also (need to) make use of child-minders, babysitters and au pairs, who are often women who have left their own children behind in their country of origin. In the West, we are witnessing a 'care drain' to our kitchens and nurseries in the private sector and to retirement homes and child care facilities in the public sector.

This reflects classic gender patterns. The dominant view of most people in the West is that migrant women are less emancipated that their

Western counterparts and that traditional patriarchal ascendancy still plays a major role in many non-Western cultures – although we should also remember that our contemporary ideal of equality between men and women is the result of a feminist struggle for emancipation that took place as recently as the final decades of the 20th century. But what happens if we view these classic gender patterns from the perspective of the countries of origin? Beck and Beck-Gernsheim have shown that migrant women in world families often make greater strides forward in social and economic terms than women from their ethnic communities who do not migrate. Migration often strengthens their position and leads to them being treated more equally by the host community. For example, divorce is legally possible and culturally acceptable in the West, whereas this is not always the case in their homelands.

Marriage migrants win prestige in the families they leave behind in their country of origin, but they often arrive in the host country at the very bottom of the social ladder.[33] Once again, however, Beck warns us against the unhealthy influence of methodological nationalism in our thinking and research. If we truly want to understand the position of world families, we cannot do so by using an exclusively Western approach. We must also learn to see the field of tension that exists between our world and the migrant's world, a tension that is reflected in these families. Only then will we be able to understand the status discrepancies that often exist in their relationships. People at the bottom of the social ladder in Belgium may nonetheless enjoy greater prestige and prosperity than their families back in their country of origin. These are the mechanisms that govern the solidarity between the migrant family here and their relations back home, which helps to explain, for example, why poor migrant families in Brussels or Amsterdam continue to send part of their very modest income back to their homeland each month by Western Union, so that their distant relatives can share in their 'good fortune'.

If we are prepared to consciously develop a transnational way of looking at things, writes Elisabeth Beck-Gernsheim, we will be better able to understand the way of life and the way of thinking of groups of people who have migrated themselves or whose parents migrated, but are still excluded from the 'majority' culture of their host country. It is only by abandoning our monocultural assumptions that we can move beyond the misunderstandings that continue to dominate the debate about migration.[34]

Towards a multiplicity of different family models?

In recent decades, it was above all the cities that won ground as the places where new forms of relationship established themselves alongside the more traditional family models. There are more singles, more LAT relationships and more same-sex couples. The growing superdiversity and transnationality that is becoming evident in our cities as a result of globalization is also leading to further changes in family structures. The position of the classic Western family model of the 20th century is no longer undisputed in our modernity – or so argue Beck and Beck-Gernsheim. Although it is still dominant for the time being, in the cities it is certain to become just one model amongst many. In this increasing multiplicity of intermediate relational forms, which vary in time and space, the differences between the national, territory-related families and the mobile, transnational families will gradually begin to fade.[35]

The world families, in which wide-ranging family networks play an ever more important role, serve as a counterbalance to the individualizing tendencies of Western family policy in recent decades. The loyalty that these world families display across national borders can sometimes clash with the loyalty to the host nation state (and its ideas) that is sometimes demanded of newcomers. Compare, for example, the expectations that Western society has of people hoping to find a partner against the expectations of families back in the country of origin.

Twenty years ago in their book *The Normal Chaos of Love*, Beck and Beck-Gernsheim examined the multiplicity of relational models that would develop if, as a result of an ever intensifying process of individualization, relationships were no longer concluded exclusively within the confines of a lasting marriage. More recently, they have extended the scope of their investigations to include the new and normal chaos of global relationships and world families. In this context, they have elaborated a new model for these families based on five key dimensions or characteristics.[36]

In the first instance, globalization and the creation of world families ensures that 'the excluded other' now becomes a part of our world and our lives. This can happen via the meeting of children at school, or through the employment of these 'others' as nannies, cleaners, painters and plumbers, or because you buy things at one of their all-night stores. All these seemingly trivial matters help day by day to bridge the gulf between North and South, between rich and poor countries, between 'us' and 'them'.

Secondly, world families rapidly become experts in cross-border communication. This does not only mean across the borders imposed by nation states or by geographical distance, which can now be bridged thanks to the developments in communications technology during the past quarter of a century, ranging from the mobile phone, through Skype, to the provision of a public infrastructure in the form of telephone shops and internet cafes. It also means communication across cultural borders. And it is precisely this latter aspect that makes world families the pioneers of intercultural networks and exchange.

The third dimension relating to the growth of world families is the fact that global inequality is suddenly given a name and a face in Western society by virtue of the presence of these families. The national family has traditionally been seen (not always justifiably) as an equalizing institution: its members usually – but not always –

belong to the same social class. They are poor, rich or middle class, with relatively slow inter-generational mobility. In world families, the growing inequality is contained within the family itself and spread over different continents. These differences help to stimulate both family solidarity and chain migration.

The fourth characteristic of world families is that they transcend national laws with increasing frequency. They are confronted with national visa and migration regulations, nationally organized social security systems, and national legislation that gives shape and form to familial solidarity. In a growing number of countries, the right to family reunification is being linked to income and language requirements. Investigations into so-called marriages of convenience are becoming ever more rigorous. At the same time, differences in national legislation also stimulate migration flows, since members of the same family will try to join each other in the countries where the prevailing laws and regulations make this possible. Intra-EU migration, the asylum regulations and the rules for family reunification all illustrate the relative shifts in the position of different countries on these matters, based on amendments to their national legislation. Divorce-related issues are a typical case in point. After a divorce, it is becoming more and more common for one of the ex-partners to go and live with family in a different country. In these circumstances, the division of property or the enforcement of alimony payments cannot be arranged within the framework of a single national legislation. In Belgium, social workers in the local Public Centres for Social Welfare are confronted daily with these legal differences, when divorced people are forced to try and pursue their right to alimony across national borders.

As the fifth and final dimension characteristic of world families, Beck and Beck-Gernsheim cite their continuing struggle to comply with the image and definition of what constitutes 'a good family'. This is an area were different world views often collide head-on. The criticism of newcomers often expressed by the majority community in the West is that the family structure of migrant families is too patriarchal, authoritarian and unequal in its treatment of women. On the reverse side of the coin, migrant families often experience the individualization of Western society as a betrayal of familial solidarity, which allows individuals too much personal freedom. This conflict of loyalties frequently persists into the second and third generations of world families, in children and grandchildren who are born and brought up here.

Although Beck and Beck-Gernsheim have devised this model based on a number of common characteristics in an attempt to better understand world families, they are perfectly aware that the prototypical world family does not exist. It is (and will remain) a collective term to describe a growing plurality of family practices that transcend the frontiers of the first, second and third worlds, even to the level of intimate personal relationships. Such families embody the field of tension between the centre and the periphery, between Western and non-Western modernity – a dynamic that it is impossible for us to understand from a purely national perspective.

Challenges for family policy

In the 21st century, there will be more and more families who are not attached to just a single country. Instead, they will be transnational, with roots in a number of different places. It is short-sighted to continue viewing this development from a purely nationalistic point of view. It is equally short-sighted to view the situation exclusively in terms of problems. If we want a better understanding of the real situation and wish to avoid moral prejudice, we need greater insights into the dynamic and the conflicts that operate within these world families.

World families are not by definition open to the outside world. Although they live across borders and across cultures, many such families are actually very closed in their approach to others, so that their attitudes are often seen as traditional and anti-modern. Hostile images of this kind within the majority community serve only to strengthen this isolation and discourage openness towards the wider society of the host country. For this reason, world families represent a serious challenge for regional and national policy-makers throughout Western Europe to develop an inclusive policy for migration, integration and family matters. For people who confuse integration with assimilation, this is a threatening prospect. For people who see integration as a process of mutual change, this can open up interesting new perspectives. In this respect, there is certainly a need for further research to empirically define the evolution of transnational family relationship.

In particular, the superdiversity of transnational families must have an impact on family policy. In recent decades, there has already been a considerable broadening of the different types of relational model. In the 21st century, it will also be necessary to take account of a growing number of world families and transnational family relationships. Current family policy fails to do this sufficiently. For example, the Flemish policy note 'Welfare, Health and Family 2009-2014' limited itself to the self-evident conclusion that the number of children in 'allochtoon' (non-native) families will continue to increase. The policy note for 2014-2019 at least goes a step further, by including the transition to superdiversity in its general analysis of the situation, but this analysis is expressed largely in terms of culture-sensitive concerns.[37] However, the challenges for family policy in age of superdiversity go much further than this.

Ethnic cultural diversity leads to an increasing plurality of family structures, with family networks operating across and beyond national frontiers. The growth in transnational families therefore demands a whole new approach in many areas of family policy. For example, there is still much work to be done to achieve a standardization of family law throughout the European Union. Greater attention also needs to be paid to the family dimension of migration policy, since this is often in direct conflict with current asylum and migration regulations. There is also considerable room for improvement in the field of social protection for families across different national borders. This includes the more efficient exchange of social security details between countries, so that rights acquired elsewhere can provide prompt and adequate assistance in the new host country. We are already familiar with the problem of securing the prompt payment of alimony within our own national borders – a problem that becomes even more difficult if the demands for payment need to be made across national frontiers, even within the EU. And which legal system will define the rights of children within a transnational family?

Meg Wilkes Karraker argues for the development of a global and inclusive concept for both the immediate and the wider family, which makes room for the multiplicity of relationships that exist between children, adults and parents and which also sets out familial rights and responsibilities, in some instances across the borders of time and space.[38] A family policy that responds to the realities of transnational and superdiverse environments can offer huge benefits to all concerned, but progress to date has been slow. Nevertheless, the demographic evolutions and the chain migration of the coming decades leave us with no other choice: we must develop measures that allow us to absorb and make best use of the dynamic inherent in transnational family relationships. It is the only realistic way forward.

Chapter 6

The hidden city

'No-one knows better than you, wise Kublai, that you should never confuse a city with the words used to describe it.'
Italo Calvino, 2003. *De onzichtbare steden* (The Invisible Cities), p. 68.

Urbanity in the 21st century means more than ever before living in diversity. However, this observation is often misunderstood. People too readily assume that this only applies to the city's indigenous inhabitants. But in an age of superdiversity this is no longer the case. In cities where more than half the population already have (or will soon have) a non-indigenous ethnic-cultural background, bringing together many different people from many different places all around the world, living in increasing diversity is something that will be experienced by *all* the city's inhabitants, irrespective of their origin and how long they have lived there.

The official city versus the real city

The population statistics show clearly that the transition to a superdiverse society is taking place most rapidly in the major cities. This conclusion is based on official statistics; in other words, the statistics that record the number of people officially registered in the city. But behind this official city there is also an unseen, unofficial city, the city where the true reality of superdiversity is to be found. If we wish to properly understand the complexity of our modern cities, we need to go in search of this real city.

The first group that does not appear in the official population statistics is the asylum seekers. For procedural reasons, they are simply not included. Instead, their presence in Belgium is recorded in a so-called waiting register, where their name remains until their request for asylum has been either granted or denied. In Belgium at the beginning of 2013 (before the actual refugee crisis of 2015), there were 62,000 asylum seekers whose applications were still pending. These people either live in municipalities that have set up (or been required to set up) asylum centres or else they gravitate towards the big cities. 4,000 of these asylum seekers were known to be living in Antwerp in 2013. The figure for the Brussels Region is thought to be over 10,000. Yet although these people live in the cities, they remain invisible in terms of the official statistics, where they will only be included when (or if) their asylum request is granted.[1]

Asylum seekers have a legal status in the city until their application is completed. But the city is also increasingly providing shelter for a growing number of people without a proper legal status: undocumented migrants or the so-called 'sans-papiers' or 'people without papers'. Officially, these people do not exist, neither for the national authorities nor for the municipal authorities of the places where they live. We all know that they are there, but they move largely in the shadows, where they remain unseen (certainly for our policymakers). Occasionally, researchers try to find out more about these undocumented migrants,[2] although the very nature of their situation means that reliable information is hard to come by.

Legally, undocumented migrants cannot work. Nor are they able to apply for social security benefits or other public welfare help. Even so, thanks to their own ingenuity, many thousands of them still find a place to live and a way to make a living in our big cities. Voluntary aid organizations, soup kitchens and food distribution centres all indicate that the number of such people has been increasing in the last decade. As a result, their importance within the city has also been increasing. They take on poorly paid and unpopular jobs on an 'informal' basis (as part of the black economy) and live in the worst rooms and buildings rented out by the secondary accommodation market. However, their children do have the right to go to school, since this is a basic right guaranteed to all children under the terms of the European Convention on the Exercise of Children's Rights. Taken together with the official migrants (asylum seekers, family unifiers, EU migrant labourers, individual regularizations, etc.), these people without papers help to strengthen the rapid increase in ethnic-cultural diversity that is taking place within so many European cities.

Most reports on migration are based on what we know, and therefore use the registered migration figures contained in the official population statistics. However, alongside the official channels of migration there are also various unofficial channels. The growing stringency of the conditions attached to legal migration means that these 'informal' channels are becoming ever more popular. In other words, there is a growing shift from legal migration towards other, less structured forms migration.[3] As a result, the differences between the legal city and the real city are becoming greater all the time. If we want to understand how European cities are truly developing and discover which dynamics are active in the superdiverse districts within these cities (which are often the arrival districts, also for undocumented migrants), then it is essential that we devote more attention to the presence of those who live in our major urban centres without a proper legal status.

'Irregular' residence of this kind can take many different forms. For example, applicants whose requests for asylum have been turned down often remain in the country, usually while they await the outcome of the appeal procedure or prepare the submission of a new request, or perhaps in the hope that they might benefit from a humanitarian or medical regularization of their situation. Others arrive on a tourist visa and then simply stay on once the visa has expired, without making any formal application for permanent residence. Yet others are smuggled in by human traffickers.

Like the migrants with legal accreditation, these various groups all tend to find their way to the big cities. There are only two ways to gain some impression of the actual numbers of these people. The first is an analysis of the number of requests for urgent medical help submitted by undocumented migrants to the Public Centres for Social Welfare of the places where they live.[4] The second is the response to the collective regularization campaigns that are sporadically held (most recently in Belgium in 2000 and 2009).[5]

The importance of regularization campaigns

The presence of large groups of people in countries and cities without papers is undesirable for a number of reasons. Some people regard this as a negation of the rule of law and argue that it amounts to an unofficial relaxation of the immigration legislation. For others, it is a humanitarianly unacceptable situation, which leads to the creation of a growing underclass without rights and protection, especially in the cities. Yet others think that it has dangerous implications for social order. Depending on the way it views the situation, a government can respond in different ways.

In broad terms, these responses include expulsion (deportation, compulsory repatriation, voluntary repatriation, etc.), the regularization of individual cases (for humanitarian or medical reasons) and (very occasionally) collective regularization. Some countries simply ignore the situation and do nothing, but in most cases national policy is based on a mixture of these three strategies, although there often remains a large grey area, where the presence of people without papers is tolerated to a certain extent, leading (as feared by some) to a de facto underclass of the stateless and the rightless.

Although deportations, voluntary repatriations and individual regularizations are taking place on a continual basis, the experiences of the past decades suggests that these have been insufficient to prevent the gradual but steady increase in the number of undocumented migrants. For this reason, governments periodically decide to allow a collective regularization, which gives the people without papers the chance for a limited period to come forward and apply for permanent residence, providing they can satisfy a number of criteria. Several countries have applied this option in recent years, including Spain (2005), Germany (2007) and the 'General Pardon' in the Netherlands (also 2007). During his second term of office, the American President Barak Obama also tried to secure an amnesty for the young undocumented Mexicans in the United States. As far as Belgium is concerned, there have been two such regularization campaigns during the past 15 years, in 2000 and 2009.[6] In both instances – as is always the case with campaigns of this kind – there was a strongly polarized debate between those in favour and those against.

For researchers, however, these collective regularization campaigns are a golden opportunity to gain deeper insights into the scale, composition and places of residence of at least a part of the population of undocumented migrants. At the same time, regularizations on this larger scale have a significant demographic impact on certain cities and city districts, since the acquisition of legal documentation opens up for the holders the possibility to bring their partners and children into the country as part of a process of family reunification. The underestimation of the effects of this chain migration after the regularization campaign in 2000 was one of the reasons why the demographers and urban watchers failed to correctly assess the level of population growth in Belgian cities during the past decade.[7]

Having said this, it is surprising (and to many incomprehensible) that so little use is made of the opportunity provided by regularizations to conduct systematic research. As far as the government is concerned, there are probably political reasons for this: there are other policy domains were they prefer to work with 'evidence based' figures. But while this might be to some extent understandable, it is less clear why the research community showed so little interest in the most recent regularization campaigns. It took almost ten years before the first modest report into the follow-up of the 2000 campaign was published.[8] There are no signs that the federal authorities intend to conduct extensive research into the outcome and consequences of the 2009 regularization.

Undocumented migrants in Antwerp

In Belgium, the lack of research at the federal (national) and regional (Flemish) levels has been compensated, in part at least, by the availability of data at city level. For the 2000 campaign, we know that the greatest number of applications for regularization were made in the big cities: Brussels, Antwerp, Liege, Charleroi and Ghent.[9] For Antwerp, sufficient data is available from both the regularization campaigns to allow a detailed analysis to be made of the official profile details of all the applicants in 2000 and 2009. This gives us a unique picture of this important group of people without papers in the city, not only in terms of their basic demographic composition, but also their concentrations and distribution. This picture is by no means complete: we must remember that it is based on two snapshots of a situation that is constantly changing. Moreover, we have no way of knowing how many undocumented migrants decided not to submit an application, because they were unaware of the opportunity, did not trust the system or did not satisfy the stipulated criteria.[10]

Notwithstanding these limitations, the regularization campaigns nevertheless allowed Belgium's major cities to be better documented than ever before. During the 2009 campaign, 7,283 applications for regularization were submitted in Antwerp, good for more than 10,000 people who had been in the city or the country without papers for a considerable length of time. In 2000, there were 4,872 regularization applications.

To measure the impact of this population on the city and its districts, we need to look at the proportional difference between the number of undocumented migrants who submitted a regularization application and the total number of officially registered inhabitants. This reveals that in 2009 there were 15 applicants per 1,000 head of the registered population (in comparison with 10 per 1,000 in 2000). In relative terms, this proportion of applicants may seem small, but in absolute terms they represent a significant group, even for a city the size of Antwerp. But to estimate the real impact of this group, we need to look behind the average figures for the whole city and examine more closely at their distribution in the city's different districts. Undocumented migrants can be found in all parts of the city, but there are clear concentrations in certain places, where this usually 'hidden' population becomes visible, as a result of both their absolute and relative numbers (see below).

In particular, two important factors determine the countries and/or regions of origin of people without papers in our cities. The first and most important factor is the presence (or absence) of people from the same country-region or ethnic-cultural group in the city in question. Unofficial migration frequently follows in the wake of official migration. The increasing level of transnationality (see chapter 5), with the accompanying development of strong familial or ethnic-cultural networks, online communication possibilities and relatively easy/cheap mobility between different lands, mean that the presence of legally regularized immigrants in a city is an important pull-factor for chain migration, both formal and informal.

In addition, the classic push factors in the country of origin also play a role; factors such as war, extreme poverty and the effects of climate change. Nor should the effects of institutional change be underestimated, such as the expansion of the European Union, which had a clear impact on migration flows and the profiles of undocumented migrants during the first decade of the 21st century.

For many years, migrants from Morocco and Turkey have been the most numerous groups of non-European migrants in Antwerp. These two countries were also at the top of the list of the countries of origin for the applicants in the regularization campaigns of both 2000 and 2009. In particular, people from Morocco used the regularization process to convert their 'informal' stays with their friends and relatives into an officially recognized right of residence. More than 2,300 of the applications in 2009 were submitted by people of Moroccan origin, in comparison with just one in five in 2000. As far as Turkish undocumented migrants are concerned, the level of increase in the number of applications between 2000 and 2009 was less dramatic, although applicants from the Turkish community still form the second largest group.

During the 2000 regularization campaign, undocumented Polish migrants formed the third largest group of applicants. However, there were very few Polish applicants during the 2009 campaign, since Poland's accession to the European Union in the interim means that Polish nationals now have the right to stay in Belgium for short periods on a tourist visa, whereas Poles in employment can legally stay here for much longer periods on the basis of the EU principle of the free movement of labour.

But the hidden city is also the home of many much smaller groups of undocumented migrants from all around the world: from Sub-Saharan Africa (with Senegal, Nigeria and Ghana in the lead), from North Africa (Algeria and Egypt), from Asia (India and Pakistan). One of the more noticeable features in the statistics for the 2009 campaign was the marked increase in the number of regularization applications from China. This was also a consequence of chain migration: there has been a Chinese community in the harbour city of Antwerp for many years, supplemented in recent decades by a further influx of political refugees from Tibet.

Without papers, but not without a job?

The large majority (80%) of the regularization requests in Antwerp were submitted by single people. Just 9% were submitted by two-person households. Larger families made up the remaining 11%. However, this does not mean that the people who submitted their applications as ' single' actually lived in the city as single or intend to stay here in the future as single. Many of them were living in accommodation provided by family or friends of the same ethnic-cultural background, and just as many have partners and children back in their countries of origin, who they hope will one day be able to join them. The granting of formal residence to one member of a family brings with it (subject to certain conditions) the right to family re-unification. In this way, regularization usually leads to an increase in chain migration. Dispatching a single migration 'pioneer' in this way is now a common tactic in migration countries to secure long-term multiple migration.

People who migrate illegally are usually of working age. Roughly 90% of the applicants for regularization in Antwerp were between the ages of 20 and 49 years. Only 2% of the applications were for children and juveniles, with just 1% for the over-60s in 2009.

The age of undocumented migrants is relevant for two reasons. Because the large majority are of active working age, this can have a considerable impact on the local job market, by providing a potential pool of extra labour. In addition, the age distribution of the applicant's is also crucial for demographic developments in the longer-term. More than 70% of the regularization applicants in 2009 were between 20 and 39 years. In other words, they were of marriageable and child-producing age. The population prognosis issued by the Study Agency of the Flemish Government predicts that the population in Antwerp will rise to some 600,000 by 2028.[11] These figures take no account of the 2009 regularization, since they were based on the official population statistics for 2008. The real increase is therefore likely to be significantly higher – as is the proportion of inhabitants with a migration background.

Hidden in plain sight

Districts with a high level of diversity usually contain a higher level of undocumented migrants. This is borne out by the regularization statistics for Antwerp, where the districts with the greatest ethnic-cultural diversity also had the highest numbers of regularization applicants. These are the districts where they can rely on family networks or networks of others who speak the same language, share the same faith or come from the same country. What is most noticeable about the statistics is the difference in the number of paperless inhabitants in each district and their high concentrations in the most deprived areas. To an even greater extent than the classic population data, the regularization data emphasizes the ethno-stratification and social layering of the city, as well as the growing polarization that this engenders.

It has already been mentioned that the average figure for undocumented migrants for Antwerp as a whole in 2009 was fifteen per thousand head of population. But in the richer (and largely white) suburbs of Wilrijk and Ekeren, far removed from the city centre and its 19th century girdle of development, this figure drops to less than one per thousand. This is in sharp contrast to the position in the superdiverse districts in the heart of the city, mainly concentrated in Antwerp-North. Here there are often fifty or more applicants for every thousand inhabitants. This means that for every twenty officially registered residents, there is at least one undocumented migrant living 'unofficially' in the same district. The only way that these districts can support this one-in-twenty population with no source of official income is by employing them in the local black economy, which is therefore a significant economic factor at district level (but also at a wider level in important parts of the city). In addition to Antwerp-North, large concentrations of people without papers are found in Borgerhout intra-muros, in Deurne-North, in the southern part of Merksem and in the impoverished areas of the Kiel and Hoboken-North.

Unfortunately, we know very little about what has happened in these districts after regularization. The research follow-up to the 2000 regularization campaign was modest in the extreme, with just a single, belated project to try and track the trajectories followed by regularized applicants. This 'before-and-after' study shows how the professional integration of the applicants often follow very different pathways: from highly successful labour market careers to a group of people who are still living on long-term benefit and are there for in a vulnerable position of dependence. After regularization, language continues to be an important threshold, particularly in Flanders, but the general level of education and health in the home country are also important explanatory factors for a person's social position.[12]

Similarly, we also know very little about the contributions made by undocumented migrants to both the formal and informal economies in the cities. During the 2000 regularization procedure, some 75% of the applicants said that they had been in some form of employment prior to their application.[13] Sadly, there is no comparable figure for 2009. An examination of the requests for supplementary assistance from the Public Centre for Sociale Welfare by regularized applicants indicates that that the employment of many of them was concentrated in specific (and often low-paid) sectors: building, catering (hotels and restaurants), domestic cleaning, fruit-picking, etc. Moreover, regularized migrants often testify that their previous 'informal' employment – frequently with a rate of pay far below the legal minimum wage – was terminated by the employer once they had acquired their legal papers. This highlights the contradiction inherent both in current policy and in the lives of people without papers: officially, they are not supposed to be here, but their unofficial presence is crucial for several important sectors of the economy.

Let us assume for a moment that at the end of next week all the undocumented migrants in Belgium will go on strike, refusing to work further on an informal basis. What would be the effect? How many building sites (large and small) would continue to operate at full capacity? How many textile workshops would be forced to close down? How many homes and offices would remain uncleaned? How much fruit would rot on the trees and which vegetables would lie unharvested in the fields? How many cars would remain unrepaired in back-street garages? How many children would have to stay at home because the nurseries and after-school care centres have closed their doors? How many brothels would have to turn away half their customers? How many dishes would remain unwashed in restaurants and how many customers would go hungry because there are no longer any waiters to serve them? In some sectors, the unofficial labour market almost seems like a pre-condition for the continued operation of the regular economy. But at the same time, we must not forget that it is also a way for some unscrupulous employers to make exorbitant profits through the exploitation of a vulnerable workforce and the avoidance of social insurance obligations.

Another bone of contention is the possible effect of undocumented migrants- who are without a reliable source of income – on public safety in the city. Most of the 'paperless ones' try to remain out of public view. As a result, some of them find their way into criminal milieus, which also thrive on the shadowy side of urban life. The dividing line between an informal survival strategy and criminal activities is sometimes very thin. This not only means a drift into petty street crime, but can also involve more serious illegal activities, such as drugs and prostitution.[14] In particular, the police in Antwerp are constantly complaining about the use of young undocumented adolescents as easily replaceable runners for the drugs trade in the city. People without papers also often remain very dependent on the organized gangs of human traffickers who smuggled them into the country in the first place.[15]

Arrival districts

Every country has its arrival cities, and every arrival city has its arrival districts – or so writes Doug Saunders.[16] These are the districts where the majority of the newcomers first settle and find a place to live. In the poorer South, these districts are often slums and shanty towns, with self-made 'housing' (if so it can be called), which later develop into integral parts of the city. In the more prosperous North, these are often the existing districts in the big cities where the newcomers can find family, friends and fellow-countrymen who can help them, or where they can find a cheap room or a mattress to hire. These are the places where the new arrivals take their first steps in a (for them) new world. This is where they must learn how to slowly climb the social ladder. These are also the districts where undocumented migrants find it easiest to adjust and survive. In each of these districts there is a 'connectivity infrastructure', which allows them to maintain various forms of contact with the homeland: telephone shops, internet cafes and offices of Western Union or MoneyGram.[17]

Superdiversity is at its strongest in the cities and, within the cities, in the arrival districts. Elsewhere in the country and in some of the more outlying areas of the cities, it is possible for people and groups of different ethnic-cultural origin to live alongside each other, in a kind of informal spatial apartheid within a white majority culture. But in the inner cities, and certainly in the arrival districts, frequent contact and (often as a consequence) confrontation with the 'other' is most people's experience of day-to-day life; in apartment buildings, on the street, in local ethnic stores, at the school gate, on the tram or the bus, in cafes or in the park.[18]

In the cities of arrival, argues Eric Corijn, writing of Brussels, the traditional institutions for the socialization of people in the context of families, schools, media, culture, etc., is insufficiently adjusted to the changing realities of a superdiverse society. As a result, a variety of 'intermediate' societies develop, informal organizations whose purpose is to ensure the necessary degree of self-regulation. These informal networks offer newcomers all the information they need to survive: about letting and sub-letting, about informal job opportunities, about free medical help and food distribution, about lawyers who can help provide papers and about the assistance offered by welfare institutions. These networks supplement what Ash Amin refers to as the 'commons' of the migration cities: shared spaces, infrastructure and services.[19] This where the first tentative steps towards integration occur at street level, months or even years before some migrants are eligible to follow an official integration course. It is in this manner that real integration often starts: with informal advice about how best to survive in the arrival districts.

More than 40 years ago, Herbert Gans published his 'classic' article entitled *The positive functions of poverty*.[20] The article was never intended to be cynical, but investigated in all seriousness the purposes that poverty could (and, to some extent still can) validly serve in a society. If a society wants to eliminate poverty, which, in the opinion of Gans, must be the objective of every just society, it is first necessary to find alternatives for the functions that poverty and, by extension, the poorest people fulfil in that society. Translated into our modern superdiverse world, this means: what do we know about the 'positive functions' carried out by people without papers on behalf of our urban economy? Without ignoring the negative aspects of the situation, such as organized exploitation and large-scale social insurance avoidance, greater insights into these matters can help us to understand the motives and mechanisms of migration in all its different forms, not only from a domestic perspective, but also from the equally important external perspective. It will also help us to understand the role that the major urban centres play in this process, particularly with regard to undocumented migrants. The regularization campaigns of the past fifteen years gave us a brief glimpse into the hidden world of our cities, but much more research still needs to be carried out into the role of this world and the way it operates, if we want to gain a more realistic picture of urban development and arrival district dynamics in this century of superdiversity.

Chapter 7

They should just learn how to integrate...

'The only annoying thing about S was her profession: intercultural communication. Who the hell dreamt that one up? During our first intercultural meeting there was no communication, just subjection.'
Anil Ramdas, 2011. *Badal*, p. 244.

'They should just learn how to integrate...' That is the expectation that a host community usually has of its migrants. But is this expectation really clear? What exactly is integration? And at what point does someone becomes integrated? It is a term that covers many different messages, not always apparent to those for whom they are intended. How do the migrants themselves understand the term? And, above all, is the concept still workable in today's superdiverse and transnational societies?

What exactly do we mean?

Migration processes are processes of alienation, according to the Dutch sociologist Paul Scheffer in his book *Het land van aankomst* (Immigrant Nations).[1] Whoever migrates automatically finds himself in a different and 'alien' society. People speak a different language, (sometimes) live according to different norms, have different customs, practice an unfamiliar religion, etc. Finding your way in a new society is not easy. If you and I were to emigrate to China tomorrow, we would carry with us our personal life history and a great deal of other cultural 'baggage': our language, our upbringing, our habits, our family contacts, ... Yet at the same time, we would also have to find a place in Chinese society, a society that knows very little about our baggage. In this respect, language is an important lever, but it is not enough by itself. There is so much more besides.

However, migration is not only a process of change for the person who migrates, but also for the host community. Sometimes, this can also provoke a feeling of alienation. People see other and often very different new neighbours in their once familiar street, district or city. What's more, these new neighbours (certainly at first) speak a different language and have different ways of doing things. New ethnic shops and restaurants begin to appear, gradually altering the streetscape beyond recognition. The composition of the classes in the local school also starts to change. Sometimes, this diversity can enrich the local community; sometimes, it leads to conflicts, great or small. From whichever perspective you view it, migration always involves adjustment. Newcomers need to find a place in the host society and the host society has to make room to accommodate the newcomers.

This process of adjustment can lead to different results in different places. Even so, in the sociological literature we can see a similar pattern of analysis with various authors.[2] They sketch a matrix with four (ideotypical) ways to deal with the adjustment. Firstly, what does the migrant identify with? Does he try to retain his own culture? Does he identify with his own ethnic group? Secondly, does he attempt to adjust to the new society? Can he identify with the majority community? These questions result in a table that shows two extreme positions, with 'yes' or 'no' as the answer possibilities in each case. Depending on the answers, the migrant will be classified into one of the four ideotypical categories: marginalization, segregation, assimilation and integration. Of course, we all know that in real world people do not function in such clear black-and-white terms along either axis: instead, the vast majority of people attempt to hold on to elements of their own culture, whilst at the same time adjusting to some elements of the host society. That being said, this categorization still provides useful way of looking at the integration debate; a debate in which the concept of 'integration' itself seems to be constantly shifting.

Processes of adaptation after migration		Retains own culture/identifies with own ethnic group	
		No	Yes
Adjusts to the host country/identifies with the majority community	No	**Marginalization**	**Segregation**
	Yes	**Assimilation**	**Integration**

When a migrant relinquishes his identification with his own culture completely but makes no attempt to adopt the norms and customs of the host country, we speak of marginalization. This person is totally isolated. He has lost his links with his past, but has made no effort to create new connections for the present and the future. Fortunately, this situation, in its extreme form, is relatively rare, although its more 'moderate' form is more commonplace. People in this marginalized category have the feeling that they have fallen between two stools. They have become divorced from their roots, but have no real sense of belonging in the host community, from which they are divided by language, lack of a job, lack of social contacts, societal position, etc. This is a clear lose-lose position: no-one benefits from marginalization.

The second response is segregation. In this case, the migrant does hold on to the culture of his country of origin, but (like his marginalized counterpart) he fails to identify with or adjust to the culture of his new homeland. In other words, he at least still has something to hold on to in his life, but he finds himself increasingly isolated on 'islands' within the city, where other people of the same background and mentality continue to live in 'the old way', without any reference to the host community. A typical example of this is the manner in which many Western managers of international companies behave when they are posted abroad to third world countries. They usually live in isolated, walled and heavily guarded compounds, along with all the other members of the privileged 'foreign' (and usually white) community.[3] Their children go to segregated international schools (where the lessons are usually in English). They spend their free time with the same group of 'ex-pats' in equally segregated Western clubs and restaurants. They only have contact with the local people in an employment context or with the staff working in their compound. Segregation of this kind can also take place on a much larger scale, with enforced racial segregation between blacks and whites, as was the case under the apartheid regimes in 20th century South Africa.

Once again, such extreme forms of segregation seldom exist in Europe, except in a limited number of very specific communities, like some elements of Roma society. Similarly, ghettos are not a feature of major European cities, which is in stark contrast to the situation in America.[4] In Belgian and Dutch cities, there are certainly districts where more people with a common ethnic or religious background (Turks, Moroccans, Jews, etc.) live together than in other districts, but this is not real segregation, not even at district level. At most, we are talking about limited ethnic enclaves, in which social deprivation often goes hand-in-hand with the development of parallel institutions (local schools, shops and restaurants) and a degree of spatial concentration. Yet even within these enclaves, there is a considerable degree of diversity in diversity, rather than the absolute domination of a single nationality. This superdiversity automatically means that everyone comes into contact with everyone else: on the street, at the school gate, in the shops and markets. The result is the creation of an 'ethnic mosaic' rather than ethnic uniformity, with increasing interaction between the different ethnic communities.[5]

There are some indications that true segregation sometimes takes place at the individual or family level. Some migrants remain so firmly attached to the traditions and customs of their land of origin that they make no attempt to make contact with the host community. A typical (and tragic) example is the isolation experienced by some of the older members of the Moroccan community. When first generation migrants decide, even for the best of reasons, to bring their ageing parents or grandparents to Europe, these elderly generations often have neither the energy nor the inclination to learn a new language and new customs. They miss the old country and the old way of life, which in many cases was also rural rather than urban. If the tension that this situation creates within the family eventually leads to a break between the older and the younger generations, the risk of segregation turning into marginalization for the older generation is very real.

The third response category is assimilation. In this case, the migrant abandons his original culture and embraces wholeheartedly the culture of his new homeland. If the assimilation is total, even the outward characteristics of difference (with the exception of skin colour) disappear. The migrant will learn to speak the language of the new country and will use this language at home. He will also adopt the dress, eating habits and other customs of the host community. Some people even expect that total assimilation should also mean rejecting of the religion of the country of origin. In this sense, total assimilation is designed to make the migrant 'invisible', indistinguishable from the local population: a Belgian amongst the Belgians, a Fleming amongst the Flemings,[6] a Dutchman amongst the Dutch – although this is to assume that there is any such thing as a 'typical' Belgian, Fleming or Dutchman.

Many people who talk about migrants 'integrating' actually want them to assimilate. They expect a one-sided process of adjustment on the part of the migrant. Moreover, assimilation expectations of this kind are playing an increasingly important role in the policies of many European governments during the 21st century.[7] This ignores the fact that complete assimilation is impossible: we were all born and raised in a certain language, culture and tradition. You can relinquish this identity up to a point, but you can never relinquish it entirely; it will always continue to exercise its influence in some way. In addition, many migrants and their children will inevitably remain 'distinguishable' as people of a different ethnic origin by virtue of their skin colour, facial characteristics or names.

Integration: a term with many meanings

Whereas assimilation places the responsibility for adjustment fully on the shoulders of the migrant, integration – in the proper meaning of the word – is a much more balanced and complex process, in which both the migrant and the host community have a role to play and in which both are expected to change. For migrants, integration involves retaining their identification with their own ethnic-cultural background, whilst at the same time accepting up to a certain point the customs and habits of the new society in which they now live. Loobuyck describes integration as participation in society without being regarded as a community apart (segregation) and without compulsory conformity with the socio-cultural characteristics of the majority (assimilation).[8] This means that identification with the culture of the new society can never be complete, since people can never entirely lose or forget their own personal history and culture. But the reverse is also true: identification with the culture of the land of origin can likewise never remain total once it has been subjected to the influence of the new homeland. Integration therefore takes place within the field of tension that exists between multiple identification and identities.

With true integration, responsibility does not rest exclusively with the person who migrates: it is a shared responsibility for a mutual process of change and adjustment. François Levrau talks of 'systemic integration': it is not only a question of whether migrants can adjust to a new society, but also requires constant monitoring of the extent to which institutions such as education, health and the labour market can deal with the needs of a constantly changing society.[9]

This means that integration is not a condition or a state, but is a dynamic process. Migrants are changed through living in the host community and at the same time the host community is changed through the presence of the migrants, who therefore become a valuable element within that changing community.

However, this does not mean that integration always runs smoothly. Precisely because it is a reciprocal process, it inevitably involves moments of conflict. For this reason, it is important to bear in mind the relative imbalance of power between the different parties: often (but not always), the migrants are in the more vulnerable position. They are usually offered a kind of 'package deal', which offers residence papers and democratic values, in return for acceptance of the hegemony of the existing national culture, according to Rainer Bauböck.[10] Newcomers are in a minority and are nearly always at the bottom of the social ladder. To make matters worse, they are additionally burdened with the expectations of the host community, which are either far from clear ("what exactly do they want me to do?") or too far-reaching ("when will I be integrated; haven't I already done enough?"). If there is insufficient equality in the integration relationship, argues Shadid, the dialogue between the parties will quickly degenerate into a one-sided monologue of compulsion.[11]

On the reverse side of the coin, some elements within the host community also experience difficulties with the change process. 'I've become a stranger in my own street' is a complaint you sometimes hear in response to the visible signs of this change. Consciously or unconsciously, these people confuse integration with assimilation. They want the migrants to change, without changing themselves.

During the last two decades, the integration debate in Flanders has also moved more in this direction: away from integration and towards assimilation. The extreme-right political party Vlaams Belang (Flemish Interest) openly argues in favour of a *Leitkultur* to which everyone should conform. Others put their case more subtly, but their assimilation message is still the same. In the Netherlands, politicians like Geert Wilders have deliberately chosen to follow the path of confrontation. This kind of polarization reduces the room for dialogue about mutual expectations and the efforts required of both sides.

Because integration also changes the host community, it acts as a mirror to reflect the norms and values of that community. What are the minimum requirements that a society can and should set? What is its underlying vision of citizenship? Does it need a citizenship test for migrants (of the kind introduced by Great Britain in 2013), in order to check that people properly understand the nature of the society they wish to join before they are granted its nationality?[12] If so, what should this test involve? Should it, for example, make use of something like the Dutch Canon of the Netherlands, a list of fifty themes that give a chronological summary of Dutch history?[13]

It is open to question whether this kind of formalized knowledge serves any useful role in the integration process, never mind whether it can make a valid contribution towards the preservation of our basic rights and the solution of societal conflicts. If we want to deal successfully with ethnic-cultural differences, we need dialogue, not schoolbook history. Moreover, this dialogue must be based on openness and mutual respect, free from all preconceptions. If we fall back on entrenched positions, from the 'our own people first' arguments of Vlaams Belang to the religious fundamentalism within some of the migrant communities, this openness and mutual respect will be very hard to find.

Integration as a controversial concept

Although to concept of integration is too often used one-dimensionally, particularly to place too much emphasis on the migrant's responsibility to change, integration is usually seen as a necessary condition for social cohesion. Flemish integration and citizenship policies (see below) are certainly based on this premise.

Nevertheless, integration as a concept continues to be contested. In particular, three fundamental criticisms are raised against the present integration approach.

The first criticism questions whether the current discourse leads to the kind of integration we want or whether it actually leads unintentionally to greater exclusion. Is integration a usable concept in this phase of superdiversity? And even if it is still useful, how long will this continue to be the case in a world of increasing transmigration and transnationalism?

Does integration actually exclude people?

According to the Dutch professor of intercultural communication, Wasif Shadid, the integration debate of recent decades has led to four undesirable side effects. Firstly, it has resulted in a strengthening rather than a weakening of the 'us-and-them' divide, with greater attention than previously now being given to religious identity. Secondly, too much attention also continues to be devoted to the claims that migrants do not integrate 'enough', which perpetuates the stigmatization of the migrant community. Thirdly, the debate has become increasingly based on the assumption of Western superiority. Fourthly, the first three points lead to an atmosphere of mutual distrust, in which meaningful integration is ever more difficult to achieve. The one-sided focus on the assimilative version of integration, on which policy in both Flanders and the Netherlands has been based in recent years, has, in the opinion of Professor Shadid, failed to provide the results we hoped for.[14]

In *#Believe*, Sihame El Kaouakibi comments that the integration debate is always about the integration of ethnic-cultural minorities and never about the integration of everyone.[15] Similarly, Paul Scheffer – who in *Immigrant Nations* argued strongly in favour of the need for integration – came to the conclusion in his recent study about Amsterdam and Rotterdam that the desire to achieve that integration can sometimes unintentionally divide a society into insiders and outsiders. He now suggests that the problems relating to migrants should be approached as 'general' social problems, rather than problems specific to a particular community. As an example, he points out how the discussion about deficient language skills amongst people with a migration background also gave rise in turn to a number of initiatives to combat reading deficiencies and illiteracy in the indigenous population.[16]

Another Dutch sociologist, Willem Schinkel, goes a step further and argues for the complete scrapping of [integration] policy. He sets the word [integration] deliberately in brackets, because for him [integration] is nothing more than a symbol. It is designed in theory to eliminate the distinction between 'members of society' and the 'un-integrated', but in fact results in the continual exclusion of those whose [integration] is regarded as 'problematical'. In this way, we arrive at a situation (created intentionally by a few, but unintentionally by the majority) that leads to the radical ostracism of people with 'another culture'. In the present social climate, this often means Muslims.[17]

What most concerns Schinkel is the fact that so many people mistakenly take as their starting point a highly organic and static view of society, as a definable entity that can be divided up and demarcated. In this way, they ignore that the people who 'need to integrate' are already a part of our society, which continues to change all the time. In this sense, Schinkel comments that the use of the term [integration] is 'highly productive', but not in the way that most people think. Instead of eliminating the problem, it actually helps to keep it alive. By devoting so much attention to [integration], we reinforce the artificial distinction between 'society' and those who supposedly still need to be integrated into it. Instead of closing the gap between the different ethnic-cultural communities and the host community, [integration] effectively makes it wider.[18]

The concept of [integration] has a strong normative effect. It helps to create an image of what our society is and should be.[19] On the one hand, the notion of [integration] has an individualizing impact: individuals must integrate. On the other hand, it also has a de-individualizing impact: a failure to [integrate] is all too quickly attributed in general terms to the culture of Ali of Mohammed. However, it is precisely on this aspect of the [integration] discourse that the debate about citizenship in being increasingly focused, with an ever greater emphasis on moral as opposed to formal citizenship. Citizenship must be active and constructive, not just a means of identifying nationality. In this manner, the concept of citizenship – like the concept of [integration] – has been reduced to a symbol that strengthens the division between those who are 'in' and those who are 'out'.

In Schinkel's opinion, this means that any discussion of [integration], even with the best of intentions, is a strategic discussion. It is never neutral and can never be devoid of power implications. This power is only productive in its ability to define the boundaries of society, but at the same time it has an excluding effect on all those who fall outside that definition. In reality, the [integration] discussion is based on an ideal picture of the way we would like society to be. The '[integration] market of well-being and happiness' is likewise based on this idealized and 'pure' dream world, which not only integrates, but above all normalizes. Put simply, it becomes a market for 'unity and order'.[20]

For this reason, Schinkel makes an (equally normative) appeal for the introduction of a whole new way of thinking and talking about [integration]. He argues that it is only through the creative transformation of the [integration] discourse that it will ever become possible to view the problems we face from a more constructive perspective. Instead of measuring one-sided [integration], sociologists should analyze the [integration] discourse and use what it tells them to reveal the mechanisms by which we 'make society', also through our use of language. Because it is precisely through this linguistic self-evidence that power speaks.[21]

It was with this kind of new thinking in mind that in 2011 the Dutch Council for Societal Development recommended the scrapping of all cultural conditions from migration policy. According to the Council, the neutrality of the state towards all its citizens is jeopardized whenever the state demands the cultural 'adjustment' of new arrivals in the country. Recognition of the freedom and the right of self-determination of the individual means accepting social, cultural and religious diversity within society.[22]

Is integration policy becoming irrelevant?

The second criticism of integration as a concept and the integration policy for which it forms the basis is that both elements are becoming increasingly less relevant as society becomes more and more superdiverse. Jan Blommaert has commented provocatively that this situation has already been reached, since current migration and integration initiatives take as their starting point a particular image of migration that no longer equates to reality.[23] According to Blommaert, the care sector, the education sector and the media all still believe in an imaginary sociological picture of a stable, resident society of people, whose background we know and understand. But in a superdiverse world, there is actually very little that we can state with certainty for any length of time about the structure of our society and the nature of the people who live in it.

This not only means that the 'integration sector' is being increasingly confronted with an escalating diversity among the people it deals with, which raises all new kinds of questions and expectations in respect of linguistic, social, cultural and religious backgrounds, but also implies in political terms that all the existing migration-related policies have lost any meaning they once had. In Blommaert's vision, terms such as 'integration' and 'citizenship' are only relevant for the smaller core of 'legal' immigrants, who enjoy the full rights and benefits of the state. These matters are of little or no relevance to the vast majority of modern migrants, since they do not intend to stay and build a life here in the long term. Consequently, they have no need of access to the more formal areas of society.

Blommaert correctly points out that the presence of a large group of undocumented migrants (see chapter 6) poses a real challenge for those who maintain that integration policy still serves a purpose. Even the government's own regulations make clear that they fall outside the scope of the citizenship programmes and in Flanders people without papers have recently been denied access to officially organized Dutch lessons. In addition, Blommaert refers to the growing group of transmigrants – people (with or without papers) who only intend to stay in the country for a relatively short time before moving on elsewhere. It is difficult – he claims – to develop an integration policy that has any relevance for this group of wanderers. There are just too many different forms of transmigration to take account of them all. Many of them are EU citizens, taking advantage of the free movement of labour within the Union. Others are only passing through on their way to some other destination (for example, England), but are sometimes forced by circumstances to stay for longer periods than they intended in countries like Greece, Italy, France or Belgium – but still for too short a period to learn the language or build up a local identity. Yet while much of what Blommaert says is true, there is no evidence in the population statistics to support his claim that this group of transmigrants will become the most important group of migrants in the years ahead. The majority of the 120,000 newcomers to Belgium each year *do* have the intention to build a new life here and the country's migration balance during recent decades has been consistently positive.[24]

This does not mean that superdiversity does not pose a problem for our vision of integration. Quite the reverse. If integration, in a social-psychological sense, is a combination of identification with the majority community and identification with your own community,[25] the question arises as to who exactly constitutes that majority community, both now and in the future. More and more of our major cities are becoming majority-minority cities, where the majority of the inhabitants belong to one of the minority ethnic-cultural groups. Do integration initiatives have any value in such a changeable context? In this new situation, with no clear majority group, we will need to evolve towards a new form of urban society in which everyone will need to adjust to everyone else, and dealing with diversity will become the new norm. As a result, the rationale for a group-focused integration policy will gradually fade away, according to Han Entzinger.[26] Although the process is a slow one, we can already see that the majority culture is beginning to change in many superdiverse cities and that a cosmopolitan hybridity is developing into a basic characteristic. In social-psychological terms, this means that the integration of the near future will no longer involve identification with the majority culture, but with the city's hybrid nature and its superdiversity.

Cities are also trying to make more positive use of their urban identity, with large-scale campaigns that seek to 'sell' the city both to the outside world and to its own inhabitants. The campaigns surrounding the London Olympics in 2012 and the 'I Amsterdam' project are typical examples. The slogan of the City of Antwerp between 2003 and 2012 was 'de stad is van iedereen' (the city is for everyone). This was also a way to try and bind local people to a city that has more than 170 different nationalities among its population. The replacement of this slogan as one of the first symbolic policy actions of the new city council under the leadership of the Flemish nationalist N-VA party can only be seen as a desperate attempt to prop up the fast declining majority culture.

Can integration work across borders?

The third criticism of integration policy is that it focuses too strongly on a homogenous image of both culture and nation. Newcomers are required to 'blend in' with the existing Flemish, Belgian or Dutch society. According to Ico Maly, citizenship programmes are too heavily reliant on an outdated Herderian ideal of one people, one nation, one language and one culture, co-located in a single and clearly defined geographical area. In today's world, this is becoming a less and less realistic way to define a modern society. Superdiversity is the new reality, yet Herderian philosophy still continues to dominate the integration debate, at least in Maly's opinion.[27] He argues with some justification for a more open and pluralistic approach to integration and citizenship.

Once again, increasing transmigration and transnationalism also have an impact on this cross-border aspect of integration policy. Whereas migrants in the 20th century only had limited technological possibilities for keeping in touch with their families in their homeland or other migration countries, the communications options available in the 21st century make it a relatively simple matter to live here and maintain networks in numerous other places. Does this transnationality result in multiple integration in multiple locations and in multiple cultural worlds? It seems unlikely, particularly with the growing phenomenon of transmigration, by which people move from place to place with increasing frequency, so that there is less need to identify with the local community.

Social cohesion in superdiversity

Does our current superdiverse society therefore signal the end for a relevant integration policy? Or do we, on the contrary, have need of a stronger emphasis on integration? Perhaps the truth, as so often, lies somewhere in the middle. A policy that provides a different, more balanced and more empowered version of integration, adjusted to the superdiversity of the 21st century, can still be of great benefit in many ways.

The strategic misuse of integration and its transformation into assimilation will work less and less well as the 21st century progresses. The demographic changes that lie ahead will transform our society, even more so than in recent decades. We are heading irresistibly towards a migration society characterized by superdiversity.

This evolution implies that it will become increasingly difficult, certainly in the cities, to identify with the majority community, never mind with the majority culture. It must also be remembered that our cities are not only displaying increasing superdiversity based on ethnic-cultural origin, but that we are also witnessing a far-reaching process of individualization, which leads to a wide variation of life styles. The dividing lines between these different life styles often cut across other social dividing lines and coincide in part with characteristics like financial position, education and age. These differences in life style run through almost every ethnic-cultural group.

The 21st century's need for integration in a society characterized by superdiversity and individualization is therefore actually a broader need for 'social cohesion'. In other words: what is the common basis on which living together in superdiversity can be organized? In this respect, the increase in diversity is a real challenge for the nature and degree of social cohesion in such societies.

According to Parekh, it would be advisable for migration societies to base their vision of social cohesion on the range of diversity present in that society, rather than on an image of equality.[28] This is something that can already be seen in some of our cities at district and school level, but it is much less evident in society as a whole. This raises questions with regard to both the legitimacy of this kind of pluralism, as well as its boundaries and pitfalls. In a superdiverse world, social cohesion will no longer be a matter of accepting and adjusting to a national identity. In a world of non-stop migration, reality will be characterized by a series of overlapping and mutually supporting identities, which continuously influence and change each other.

This means that we will be systematically less able to hold on to our static image of nationality. Many people still behave as though there is such a thing as a Flemish, Belgian or Dutch identity, which has remained unaltered from the 19th to the 21st century and will continue to persist far into the future. Such an identity does not exist. Similarly, there is no such thing as a permanent Moroccan, Turkish or Chinese identity that will remain immune to the passage of time. Richard Sennet has quite rightly stated that society becomes more primitive in relation to the extent that its people see themselves more categorically in terms of a fixed identity.[29] Likewise, the French sociologist Jean-Claude Kaufmann argues in his work on identity politics that we should not confuse the history of a country with its national identity. This applies equally to our individual identity. Neither our national nor our individual identities are to be found in our roots, origins or memory; instead, these identities are a reflection of the constructed sense of meaning that we give to the present.[30]

Only a dynamic vision of identity that is pluralistic and changeable – albeit slowly – can do justice to the complexity of our modern society. Superdiversity has become a part of our urban environment, so that dealing with superdiversity must henceforth become part of the identity of every city dweller.

Integration in an age of multilingualism

'The Language is the People' was the name of the movement set up in Flanders by Prudens Van Duyse in 1836.[31] For the past two centuries, this has been the fundamental idea of the Flemish movement and its echo is still found in our thinking about integration. Even within the framework of an open and dynamic vision of social cohesion, knowledge of the language of the country where you are living remains an important element in any society. The possibility to communicate with each other always brings people closer together or, at the very least, is useful in terms of everyday interaction. Linguistic knowledge is a consequence of education, but for children it is also an important precondition for performing well within that education and for developing their capacities to the full in later life. The attention given to the importance of language is therefore justified.

Does the advent of superdiversity change anything in this scenario? The answer is 'yes', in two distinct ways. Firstly, if the number of different languages present in a city increases, the importance of Dutch (in Flanders and the Netherlands) as a common language also becomes increasingly important. If ten or fifteen different languages are spoken in the homes of children who sit together in a superdiverse class, Dutch is the only language that can be used in class to teach them and the only language that can be used by the children themselves in the school playground to talk to each other. Much the same is true of superdiverse teams on the work-floor or in offices. There is a need for a common language.

However, the situation is more complex than it seems. Within the cities, there are many ethnic communities that are now sufficiently large to build up their own strong networks in their own language. Whereas the need to use a common language to communicate beyond the boundaries of different communities increases the value of Dutch, its value as a means of communication within the local ethnic networks declines. Newcomers often first establish themselves in their own linguistic community. They find informal work through their fellow countrymen or in ethnic shops, restaurants and small businesses. They meet each other in Moroccan tea houses, Turkish coffee bars, Polish or Bulgarian community centres, Spanish diners, or in mosques and churches with sermons in their own language. Superdiversity inevitably means a transition to more multilingual cities.

This factual conclusion is politically very sensitive, particularly in Flanders. Brussels and Antwerp are already de facto multilingual cities. For Brussels in recent decades, the linguistic issue has not only been about the intercommunication of French-speakers and Dutch-speakers, although this continues to dominate the political agenda. The third Brussels Language Barometer in 2011 showed that multilingualism in the city was gaining ground fast. The superdiversity of the inhabitants is increasingly reflected in the number of languages being spoken. The Language Barometer asks people to identify the languages they can speak well or fluently. The total number of languages increased from 72 in 2000, to 96 in 2005, to 104 in 2011.

French continues to be the best known language, and is spoken well by 89% of the city's residents. This is followed by English (30%) and Dutch (23%). There is also a clear upward trend for Arabic (18%), with more than 100 other languages used in smaller ethnic communities bringing up the rear.[32]

Knowledge of a language is one thing, but the circumstances of its use are equally important. What languages are spoken in the homes of Brussels residents? In 2011, single-language French and Dutch families made up just 40% of those questioned. In others words, families that use French as their means of domestic communication are no longer the norm. A third of the city's current population of young people are growing up in families where neither French nor Dutch is spoken at home.

According to Rudi Janssens, the results of the third Brussels Language Barometer show that the number of single-language inhabitants is not only declining but also decreasing in importance. Linguistic diversity is now a fact of life and will continue to increase, further encouraged in part by the current trends in family formation. The number of 'Brusselaars' with a different language background is on the rise and this linguistic richness will be passed on to following generations. Partners in mixed-language marriages often wish to pass on both their languages to their children. As a result, more than half of the current generation of Brusselaars under the age of 25 grew up in families where two or more languages were regularly spoken. Moreover, the primary language acquisition of the very youngest members of society is also characterized by an ever growing diversity. Brussels is not developing in the direction of unilingual or bilingual assimilation, but is moving in the direction of multilingualism, with a highly complex language repertoire. More and more Brussels families are mixed-language families, which not only means that different languages are passed on within the family, but also that the knowledge of those languages allows the members of the family to function better in the wider multilingual society of the capital city. In other words, language in Brussels is becoming less an 'either...or' story and more an 'and...and' story.[33]

Similarly, the image of Antwerp as an almost homogeneous Dutch-speaking city urgently needs to be adjusted to reflect the realities of the situation. Of course, the starting point for comparison purposes for the largest city in Flanders is different than for Brussels, which has an official two-language status (French and Dutch). Nevertheless, in Antwerp we find most of the same trends. The migrations that resulted in almost 170 different nationalities living in Antwerp have also moved the city firmly in the direction of multilingualism. This is not yet evident to the same extent as in Brussels, but there is little doubt that in the future increasing superdiversity in Antwerp will also lead to ever greater linguistic diversity. One indicator for this claim is the languages spoken at home in the families of children currently in primary education in the city. In 2012, 39% of primary school-goers spoke a language other than Dutch at home. This percentage is increasing quickly: the comparable figure for 2008 was just 32%.[34] Even if these figures give a slightly distorted picture, because many of the indigenous inhabitants prefer to send their children to 'whiter' schools in municipalities outside the city, they are nonetheless clearly indicative of the scale and the increase in multilingualism within the city as a whole. Moreover, the range and size of the ethnic communities in Antwerp mean that their members can quite easily conduct large parts of their daily lives in their own native tongue – a phenomenon that is also evident in other major cities.

The question is therefore how we should now deal with this growing multilingualism. In these high days of nationalist sentiment many politicians, not only in Flanders but elsewhere, react defensively and attempt to cling to the whole unrealistic fiction of unilingualism. This is in stark contrast, for example, to the approach shown by the world city of London during its successful candidacy for the Olympic

Games in 2012, when it make a strong selling point of the fact that more than 300 different languages are spoken there.[35]

But let me be clear on this crucial matter: although unilingualism is a fantasy, the growth of superdiverse and multilingual cities means that it is more important than ever before to emphasize the need for people from other ethnic communities to learn Dutch in Flanders. The key question is how and from which perspective? Linguistic knowledge must become a lever for emancipation and must never be an excuse for exclusion. The language struggle waged by the Flemish people in the 20th century against the dominance of French in Belgium was a necessary struggle. The right to speak and use Dutch in official contexts had to be wrestled from the French-speaking ruling class. The Flemish struggle in the 20th century was largely a social struggle.

Some of today's Flemish nationalists, who argue most stridently for the supremacy of the Dutch language, seem to have forgotten what it feels like to be disadvantaged in so many different areas of life, simply because of the language you were born with. The language struggle that some Flemings now wage against the migrants who do not (yet) know sufficient Dutch is not dissimilar to the reaction of the French-speakers toward the Flemish community in the 20th century. This kind of reaction always works to the detriment of the weakest party. Surely it cannot be our intention in a superdiverse city like Antwerp to maintain the exclusivity of Dutch as the sole language, at the expense of the socially vulnerable members of society who do not yet have sufficient command of that language?

Instead of adding further linguistic requirements to the list of conditions that make people, including migrants, eligible for scarce social housing, we should instead be investing more in an adjusted form of Dutch-language training without waiting lists. We need to take reality as our starting point: while Dutch will continue to be the 'lingua franca' of the majority (but never the totality) of the people living in the superdiverse Flemish and Dutch cities, it will only be so alongside a wide range of other languages spoken by a multiplicity of ethnic communities. Recognizing that we live in a superdiverse society means that we must stop regarding multilingualism as a problem. In the second decade of the 21st century, the time has come to start promoting multilingualism as an advantage, rather than trying to enforce an outdated unilingualism by limiting the social rights of non-Dutch-speakers.

To achieve this goal, we need to follow a twin-pronged policy. The first prong, as already mentioned, is further investment in language training. Budgets have been increasing in recent years, but they are still woefully inadequate. Politicians who claim that Dutch is important will need to put their money where their mouth is, so that more people can learn the language more quickly. The waiting lists (depending on the mother tongue of the trainee) are just too long. More resources would also allow greater diversification of the training to reflect the different levels of ability of the trainees (elementary, advanced, etc.). This would also allow some groups to follow more intensive courses than the current two or three half-days each week.

Moreover, current language training is frequently too far removed from the real lives that people lead. Some good results have already been achieved with mother and father projects at local schools, where the parents can follow language lessons at the schools their children attend. If research confirms the initial impression that this more informal (and therefore more realistic) method of language training really works, similar initiatives of this kind can and should be developed.

Running parallel with this, there is also a need for innovation in terms of methodology, both from the policy-makers and from the training sector itself. The current approach is too 'scholastic', too school-like, certainly for adult newcomers. Notwithstanding the enthusiasm and dedication of the trainers, the setting is too 'classical' for people who are often illiterate even in their own language. These people are more likely to learn the language effectively through doing things; for example, while working. However, the current system in Flanders is not geared for this. During their first years in the country, we require people to pass through a 'dependency' process (citizenship programmes, waiting lists, a number of years of Dutch lessons, etc.) before they can become eligible for social employment via the Public Centres for Social Welfare.[36] Many migrants are keen to make progress, but learning is often slow. Perhaps it would be useful to introduce foreign-language work teams, such as an ironing workshop staffed exclusively with Berber women or a renovation project with Iraqi or Tibetan construction workers, under the leadership of a supervisor who speaks both Dutch and the other relevant language. In this way, people will learn practical Dutch in a practical context, which will make it easier for them to find work more quickly, thereby reducing their period of dependency. Experiments of this kind are surely worth a try?

The second prong is to place greater emphasis on multilingualism as something positive, which can be used as a lever for social and professional advancement. The number of children with a migration background leaving school without a diploma is currently at an unacceptably high level and continues to rise. One of the main barriers to academic success is language. Multilingual schools – with lessons in a limited number of subjects being given in the pupil's mother tongue – should not be seen as a block on language development, but rather as a stimulus for the wider acquisition of knowledge.[37] In view of the growing number of children being brought up in families where no Dutch is spoken, this also has to be an experiment worth trying. The results of the school would need to be evaluated independently and scientifically, since this will be the only way to convince people who regard measures of this kind as a political taboo.

Multilingualism requires the creation of an infrastructure in cities that will allow newcomers to overcome language barriers, where necessary. Attempts to make savings on official translation services or to charge (some) people for the use of these services, as is the case in Antwerp, demonstrates an ideological blindness to the realities of the situation. Of course, translation services are not intended to hold people's hand throughout the rest of their lives, but for many newcomers these services fulfil a crucial bridging function during their early years in the country (and sometimes even longer for poorly educated). Removing translation services or making them chargeable clearly works to the disadvantage of people who are already disadvantaged enough, but also significantly increases the linguistic load on schools, welfare organizations and other city services. It is difficult to see this as a constructive way forward.

From integration to emancipation and participation

Half a century ago, during the 1960, Belgium actively sought to attract migrant workers from Morocco, Turkey and Southern Europe. During the subsequent 50 years, the country has evolved into an immigration society living in superdiversity. Yet throughout those five decades integration has always been – and still remains – a controversial concept around which it is difficult to form a consensus.

The problem began right at the very start, back in the 1960s. Both the Belgian government and the migrants themselves saw the new arrangement as a temporary one. The government continued to believe in this myth, even when it became clear after several years that many of the migrants, for whatever reasons, were here to stay. As a result, a golden opportunity was missed to emphasize the importance integration and language training at an early stage. It was only much later – too late, in fact – that facilities for the migrants to learn Dutch were introduced. The damage was done and the language deficiencies of the first generation were passed down to subsequent generations, so that the problem is still with us. The low general level of parental literacy continues to be a major barrier to scholastic success for children with a migration background.

Whereas the need for integration now strikes us as something self-evident, this was not always the case. It was only relatively recently – in 2004 – that the obligation to integrate became a general one in Flanders. After experiments in the field during the 1980s and 1990s, in 1996 the Flemish Government finally recognized for the first time in the strategic plan for its Flemish minorities policy that there was a need for some kind of reception programme for newcomers to the region. In 1998, this programme was formalized in the Flemish Minorities Decree. The objectives of the decree were to help newcomers find their way in their new home and to stimulate them to take part in local society. In February 2003, the Flemish Parliament finally approved the Citizenship and Integration Decree, which set out the aims and target groups for Flemish integration policy and also stipulated the content of the integration trajectory. Just over a decade ago, on 1 April 2004, the provisions of the decree came into force.[38]

Amendments to the decree in 2007 extended the obligation to integrate to a wider group of newcomers, with administrative sanctions foreseen for those who did not comply. The 'social norms and values of our society', said the amendment, must now be made more clearly understood by a requirement for the newcomers to follow a social orientation course. At the same time, the door was opened for the assessment of performance. Newcomers were not only obliged to follow all the elements of the integration trajectory, but were increasingly expected to achieve a certain level of results; for example, by passing a test.

On 29 May 2013, the Flemish Government approved a new Citizenship and Integration Decree to create a policy framework that merged together the two constituent elements.[39] As a result, all the organizations from both sectors were now amalgamated in a single government authority: the Agency for Integration and Citizenship. This considerably weakened the role of the social midfield, so that more than ever before the integration sector became dominated by the government's vision of integration.

In other words, following the false start in the 1960s, a number of measures have been taken to try and improve the situation, but there is still no clear consensus about the value of these measures or about the concept of integration per se. Whether consciously or not, integration is becoming confused to an increasing degree with assimilation and the responsibility for integrating is being placed more and more on the shoulders of the migrants themselves. The fact that integration is actually a mutual process that needs to be actively stimulated by an effective policy from within the host society is something that is being systematically overlooked. This short-sighted policy means that the government has put all its eggs in one basket. We still need to make much greater efforts in several other fields: bringing down the level of coloured poverty, eliminating the educational disadvantages of migrant children, reducing unemployment and discrimination in the labour market, combating racism. Integration that opens up the perspective for social advancement can have a stimulating effect on the migrant community, but this perspective is currently lacking for too many people of a different ethnic background, particularly those who are poorly educated.

Notwithstanding the criticism of the way we deal with integration today and the potential risks that this involves for the future, the abolition of the concept – as argued, amongst others, by William Schinkel – is not a viable option. In our superdiverse cities there is a greater need than ever before for social connectedness and solidarity, based on a commitment to a common society. At the same time, social improvement will only be possible if the necessary levers are present, including a basic knowledge of the language and social customs of the host country. However, the measures taken to provide these levers must be conceived within an emancipatory framework, which empowers newcomers and gives due recognition and value to their efforts and competencies. All too often, the host community seems to think that integration needs to be 'forced' on the newcomers, whereas most of the new arrivals would like nothing better than the opportunity to play a positive role in society and build a new life for themselves and their families.[40] Put simply, we need to see integration less as an objective in its own right and more as a tool for social emancipation. But this will only work if it is experienced as such by those involved. For this reason, Jozef De Witte suggests that we should no longer use the term 'integration policy', because it makes people think too much in terms of cultural integration (see chapter 9). He puts forward 'participation policy' as a possible alternative, which must guarantee that everyone in the country, irrespective of their origins, is able to take part in society.[41]

Thinking about integration in terms of emancipation also implies that we must abandon our monocultural vision and embrace the reality of superdiversity. In their book *Superdiversity, a new perspective on integration*, Maurice Crul, Jens Schneider and Frans Lelie indicate a possible trajectory for a new approach. Their starting point is that emancipation cannot be forced, but can be stimulated and facilitated by society. According to their hypothesis, the embracing of progressive values comes not through compulsion, but through socio-economic improvement. This process must make use of the power and energy that can be generated by the emancipation of the second and third generations of migrants. The question is therefore how, where and under what conditions this emancipation of the second and third generations can most profitably take place? Their conclusion is that a positive outcome can best be achieved by playing the social improvement card. Consequently, their emancipating integration policy is partly dependent on choices that are made in other policy domains, such as education, the labour market and housing.[42]

Last but not least, it is also vital that sufficient steps are taken to allow the cities to function as frameworks for integration. In a superdiverse society people have multiple identities, which means that their identification with the city where they live is sometimes more important than their identification with the wider region or country. It is in the reality of urban life that all the different policy lines come together. It is at local level that superdiversity is given concrete shape within an increasingly multilingual context. Integration through emancipation means that the cities must work as emancipation machines. This means in turn that the integration we desire can only be achieved by far greater investment to strengthen urban structures and urban policy, based on an open, inviting and pluralistic attitude toward diversity.

Chapter 8

Multiculturalism 2.0

'The spread, speed and scale of diversification processes, and the conditions of superdiversity that arise with them, are inherently tied to power, politics and policy.'
Fran Meissner & Steven Vertovec, 2014. Comparing *superdiversity*, p. 552.

In Europe, we have never been able to live together so relatively peacefully with so many people of different ethnic-cultural backgrounds as we have in the 21st century. Cultural diversity and multiculturalism are a social and societal fact. Paradoxically enough, it is precisely at this moment in time that it is becoming fashionable to talk about the failure of the multicultural society. We are surrounded everywhere by a growing diversity, but the prophets of doom would have us believe, to paraphrase the title of René Magritte's famous painting, *'ceci n'est pas une société multiculturelle...'*: this is not a multicultural society.

We need to make a distinction between the current multicultural reality and multiculturalism. Multiculturalism is not concerned with diversity in society, but is the totality of political-philosophical ideas and policies for dealing with that real diversity.[1] According to François Levrau,[2] multiculturalism is a controversial and questionable concept. On the one hand, it is a policy option that wishes to make good the desire of minority groups for proper recognition in society. A policy based on multiculturalism therefore seeks to combat the economic inequality, political under-representation, social stigmatization and cultural invisibility of ethnic-cultural minority groups.

Following Kymlicka, Levrau argues that this can be achieved by pursuing a multicultural policy that embraces diversity, removes or reduces the legal limitations that apply to minority groups and replaces them with active measures to support those groups. Running parallel with this, multiculturalism is also a political philosophy that has the desire for social recognition as its central pillar, rather that social-economic justice (see chapter 9).

So why is there now suddenly so much criticism of the multicultural society and/or multiculturalism? Where does this criticism come from and is it justified? Of course, it is impossible to make the transition from a majority culture with a minimal presence of migrants to a new urban culture in superdiversity without expecting some problems. Even in cities where hundreds of thousands of migrants have found a place to live and have become members of society, we are still faced with problems of social deprivation, racism, discrimination and inter-community disputes at district level. There are also problems of social fraud and criminality. There is likewise the problem of radicalization in some Muslim communities and the problem of the strong Islamophobic reaction that it provokes, not to mention the many other important social and political reactions to the growing presence of migrant communities. At the same time, we must recognize that we live in one of the richest parts of the world, notwithstanding the crisis of recent years, where there are relatively few social and ethnic conflicts. Should we therefore conclude with Rainer Bauböck that multiculturalism, like history and democracy, will survive the premature announcement of its death?[3]

The multicultural drama?

Has the multicultural society failed? Has multiculturalism failed? This is what a number of critics and politicians throughout Europe have been claiming in ever more strident tones during the past decade.

Why does the term 'multicultural' excite so much emotion and controversy? During the 1980s and the 1990s the criticism of the multicultural society was largely the preserve of the extreme right and usually had a strong racist tone. In different European countries extreme-right parties had significant electoral success with programmes that were openly anti-migration. Examples include the Vlaams Blok in Flanders, the Front National in France, the FPÖ of Jorg Haider in Austria and the Republikaner in Germany. The inevitable and justified response to this growing racism led to a strongly polarized social debate about multiculturalism in all its aspects. Racially inspired attacks on migration were countered by the adherents of a multicultural society, who saw diversity as adding something rich and vital to our local communities. The debate was so intense that for almost two decades the focus was fixed on 'whether or not' we want a multicultural society, rather than 'how' we can make that society work.

The end of the 20th century saw an important widening of the debate, with criticism of multiculturalism now being made by larger, more mainstream groups, sometimes even from the 'progressive' side of the political spectrum. In the Low Countries, the essay *Het multiculturele drama* (The multicultural drama) by Paul Scheffer, written in 2000, marked a symbolic turning-point in this process.[4] In a reasoned and eloquent manner, the essay put into words many of the criticisms that were starting to be raised more generally against the multicultural society. Scheffer's arguments generated a broad discourse on multicultural themes and many people were in agreement with his critical stance, including many moderates and progressives who until then had provided the main opposition to the more virulent criticisms of the extreme right. Scheffer himself also had a social-democratic background and between 1986 and 1992 had worked for the Wiarda Beckman Stichting, the research bureau of the Dutch social-democrats. The main thrust of his essay was that multiculturalism was creating a dangerous underclass in society: '*In contrast to the energy with which the Netherlands approached the "the social question" in days gone by, the current reaction to the continuing social and economic decline of entire generations of people with a migration background, with the creation of an ethnic underclass as a result, is one of apathy and indifference. We seem unconcerned by the multicultural drama that is taking place before our very eyes.*'

At the same time, he argued that part of the problem was the intractable nature of certain cultural differences, focusing primarily on what he saw as the uncompromising stance of the Muslim communities: '*The main issue is that the separation of church and state in not accepted in Islamic circles (...) It is above all in family culture that there is a wide gulf between current Dutch practice and the ethical values of the Islamic communities. We now live alongside each other rather than with each other, preferring to look the other way rather than look each other straight in the eye. But the problem will not go away and we need to recognize that there are some cultural differences that cannot be smoothed over, ironed out or bought off.*'

He went on to reject the 'culture of tolerance' and suggested that the host community in the Netherlands should be much more forthright about what it expected from the migrant communities in terms of integration. '*The culture of tolerance, which has now reached its limits, goes hand in hand with a self-image that is essentially untruthful. It is necessary to leave behind once and for all the cosmopolitan illusion in which so many of us seem so comfortably wrapped. The almost dismissive manner in which the Netherlands has dealt with its own national awareness does not work in the inviting manner that its proponents expect. (...) The limitless tolerance of the Dutch people does not lead to integration, because behind the facade we are often dealing with communities that are aloof and unappreciative. An easygoing and self-indulgent multiculturalism continues to make ground, because we fail sufficiently to put into words the things that actually hold our society together. We do not say enough about our limits, we fail to cherish our own past and we treat our language with nonchalance. A society that denies itself has nothing to offer newcomers. A majority that refuses to accept that it is a majority has lost sight of the hard compromises inherent in integration, which always work to the detriment of existing traditions.'*

Scheffer wanted to promote debate and policy change (and he eventually got both). He ended his essay with an appeal: '*A parliamentary commission of inquiry is necessary to investigate immigration and immigration policy, because whole generations are currently being written off in the name of tolerance. The current policy of broad acceptance and limited integration magnifies rather than reduces inequality and contributes to a feeling of alienation within our society. Tolerance is creaking under the weight of the economic and social burden it must carry. The multicultural drama that is being played out in our streets and cities is the biggest threat to social peace in our country.*'[5]

Seven years later, he published a more developed and more nuanced version of his ideas in his international bestseller *Het land van aankomst* (Immigrant Nations), which was seen by some as an appeal for citizenship and integration, and by others as a classic example of the culturalization of the migration debate. The book is characteristic of the so-called 'new realism' approach to this debate, which says that we must dare to give a name to integration-related problems. Yet while it is true that recognizing problems is an important first step towards solving them, the 'new realism' gradually became more and more negative in its attitude towards the key issues. Its basic premise is that integration has been a failure, not only in socialeconomic terms, but also (and perhaps primarily) in cultural terms.

Under the pressure of this new realism, policies were developed that placed a greater emphasis on the responsibility of the migrants to make integration work.[6] This was matched in the public debate by a growing popular resistance to the so-called 'political correctness' of multicultural thinking. Under the pretence of 'facing up to the facts', the migration discourse gradually slipped back into polarization, with a renewal of negative 'us-and-them' thinking as a result.

Of course, the debate in the Low Countries about the merits of a multicultural society has also been influenced by international events, such as the terrorist attacks on the World Trade Centre in New York on 11 September 2001, the train bombs in Madrid (March 2004) and the similar attacks on public transport in London (July 2005). In the Netherlands, the politically inspired murders of the politician Pim Fortuyn (May 2002) and the filmmaker Theo Van Gogh (November 2004) led to a further polarization within Dutch society. Nor are such problems wholly a thing of the past. The demonstrations by the anti-Islamic movement Pegida in Germany, the mobilization in many European countries of young Muslim men to fight in the Syrian civil war, the attack on the offices of Charlie Hebdo in Paris in January 2015 have all served to further polarise the migration and multiculturalism discourse, with a particular emphasis on the seeming incompatibility of the Western and Muslim worlds – and this in an age of superdiversity, which sees more Muslims in Europe than ever before.

The arguments of new realism

For those who had long been proclaiming the death of multiculturalism, the above events were the final nail in its coffin – or so write Steven Vertovec and Suzanne Wessendorf.[7] They analyzed the various criticisms relating to the supposed failure of the multicultural society and made an inventory of the elements in the integration discourse in different European countries. They concluded that there are five basic criticisms that recur regularly in different places at different times. The first of these criticisms is that multiculturalism is a one-dimensional ideology, doctrine or dogma. The second criticism claims that this one-dimensionality has had a censuring effect on political debate. In the name of political correctness, the real problems have been swept under the carpet for years. The third criticism argues that multiculturalism has contributed to (rather than reduced) segregation, by paying too little attention to national values and the need for social integration, thereby promoting the development of parallel communities living alongside each other. As a consequence of this short-sightedness, multiculturalism has rejected the need for common values of any kind – the fourth criticism. At the same time, its cultural relativism makes it blind to practices such as the unequal treatment of women, forced marriages, honour killings, female circumcision, etc. Fifth and finally, in recent years multiculturalism has become a breeding ground for terrorism.[8]

The so-called new realism, which broadly concurs with most of these same criticisms, has now become widespread in mainstream political circles. The extreme right has lost its monopoly of denigrating multiculturalism. In recent years, new realism has become the dominant discourse throughout Europe, cutting across national borders and party differences. The German Minister-President Angela Merkel has in 2010 openly stated that multiculturalism in Germany has failed.[9] Former German SPD politician Thilo Sarrazin -a member of the board of directors of the powerful German National Bank – has said that Germany is in danger of abolishing itself by allowing excessive migration.[10] The British Prime-Minister David Cameron talks of the need for a 'shared national identity' to replace a 'doctrine of state multiculturalism' that demonstrates too much tolerance.[11] A week later his sentiments were echoed by the former French president Nicolas Sarkozy, who similarly claimed in a television interview that the multicultural society in France had failed.[12]

In short, this era of new realism is dominated by integration pessimism.[13] The pendulum has swung completely the other way and very little now remains of the positive discourse of the past, including its naive expectation that diversity would only enrich society and not bring conflict in its wake. Instead of naming the real problems as a precursor to finding effective solutions, the debate now seems to have become bogged down in a hopeless negativism, which places most of the blame for the failure of multiculturalism on the shoulders of people with a migration background. According to David Pinto, a former professor of intercultural communication, Dutch society has gone from one extreme to the other in its approach to the migrant community: 'from cuddling them to death to clubbing them to death'.[14] Baukje Prins and Sawitri Saharso talk of a similar shift from tolerance to repression.[15] Allesandro Silj comments that multiculturalism has become a negative value, rather than being one of the fundamental principles of Western democracy, as it previously was. Assimilation is the new base line in migration policy in most of the countries in Western Europe, which only serves to slow down the rate of real integration.[16] This translates into an increasing element of compulsion in government-sponsored integration initiatives.

Which multiculturalism is bankrupt?

One of the most interesting features of this whole debate is the remarkable absorptive capacity of the concept of multiculturalism, which covers just about every element of policy and every approach to diversity. It is certainly true that the superdiverse reality in our cities is extremely complex, with many different components and their variants. To help us to see more clearly through this maze of diversity, Rainer Bauböck distinguishes three different kinds of multiculturalism.[17] 'Celebration multiculturalism' takes as its starting point the positive evaluation of cultural, ethnic and religious diversity as a public good that enriches our society. Authenticity and the preservation of culture and cultural differences are often central to this approach. At the same time, however, there is a risk that people's attention will remain focused on the things that divide us rather than the things that unite us, while the framework itself offers insufficient levers to help solve potential conflicts between different groups.

Bauböck's second classification is 'toleration multiculturalism'. This takes as its starting point the realization that differences can indeed lead to conflicts. However, an attitude of mutual tolerance must allow different communities to live harmoniously alongside each other. Through a minimally invasive approach, tolerance must keep conflicts within reasonable bounds, whilst at the same time allowing underlying differences in values to be preserved. The crucial question for this type of multiculturalism is just how far the limits of tolerance can actually be stretched. Just how tolerant can we be when faced with the intolerance of others or the denial of basic human rights? The answers to these questions expose the differences within society to a degree that is not always easy to cope with.

Bauböck's third variant is 'recognition multiculturalism', which responds to the desire of the different minorities and communities to be recognized within the society where they live (see chapter 9). Public acceptance and valuation of differences within this type of multiculturalism is often seen as a source of self-respect for individual members of ethnic communities.

Which of these three different types of multiculturalism are supposed to have failed, according to the critics? If we link the analysis of Steven Vertovec and Suzanne Wessendorf[18] to the Bauböck classification, it soon becomes clear that celebration multiculturalism and toleration multiculturalism are the variants most under fire. The discourse for both variants has become much more critical in recent years. The question is whether this negative discourse has also led to a change in policy. It is indisputable that in political debates multiculturalism is seldom praised these days. Many politicians fear that the concept has lost the support it once had. But has this basis really been significantly reduced? Be that as it may, there are very few politicians today who are prepared actively to make efforts to widen that support. On the contrary, we increasingly see a new kind of assertiveness, with a stronger emphasis on citizenship and integration programmes, linked in both cases to the importance of learning the local language. The general tone of the debate has become more negative. We are more frequently hearing phrases like 'enough is enough', 'it's time to stop the pampering' or 'what about *our* rights?' This is reflected in the behaviour of those politicians who tend to follow the growing reluctance in public opinion to support multiculturalism, rather than trying to prepare society (and their voters) for the transition that is already taking place. This downward spiral in the multicultural discourse is not necessarily inspired by racist thinking, but it does give extra ammunition to the real racists in society, say Vertovec and Wessendorf.[19]

While these developments are taking place, diversity continues to grow. Fortunately, there is at least a greater continuity in public policy than in the public discourse. Vertovec and Wessendorf conclude that while many legislative texts no longer refer directly to multiculturalism, they do refer increasingly to diversity. However, in practical terms the two concepts are used interchangeably in what has now come to be known as diversity policy, which is effectively multiculturalism under a different name. However, the accent within the legislation has changed, with a greater emphasis on the individual nature of inclusion: it is up to the migrants to make sure that they integrate properly. This shift perfectly reflects the neo-liberal spirit of the age, in which individuals are increasingly held to be responsible for adjusting to the structural changes taking place in our global risk society.[20]

The Canadian politocologist Will Kymlicka has commented on the fact that there are many differences of opinion about what comes after multiculturalism, but that there is a remarkably uniform consensus that we are already living the post-multicultural age.[21] Bearing this in mind, he has reached three conclusions as a result of his analysis of the 'rise and fall of multiculturalism'. In the first place, he argues that many contemporary analyses are based on a fundamentally wrong initial premise, focusing too strongly on what is almost a caricature image of multiculturalism during the past 40 years; namely, the 'feel-good glorification' of ethnic-cultural differences as an enriching factor in society. In addition, these analyses nearly always refer to the recognizable cultural characteristics of ethnic groups, such as their cooking, their clothes and their music. If this celebratory variant was indeed the core of multiculturalism, then much of the present-day criticism of the concept would be justified, says Kymlicka. Fortunately, multiculturalism is about much more than that.

In essence, it is a part of the human-rights revolution that took place after the Second World War in the field of ethnic and racial differences. This revolution happened in three phases: the struggle of the countries in the South to achieve decolonization; the struggle against racial segregation and discrimination in the developed world; and the struggle for multiculturalism and rights for minority groups. Multiculturalism is therefore about developing new models of democratic citizenship, based on the ideal of human rights, in replacement of the older undemocratic relationships of hierarchy and social exclusion. In other words, multiculturalism as part of the struggle for greater human rights throughout the world is far removed from the image of multiculturalism as the undynamic exaltation of the culture and folklore elements of various ethnic communities. On the contrary, multiculturalism is a dynamic process that seeks to achieve cultural recognition, economic redistribution and political participation within a framework of societal change. It is in line with this vision that Vimla Nadkarni, chairwoman of the International Association of Schools of Social Work, recently warned against the danger of 'human rights fatigue'.²²

Kymlicka's second conclusion is that we have overestimated the actual depth of multiculturalism's 'fall'. While there has indeed been a decline in the use of the term, combined with a negative trend in the public discourse, in many countries that supposedly no longer wish to implement multicultural policies we nevertheless see a continual strengthening of measures designed to recognize ethnic-cultural differences within society. These measures can take a variety of different forms, such as school programmes, training courses, artistic expression, etc.

His third and final conclusion – which brings us to the heart of the matter – is that we are looking the wrong way at the difficulties and limitations with which we are confronted. The question we should be asking is not whether multiculturalism is dead, but rather why multicultural citizenship seems to work in some places but not in others. This realization will require us to move away from the idea that the road leading to a multicultural society is always smooth and linear. According to Kymlicka, multiculturalism should focus more fully on the problems and risks inherent in that journey. In his opinion, a form of liberal multiculturalism is the only constructive manner to deal with diversity in superdiverse societies. As a liberal himself, he wishes to arrive at a situation where everyone is free to pursue his or her own image of the good life. This freedom requires that people have access to their own culture, as a primary social good that makes it possible for men and women of every ethnic background to live their lives as autonomous individuals.²³

Multiculturalism 2.0

The resistance to multiculturalism in recent years is partly inspired by ideological reasons and partly as a reaction to the real tensions and conflicts that accompany the transition to superdiversity. At the same time, it is also part of the adjustment from a relatively homogenous society with a dominant majority culture and a small group of migrants to a society increasingly characterized by majority-minority communities. The question is no longer 'whether' we want to live with numerous other nationalities and cultures. This is already the case, and superdiversity will ensure that the process is pushed further and further, even in smaller towns and municipalities. Consequently, the question now becomes 'how' can we all live together in the best possible way. Or to express it differently: how can we move beyond the 'us-and-them' mentality in a manner that is compatible with urban structures and urban living in the 21st century?

This kind of social change demands an adjusted form of multiculturalism. David Ley speaks of post-multiculturalism,[24] but we can just as easily call it multiculturalism 2.0. Without bowing to popular pressure and prejudices, the process of social change requires us to find a new way to deal with the daily realities of superdiversity.

The first adjustment is the need for a more balanced view of the multicultural concept. The progressive discourse of the 1980s and 1990s about the richness of a multicultural society and the best ways to relate to that society was too euphoric for too long. In an attempt to offer a positive alternative to growing racism, it turned a blind eye to the very real social problems and conflicts inherent in integration, problems that led to increasing uncertainty on both sides of the ethnic-cultural divide. Unfortunately, the so-called new realism of the first decade of the new century took matters to the other extreme, with a highly negative view of migration and integration.

What view of multiculturalism should we take now? The original concept foresaw a society in which different cultures would live peacefully alongside each other in a process of mutual enrichment. This is still possible, but it will not happen by itself and it will not happen without conflict. Every migration process involves conflict of one kind or another, ranging from serious clashes about core values to minor irritations about strange and unfamiliar customs. These kinds of tension were evident in the transition to cosmopolitan cities and a cosmopolitan society that has taken place across Europe during recent years. This transition radically altered the streetscape and provoked reactions of uncertainty, fear and even resistance among many members of the indigenous community. This will not change immediately in the years ahead. Having said this, there are many other people for whom diversity is perfectly normal and acceptable. Today's children and young people are growing up in an urban environment that is irreversibly superdiverse. For them and for their own children, this superdiversity will be something self-evident.

A second necessary adjustment in our way of thinking is the requirement for a more dynamic view of culture and ethnic-cultural differences. One of the problems in the past with some forms of multiculturalism was that they threatened to essentialize cultural differences. For many years, too much emphasis was placed on the inalienable nature of the newcomer's own cultural identity, which he was encouraged to retain at all costs, according to the Dutch essayist Bas Heijne.[25] This static approach, stimulated by a narrow view of the multicultural ideal, came to dominate thinking about the way different groups should live together, without any real appreciation of the evolution that people inevitably undergo in different communities and cultures.

In this instance, the cosmopolitan vision of Ulrich Beck can help us to bypass the short-sighted 'either...or' approach and leads us to a more constructive 'and...'and' approach, which foresees that people can combine different roles, positions and identities. This also implies a dynamic view of culture (see chapter 9), which in turn implies a willingness to seek out the elements that can bind together all (or nearly all) the inhabitants in our cities. Living together harmoniously must take as its starting point a respect for the 'otherness' of others and a recognition of the conflicts that this can sometimes create. This recognition is a precondition for (finally) creating a consensus to deal effectively with discrimination in education and in the labour and accommodation markets.

The third change requires us to give the city as a context a much more central position in our thinking, which needs to be reflected in a much stronger urban policy. The Dutch sociologist and professor of migration studies Han Entzinger has rightly pointed out that a good integration policy is nothing more and nothing less than a good urban policy.[26] In this respect, we need to understand that we are not currently experiencing the failure of our multicultural society, but are in fact living through the last days of the monocultural nation state. In these circumstances, the city will become a more central base and anchor point in an ever changing globalized world. It is from within this urban context that the importance of self-chosen networks will grow. According to Ulrich Beck and Elisabeth Beck-Gernsheim, the processes of globalization, climate change and the increase of world families living across national borders and geographical distances has resulted in the creation of what they call *Schiksalgemeinschaften*, loose communities of common interest and solidarity. In this way, the 'global other' will increasingly become a part of our lives. The age of closed communities and nation states is over.[27]

Fourthly, we need to find a new balance that will return the human rights issue to a central position in the multicultural debate, while at the same time having due concern for the quality of real life in the cities. A narrow version of multiculturalism, which only recognizes demographic evolutions as the core reality of superdiversity but fails to focus on human rights as an essential element of the changing demographic situation, is not an option. Unfortunately, this is what often happened in the past and in some cases still happens today.

Fifthly, we must be much more active in combating racism and discrimination, as well as forms of victimization. All too frequently, discrimination and even racism are minimized, relativized or even condoned. Resistance to so-called 'political correctness' has in some cases opened the door for people to make comments that are openly racist or to support actions that are blatantly discriminatory. Living together with others demands a minimum of mutual respect and, preferably, mutual recognition.

On the other side of the coin, it helps no-one to systematically adopt the role of 'victim', since this leads first to frustration, followed by apathy and even aggression. Accepting victimization is a denial of the role that people can play in working for change and exploiting the options at their disposal. The Swiss-Egyptian philosopher and Islamicist Tariq Ramadan is also critical of the way some young Muslims choose to take on the role of victim. This 'minority mentality' must be resisted and instead migrants must take the necessary steps to become full citizens in their own right on a basis of equality. This, according to Ramadan, should make it possible within the Muslim community to avoid the temptation of assuming the victim's role. He encourages his fellow Muslims to reject this role and to stop blaming their position on 'a society that doesn't want us', 'Islamophobia' or 'racism'. He does not doubt that these negative attitudes towards Muslims exist, but they must be combated by citizens, including Muslim citizens, who are prepared to oppose the forces of injustice, discrimination, hypocrisy and stigmatizing popular opinion. Recognizing that victims exist is one thing, but deliberately assuming the role of a victim is something altogether different, concludes Ramadan.[28]

Last but not least, we need to develop a new and emancipating vision of citizenship, based on a human rights approach. Emancipating citizenship does not mean citizenship that provides a migrant with the right papers or can be obtained by following citizenship and integration classes. It means citizenship that people of different communities can build up together, in 'co-production'. Citizenship is by definition dynamic and cannot be imposed in a static or normative manner. It is a reciprocal and interactive process. It is only in this way that a shared citizenship can be created, based on the belief that the lives of all the people living here, irrespective of their origin, take place within the same social space.[29] This requires a process of common search, dialogue and conflict to arrive at an agreed set of conditions attaching to this shared citizenship, which in many ways will be a more socially responsible and urban form of citizenship than the citizenship of the nation state.

In search of a shared citizenship

This kind of shared citizenship is diametrically opposed to the process of polarization that has been taking place on both sides of the cultural divide in recent years. This is yet another of the curious paradoxes surrounding the heated debate about multiculturalism: if we are not careful, the continual criticisms about the failure of integration will become self-fulfilling prophecies, since they will continue to provoke further reciprocal polarization. Even though the number of people between 'us' and 'them' is growing all the time, polarizations and provocations of this kind encourage the renewed strengthening of 'us-and-them' thinking. Islamophobic reactions force a part of the Muslim community to fall back on their religion and its symbols. It is no coincidence that more headscarves are currently being worn in Belgium than ever before, not only as an expression of faith, but also as an outward sign of 'being different', as part of a constructed identity. It is equally no coincidence that conservative tendencies in Islam, such as Salafism, are also starting to take root in Belgian cities,[30] which in turn further heightens the fears of the Islamophobes – and so the vicious circle continues.

These extremes strengthen each other. And just as polarization intensifies the hostile image of 'the other', so the process of social exclusion strengthens the self-withdrawal of people into their own ethnic-cultural communities. Satellite television, the internet and small, segregated networks make it easy for these people to live in their own little world. They are still here in a physical sense, but at least in part they live virtually in their country of origin.

Searching together for forms of shared citizenship is a way to break through this spiral of polarization, so that we can all move forward together. This requires us to have an eye for the diversity in diversity. It also requires a reconsideration of categorizations such as 'autochtoon' (native) and allochtoon (non-native). Very different generations of migrants are often lumped together under the same terms, which are becoming less precise every day. We define today's children in terms of their origins, instead of preparing them as well as we can for the future.

If we want to move beyond 'us' and 'them', we need a shared future and a form of shared 'we'. This is by no means evident in a world where individualization is resulting in more personal freedom than ever before, which in turn promotes the development of individual rather than shared identities. But unless we can somehow manage to find these forms of 'we', we will not succeed. Without critical commitment, the fabric of society will crumble. The realization that we are mutually dependent on each other must be strengthened and must be based on more than gestures and symbols alone. Citizenship is about the extent to which people feel a sense of responsibility for their wider environment and are prepared to take account of others outside their immediate family. The individualization and migration processes of recent years mean that this new 'we' must be open and pluralistic, so that it can include all the newcomers. After all, the newcomers of today are the 'old hands' of tomorrow.[31]

Towards a scenario of hope and empowerment

It is clear that we need a new perspective that will allow the development of a new vision of multiculturalism within the context of the superdiverse reality of the 21st century. In their study of superdiversity, Maurice Crul, Jens Schneider and Frans Lelie offer two challenging scenarios for the future, building on the work of the French politocologist Dominique Moïsi in his book *The Geopolitics of Emotions*.[32]

If we fail to organize superdiversity properly; if we cultivate 'us-and-them' thinking; if we continue to think in terms of a disintegrating majority culture; if we do not regard people with a migrant background as equal citizens; if we allow superdiversity to develop in a context of growing ethnic inequality and coloured poverty; if we do all these things, we risk being confronted with a 'scenario of fear and humiliation'. This is a scenario in which the different ethnic groups will continue to withdraw further and further into themselves, leading to the ever greater polarization of society. This disastrous scenario is likely to manifest itself most strongly in cities, where new arrivals and their families are denied the opportunities of upward social mobility and where racism and exclusion are rampant. The populations in these cities will increasingly look inwards and isolate themselves within their own ethnic group. Inter-ethnic contacts will be difficult and friendships between the young people of the old majority community and the second generation of migrant youngsters will be the exception rather than the rule.

At the opposite end of the spectrum, there is also a 'scenario of hope and empowerment', in which different ethnic groups are able to address the issues that divide them. Equality and emancipation are the most important outcomes of this optimistic scenario, which will only be possible in cities and societies that offer equal opportunities to the newcomers and their children; that actively combat racism; that develop and open and outward-looking climate. Within this scenario, migrants and their families will be able to identify with their new homeland and (perhaps primarily) their city of residence. In this respect, social trust – not least for the migrants – is essential.[33]

For Crul and his colleagues the power and energy of the emancipation process of the second and third generation of migrants will be the motor for this scenario of hope and empowerment. In European countries where the second generation are given opportunities in education and treated equally, a process will be set in motion that leads to a strong and visible emancipation movement amongst this second generation. Emancipation is seldom the result of compulsion to adjust to the norms of the majority group, but it is possible as a consequence of upward social mobility within your own social group. In all countries, it is the highly educated second generation of young adults that propagate the most progressive opinions within their own communities. In this respect, the social-economic emancipation of women can also play a crucial role.[34]

Polarization increases fear; emancipation and empowerment increase hope. This is the tipping point at which we currently stand. The manner in which the transition to the majority-minority city takes place will influence to a significant degree the direction that our future will take. It is precisely because the indigenous community will lose its dominant position that opportunities will occur to move towards a more equal society.[35]

Chapter 9

Dancing around culture

'The identity she wanted to reduce to a simple administrative matter was still alive and well, and refused to be suppressed. In spite of all her efforts – her long self-convincing talks with herself, the way she changed her habits and tried to acquire certain characteristics, such a speaking with a rolled R – her adopted nationality, the identity she had assumed of her own free will, remained subordinate to the foreign, ethnic one of her birth.'
Rachida Lamrabet, 2007. *Vrouwland* (Woman's Land), p. 127.

Superdiversity is changing our society, most rapidly and most strongly in the cities. Many professionals experience this daily: child minders, teachers, youth workers, social workers, doctors and nurses, local government officials, policemen, bus and tram drivers, etc. The interculturalization of sectors like education, social work and health care are well under way. In the labour market we are also becoming increasingly familiar with superdiverse companies and organizations, although ethnostratification plays an important role here, so that the differences between individual companies and sectors are often great.

For many people interculturalization is a search process, a matter of trial and error. You hear this from social workers in the city, from child minders and nursery workers, and from teachers in primary and secondary education. You hear it from policemen, recruitment bureaus and staff working in town halls. But you also hear it from people with an ethnic background, who are the first 'pioneers' to work in a company where diversity has been limited until now. Or from Turkish and Moroccan workers who have to serve Congolese or Kurdish customers. The diversity in diversity makes intercultural competencies more necessary than ever before – for everyone.

In this age of superdiversity, there is no longer any question of a single discourse or a single model of interculturalization. Workable methods in a complex urban reality are dynamic and combine different approaches. This can range from structural measures against oppression and discrimination to models for intercultural communication and the development of modified visions of culture.[1] Rather than searching for a single methodology of interculturalization, it is more useful to investigate a multiplicity of different possibilities, as a 'tool-kit' that will allow us to offer 'made-to-measure' solutions specific to the circumstances.

In diversity policy, but also in the processes of interculturalization, we are regularly confronted by different fields of tension. One of the characteristics of fields of tension is that they cannot be resolved by choosing a position and sticking to it. Both sides of the field have value and this value must be respected. It is more challenging (and more fruitful) to investigate how you can reconcile the different (and often opposing) views. In this chapter I will discuss two related fields of tension that are relevant both for policy and for day-to-day work in the social sector and education: the field of tension between redistribution and recognition, and the field of tension between structure and culture.

Between redistribution and recognition

The first field of tension is connected with the extent to which diversity policy is focused on redistribution or recognition. This is a discussion that already dates back several years. In this context, reference is often made to *Redistribution or Recognition? A Political-Philosophical Exchange* by Nancy Fraser and Axel Honneth, but the theme was already being explored in the 1990s by the philosopher Charles Taylor.[2]

The 'politics of redistribution' aims to achieve a maximum of socio-economic justice. To make this possible, policy is based on the need to tackle structural inequality as the central issue. Measures and assistance initiated on this basis therefore seek to reduce inequality and combat structural discrimination. This is not only relevant from a political-philosophical perspective. In their book *The Spirit Level. Why more equal societies almost always do better*, Richard Wilkinson and Kate Pickett demonstrated how countries with less inequality systematically score better on welfare and well-being indicators.[3] The politics of redistribution always takes as its starting point the belief that every person is equal and of equal value, and that consequently policy must seek to ensure a set of equal (basic) human rights for everyone.

The 'politics of recognition' involves a different approach. Here the focus is set on the claim of certain groups, usually minority groups, to be recognized (and preferably valued) for their specificity. While the politics of redistribution starts from the premise of an unacceptable inequality and therefore seeks to create greater equality, the politics of recognition reverses this process, by taking as its basic premise the need to first rectify a lack of recognition for inequality and difference. The claim for recognition is based on opposition to all forms of cultural discrimination and lack of respect for groups and/or cultures. In this way, for example, poor relief organizations ask for the recognition of the deep wounds that poverty can cause. Similarly, migrant organizations call for the recognition of their uniqueness, individuality and otherness. Some people talk of recognition multiculturalism, which seeks to rectify the imbalance of power between the minorities and the dominant culture. The public affirmation of cultural diversity is therefore seen as a source of individual self-respect for members of minority groups.[4]

Charles Taylor has sketched how the claim for recognition and identity has grown through the years. It is a relatively modern claim, which is closely related to the notion of dignity. Taylor places the emergence of the recognition of individual identity as a phenomenon towards the end of the 18th century, in conjunction with a wider ideal of authenticity. It is a feature of our modern age that identity and recognition are no longer as self-evident as they once were and are, in fact, often problematical. Precisely because recognition has been thematized in recent years, it can now either be granted or withheld. Recognition requires the participation of a relevant other, who can and must grant recognition, but who does not necessarily do so. We always define our identity in dialogue with the identities that others wish to recognize in us. Even argument and dispute about these matters is a form of dialogue.[5]

Recognition in the public domain is based on the principle of equal citizenship, but at the same time adds recognition of difference. This implies recognition of the unique identity of an individual or group, which may or may not be different from all others. In other words, recognition takes as its starting point the right of everyone to be different and 'other', and for this reason sometimes asks (in part, at least) for the unequal treatment of the person concerned. The key question then becomes: which differences can be recognized or regarded as legitimate? For example, the right to wear a headscarf is currently the subject of an increasingly polarized debate in Flanders. No-one disputes the right to wear it at home, but what about in public, or at work, or behind the counter in a bank or town hall?

The desire for recognition often has its origins in the struggle against a perceived cultural-symbolic injustice. According to Levrau, this perception is rooted in the social patterns of presentation, interpretation and communication.[6] Minorities are constantly confronted with the culturally dominant images of the majority community, so that they feel invisible from a communication perspective or are repeatedly challenged by stereotypical presentations. A policy of recognition seeks to positively endorse undervalued differences between groups via a process of cultural-symbolic change, based on a positive appreciation of cultural diversity. In this way, the politics of recognition is really a kind of politics of identity, since it involves the reassessment and revaluation of the cultural identity of groups that do not belong to the majority culture. In other words, differences between groups are (partially) confirmed and accepted.

Do we overestimate the importance of identity and recognition? Or do we underestimate it? In the debate about headscarves in Flanders, for example, it is noticeable that the fight for the right to wear a headscarf often occupies a more prominent position in the social agenda than the problem of limited educational opportunities for many children from poor families or families with a migration background. For both sides of the headscarf debate the crucial issue is one of recognition and for both sides it is a matter of principle and emotional commitment. For the wearers of headscarves, it is an important part of their religious faith, which in turn is an important part of their identity. Opponents see the wearing of headscarves as a breach of the principle of social neutrality and fear a return to the 'bad old days' of religious dogma, with all that this entails. The escalation of the recognition debate is often the result of a lack of appreciation of the importance of the issues at stake for the persons concerned.

In a superdiverse society there is a need for both the politics of redistribution and the politics of recognition. However, it is no easy task to combine the two, since there is a very clear field of tension between them. Redistribution is based on the ideal of equality between people, whereas recognition is based on acknowledging the differences between people.[7] Redistribution wants all people to be treated equally. It demands an equal share in prosperity, public assets and opportunities for everyone. Recognition, however, presupposes that different people should be treated differently, and therefore sometimes unequally, since this is the only way to do justice to the relevant difference for the people involved.

Notwithstanding the paradoxes inherent in this field of tension, policy and social work in the 21st century will need to be founded on a combination of both concepts. The politics of redistribution needs the support of the politics of recognition, and vice versa. Without redistribution, there can be no reduction in inequality and no granting of fundamental human rights for all. But without the recognition of identity and the otherness of others, there will be insufficient consensus to push through a policy of redistribution, so that the most vulnerable groups in society will continue to regard themselves as 'second-class citizens', even if the structural gap with the majority community is narrowed.

Two decades ago, Nancy Fraser was already warning us that the struggle for recognition should not overshadow the continuing need for redistribution. From the 1980s onwards, the emphasis in justice thinking moved towards themes like dignity, respect and identity.[8] For example, in the General Report on Poverty in Belgium during the 1990s the demands for greater dignity and recognition in the lives and daily struggles of people in poverty were much more forceful than the demands for a structural approach to growing social inequality.[9] In the campaigns of the women's movement and (even more so) the holebi movement there was a similar clear focus on the desire for recognition. This same desire still plays an important role in ethnic-cultural minorities today.

At the same time, we must also realize that there are limits to recognition. The politics of recognition is not a license to recognize every characteristic of every culture, religion or element that go to make up people's identities. This recognition still takes place within the limits set by society, preferably based on a clear human rights perspective. Consequently, there are boundaries to recognition, but these boundaries are variable and must be discussible in a world of superdiversity. In other words, we must see the recognition of identity and culture as something changeable, as something that is the result of a continual process of dialogue. It is not simply the one-sided recognition of a fixed identity by the majority culture.[10]

This is the essence of integration as a reciprocal process. It not only requires adjustment on the part of the migrant or person who comes from a different culture, but also requires change on the part of the host community, so that a new synthesis is created. It is for this reason that Thomas Faist describes the struggle for greater recognition and redistribution as a form of democratic engagement and an expression of active citizenship.[11] It is a fundamental element in the democratic nature in our society.

Between structure and culture

A second field of tension exists between the conflicting needs of structure and culture. This second field is closely related to the first field of tension between redistribution and recognition, and broadens the debate about the latter. Dealing with culture and cultural differences is not only important from the perspective of policy and interculturalization, but also for practical applications in the social sector. Traditionally, social work is a combination of individual actions and structural measures. Inequality, poverty, social exclusion and discrimination all affect individuals, but they are not purely individual problems. They are also societal problems, which cannot be solved by occasional language courses, sheltered employment opportunities and personal integration/activation contracts alone. These are all useful instruments, but they can only have a positive effect if they are implemented within a framework of structural measures to reduce poverty, inequality and discrimination as a whole. This was true even in the days before our society became more diverse. It is doubly true today.

Structural measures to reduce deprivation in all its forms mean a stronger social policy that takes account of the need to improve the income position of people in poverty, by providing these people with the opportunity to earn that income through proper employment, with the safety net of a sufficiently high and index-lined benefits system for those whose income from labour is inadequate. Structural measures mean adjusting our social structures, so that education no longer simply reproduces inequality in new generations, because of the social-economic position or ethnic background of the parents. Structural measures mean providing access to good quality health care for all, so that inequality in illness and even in death is eliminated. Structural measures mean ensuring the provision of sufficient good quality accommodation at affordable prices, even if this requires direct intervention in the housing market to make this possible. Structural measures mean introducing a policy to tackle racism and discrimination root and branch, so that people really are given effective equal opportunities.[12]

These kinds of structural change are usually, but not always, related to redistribution. Such changes frequently encounter resistance from vested interests and are also sensitive issues for the mass of the general public. As a result, structural change is seldom conceded easily but usually needs to be forced through as a result of social action or (increasingly in this day and age) legal action.

However, we must remember that society is not determined by its structures alone. Culture and cultures also play an important part. In recent years, the debate about the role of culture in migration and integration has become highly polarized; in fact, there are few subjects that generate so much emotion. To some extent, this is a consequence of the struggle of the migrant community to secure recognition and acceptance for the interconnectedness of culture and identity.

The advancing tide of culturalization

The reality of the transition to a superdiverse society had made clear that assimilation is no longer an option (if it ever was). This leads to frustration amongst those who have always equated integration with one-sided assimilation of this kind. The discourse about the supposed failure of integration (meaning assimilation) and the multicultural society has been reflected during the past decade in dozens of different books and articles, and the basic arguments have been reinforced by the comments of many politicians of all persuasions (see chapter 8).This so-called failure has often been expressed and explained in cultural terms.

Increasing culturalization of this kind means that the diversity debate in the 21st century is likely to be increasingly a debate about the struggle between different cultures. At world level, Samuel Huntington has already set the tone with his geo-political analysis about civilizations that are incompatible or even likely to clash.[13]

At the micro-level, the debate is often about the cultures of some groups of migrants. Consequently, it is not the social-economic deprivation of these groups, with their high levels of poverty and unemployment, that is the main subject of discussion; nor is it the discrimination they face as a result of the lack of democratization in the education system or the terrible housing conditions they are often forced to endure. Instead, the focus is set firmly by the host community on their social cultural integration.

People who culturalize the debate in this manner place the blame for our current social problems fully (or largely) on the shoulders of the ethnic-cultural elements, without taking any account (or doing anything about) the structural disadvantages these elements face. This results in the creation of a 'cultural guilt model', in terms of which the migrants' situation – unemployment, poverty, bad housing – is viewed as being their own fault and their own responsibility, simply because 'they are migrants, are Muslims, are Romas, are people from Central Africa, etc.' People who culturalize, reason as though cultural identity is monolithic, unchangeable and indivisible. Based on the clear distinction between 'us' and 'them', both sides identify the essential elements of (their) culture that need to be preserved as a kind of 'cultural nature'.[14]

In Flanders, knowledge of the Dutch language is a particularly sensitive issue in this respect. An insufficient knowledge of Dutch is seen less and less as a barrier to integration that still needs to be overcome, and more and more as a sign of the unwillingness of the migrants to integrate properly. Intention processes are becoming dominant in this debate: whoever is unable to speak Dutch or speaks it badly, is now presumed to have made insufficient effort. This is also being increasingly reflected in the judgements handed down by the labour courts in relation to public welfare support, where the conditions attached to this support are becoming ever more burdensome for the migrants, certainly in Antwerp. We are gradually moving towards a situation where it is no longer a question of the migrants making sufficient efforts to learn the language (intention orientation), but has become instead a question of their ability to make those efforts successfully (results orientation), even for people who are illiterate in their own language. In other words, behind the reasonable expectation that migrants should learn Dutch – which can indeed be a lever to emancipation and upward social mobility – there is also a hidden assimilation agenda.

Not culture but structure?

Increasing culturalization is provoking increasing opposition, which has led to abroad debate about the role of culture and the impact of cultural differences. Most of these dissident voices reject the too one-sided focus on culture and continue to concentrate instead on the problem of structural discrimination. Mark Elchardus calls this the conditioning thesis, which posits that the attitudes of people are largely determined by material and socio-economic conditions. The proponents of this thesis regard cultural explanations as the misplaced culturalization of social and economic differences.[15] In their opinion, the core of the problem is not culture, but rather poverty and unemployment amongst people with a migration background. The causes of social vulnerability in the non-native migrant community are therefore the same as the causes of social vulnerability in the native host community. In other words, people at the bottom of the social ladder are all in the same boat, irrespective of origin. In addition to structural exclusion, some groups are also confronted with the additional problem of racism. However, the focus on culture distracts attention from structural inequalities and the social exclusion in which they result.

Arguments of this kind characterize the work of (amongst others) Ico Maly and Jan Blommaert. They sharply criticize the culturalization and individualization of societal problems, because this means that the increasing polarization of society is no longer seen as a problem specific to the structure of that society and the mechanisms of its political-economic system.[16] Jan Blommaert describes a paradigm that focuses on culture as a 'rightist' paradigm, while a 'leftist' paradigm concentrates instead on socio-economic differences. These different paradigms are defined by a different inter-textuality. A focus on religion and cultural differences reflects the tradition of the rightist discourse of ethnic or linguistic chauvinism and nationalism. This discourse valued homogeneity as the 'recipe' for an ideal society, in which peoples and cultures where segregated off into self-contained entities (nation states), which were deemed to have an absolute existence throughout time. According to this hypothesis, cultural differences are the most important differences, the differences which dominate all others. This leads to a fundamental narrowing of the concept of 'integration', reducing it to a purely ethnic-cultural matter, so that the equally important need for social and economic integration is lost from view – dixit Blommaert.[17] In much the same way, Bleri Lleshi also places culturalization within the context of a rightist discourse that contributes to the 'abnormalization' of foreigners.[18] For this same reason, Renée Frissen and Sadik Harchaoui argue that migration should no longer be framed as an integration issue but as a socio-economic issue.[19]

The Dutch sociologist Willem Schinkel has also warned that structural discrimination against migrants in relation to income, labour market position, educational opportunities and housing are being increasingly treated as cultural problems.[20] We are gradually moving towards a more extreme and perverted form of culturalism, which Schinkel refers to as 'culturism'. This leads to a form of racism, where the concept of 'race' is replaced by the concept of 'culture'. Characteristic of this situation is the tendency to regard the culture of the migrants as the underlying cause of the most diverse problems, simply because this migrant culture does not fit in with the dominant culture. This in turn strengthens the distinction between 'society' and the 'un-integrated'.

People with a migration background experience this culturalization as a lack of recognition for their identity or even as a blatant attack on their culture. They rightly point out how the process of culturalization continually pins people to their country of origin. Culture is interpreted and essentialized as something static rather than something dynamic. The Ghent politocologist Sami Zemni has said that in many cases the culturalization of societal issues is simply a pretext for not discussing other aspects of the situation.[21] In this way, social and political problems are transferred to the fields of culture and religion, with dire consequences for the development of a harmonious society. It leads, for example, to growing Islamophobia and reduces the broad challenges posed by globalization to a matter of narrow cultural differences. For Zemni, culturalization is the easiest response to the lack of political will in the core domains of inequality and discrimination.

Tariq Ramadan similarly argues that societal problems should not be 'Islamatized'. Unemployment, marginalization and other problems must be dealt with as political issues. Instead of placing the 'migration question' within the proper framework of human rights and economic reality, it is all too often viewed from the perspective of identity, religion and culture.[22] In much the same vein, Yamilla Idrissi, a member of the Flemish Parliament for the social-democratic party, opposes the increasingly fashionable explanatory model that seeks to use culture, and Islam in particular, as an explanation for all the ills of society. Although she concedes that "in the past, the Left has paid too little attention to the cultural dimension of some societal problems", she nonetheless criticizes the one-dimensional thinking of the Islam debate and focuses on what she believes we have to lose by our increasing fixation with cultural identity.[23]

Yet notwithstanding all these warnings, culturalization still seems to be gaining further ground in society as a whole. Even in the field of social work, Bea Van Robaeys and Kristel Driessens have noted the clear presence of a 'cultural guilt model' in dealings with people with a different ethnic origin. Some social workers have a tendency to see cultural differences rather than poverty as the root of the problem, believing that the former is the cause of the latter. This thinking is based on a perception amongst (some) social workers of a 'culture gap', which makes it harder for them to view the problems of their migrant clients in multi-dimensional terms. As a result, complex issues are oversimplified and reduced to a matter of culture – for example, classic gender patterns – rather than being placed in a broader structural framework.[24]

Dancing around culture

In a world of growing superdiversity, culturalization is not the answer. It is a culpabilization approach, which defines people exclusively in terms of a background based on a too static view of culture. Having said this, we must also be careful not to lose sight of the importance of the growing diversity of cultural backgrounds. The question therefore remains how can we best deal with the field of tension that exists between structural issues and cultural issues in a vigorous and positive manner?

The strong polarization of the debate between the structuralists and the culturalists has left little room for manoeuvre in recent years. As a result, we tend to dance around the cultural problem, rather than confronting it head on. This is unfortunate, since dialogue between the different schools of thought is essential, if we wish to develop effective policy and provide effective social assistance. All too often, the justified rejection of culturalization and cultural guilt models has the undesirable side-effect that discussions about culture itself become taboo. However, it is not possible to correctly understand the position of minority communities on the basis of their socio-economic characteristics alone, without taking account of the cultural specificities of individuals and groups.[25] Culture is relevant, conclude Kasinitz and Mollenkopf in their study of New York. Notwithstanding the large differences that exist within different ethnic groups, the differences between the different ethnic groups in terms of their organizational response to the city remain relevant.[26]

If we want to tackle structural deprivation and discrimination, we not only need to modify our social structures, but also need to strengthen people's ability to improve their own position within that society. This latter aspect can only be successfully accomplished on the basis of proper insights into the living environment of the people in question – and this inevitably brings you into contact with their culture. Culture often invests people with energy, self-esteem and identity. On the reverse side of the coin, culture can sometimes act as a break or hindrance to progress. We therefore need to urgently develop a new and powerful policy for social improvement that combines the tackling of structural discrimination with an open approach to cultural differences.

An important part of the assistance that we need to provide for the migrant community cannot be successfully implemented without explicit attention for the cultural context. A poignant picture of the impact that the cultural environment can have on social assistance was given by Birsen Taspinar in her book *Moeders van de stilte* (Mothers of silence), the story of three women living in a foreign land.[27] Good social assistance in response to intra-family violence needs to take account of the culture and the cultural perceptions of the people involved.[28]

Similarly, the health sector needs to develop 'culturally competent care', which goes further than the use of intercultural translators and mediators.[29] This is equally true for the growing number of people with a different ethnic origin who in years to come will increasingly find their way into care homes for the elderly, where it will be crucial for their quality of life that due attention is paid to their social and cultural ties. Simply approaching the elderly as 'biomedical beings', devoid of significant cultural and social attachments, removes their human dignity.[30]

At the same time, we should also realize that cultural characteristics can sometimes create a serious threshold in assistance relationships. When families argue that it is normal in their culture for women to play a subordinate role and that consequently they should not be allowed out of their home alone, this makes it extremely difficult for them to follow Dutch lessons or to find non-domestic employment, which in turn makes it doubly difficult for the social services to develop a successful integration trajectory for that family. For this reason, the classic human-rights and emancipatory approach to social work in Europe can often run into difficulties when confronted with the cultural imperatives of some migrants. Sometimes these difficulties are legal in nature. For example, the claims of some families that it is the custom in their culture for young people to marry at the age of 14 contravenes Belgian marriage legislation, which seeks to safeguard the educational opportunities open to teenagers and sees marriage as the freely chosen union of adult partners.

Dealing vigorously and effectively with culture

If we want to see culture as a positive force, whilst at the same time seeking solutions for the 'threshold' effect it can sometimes create, we need to develop an approach that accepts culture as something dynamic and heterogeneous, and therefore capable of evolution. Aleidis Devillé and Jurgen Basstanie have rightly pointed out that both in the field of social work and in society as a whole we far too often maintain an unnecessarily static view of culture, a view that is now long outdated. Almost 20 years ago, Eric Corijn was already arguing that in the confrontation with the right and with other traditional forces, it is necessary to emphasize that culture is a construction, a product of human interaction. For this reason, culture needs to be divested of every essentialistic interpretation.[31] We need to recognize that culture can change, can contain inconsistencies and can be shaped by individuals through their interaction with their own social-economic position and their relationship with important social institutions, such as education, the media or politics. Culture is therefore a 'constantly moving balancing act'.[32]

Culture is also much wider than a focus on values and norms, which people adopt and adjust. Stijn Oosterlynck has identified five broad dimensions in culture.[33] While he generally applies this model to the struggle against poverty, a number of his insights also apply for dealing effectively with ethnic-cultural diversity. According to Oosterlynck, culture works first and foremost as a 'frame', a way in which people can perceive themselves and their surroundings. Working in and around culture therefore means gaining insights into the frames that people use for dealing with diversity and then exploring together the possibilities for changing those frames.

His second dimension sees culture as a 'practical guide' or 'technical repertoire', a kind of toolkit of experiences from which people can choose when reacting to certain situations. Working effectively with culture is therefore a question of increasing the scope of this toolkit, so that people have more options open to them. At the same time, culture is also a narrative, a way of thinking that allows people to construct a story (coherent or otherwise) of their lives. Giving linguistic expression to their dealings with diversity and cultural differences makes people stronger, but also makes them more aware of the conflicts that cultural differences can sometimes generate.

Symbolic boundaries are the fourth dimension of culture, which people use to divide themselves and others into different social categories. These boundaries are a source of constant discussion and dispute, as a result of which they are sometimes shifted, lifted or even removed altogether. Not everybody has the power to define these boundaries for themselves. Many people have boundaries forced upon them by others; for example, the way that children born in

Belgium from Belgian parents with a different ethnic origin are still frequently referred to as 'migrants'. Even so, the debate about the symbolic boundaries that define which groups are 'in' and which groups are 'out' can sometime help people to adjust their own position. This is crucial to the development of ethnocentrism, according to Mark Elchardus and Jessy Siongers.[34] Their research has shown that ethnocentrism – the judging of one culture by the norms and values of a different culture that is regarded as superior – is one of the cultural elements that people use to define the symbolic boundaries of the group to which they belong or wish to belong.

Access to cultural capital is the fifth and final dimension of culture.[35] For the French sociologist Pierre Bourdieu, this essentially means the social stratification resulting from taste, style and cultural practices. In this way, for example, many of the children with a migration background mentioned in the previous paragraph do indeed feel out of place in the 'white' middle class culture that they experience both at school and in society at large. Culture makers, such as the choreographer Sidi Larbi Cherkaoui and the pop singer Stromae, are still very much exceptions in Belgium. However, there are some encouraging signs. The Antwerp urban culture organization *Let's Go Urban* has recently received praise and recognition, not only for its general success, but also for the range of cultural productions that it brings.[36] That being said, the interculturalization of culture still has a very long way to go.

Structure and culture

Efforts to work effectively and empoweringly with structure and culture can and must go together, based on an emancipating vision and a human rights approach.[37] According to Paolo Boccagni, the new perspective of superdiversity can help us to move beyond the outdated debate about the respective merits (or otherwise) of the culturalized versus culture-blind approaches of the past. A dynamic view of culture and a vigorous but constructive approach to the field of tension between structure and culture is relevant for policy and for society as a whole. Nowhere is this truer than in the field of practical social work. In the age of superdiversity, social work must search for empowering combinations that can deal with the structural factors of discrimination, whilst at the same time maintaining an open approach to cultural differences. These differences can be both a force for progress and a source of obstruction. This means that in addition to providing individual assistance and working for structural change, we must also have the courage to work for social change in an empowered and diversity-sensitive manner, without culturalizing the social problems we may encounter along the way.

In short, empowering social work must take structural discrimination as its starting point and must seek to secure individual and structural improvements, while also taking due account of the culture and living environment of the people involved. When dealing with people of a different ethnic-cultural origin, this means entering into dialogue about sensitive cultural elements in a respectful manner, recognizing those elements as a strength whenever possible or making them discussable as an obstacle when not. Bea Van Robaeys and Kristel Driessens talk of a diversity-sensitive approach. This requires social workers and other professionals to suspend their moral judgements about cultural differences. Diversity-sensitive social workers are conscious of the fact that differences between people are socially constructed and they reflect this in their thoughts and actions.[38]

Diversity sensitivity has much in common with intersectional thinking. Intersectionality seeks to approach people in their uniqueness, bearing in mind their cultural and other differences. People combine primary and secondary characteristics. Primary characteristics are inborn, but not neutral; these include gender, age, class and ethnicity. Secondary characteristics can be influenced and therefore changed, and are also subject to personal preferences and circumstances; these include place of residence, place of work, relational status and choice of life philosophy. Taken together, they are the axes of identity formation. The intersectional approach regards diversity as a multilayered concept and places culture within a context. Consequently, in this vision identity is multiple and dynamic, and it repositions the individual in his or her own living environment.[39] Due attention is paid to culture from a structural perspective, without lapsing into a one-dimensional view of diversity. According to Boccagni, a superdiverse approach can be distinguished from an intersectional approach by virtue of the greater importance it attaches to the individual trajectories that people need to follow. At the same time, too strong an emphasis on individualization is a poor substitute for traditional frameworks like gender, handicap, sexuality or even ethnicity, on which social action has, to a large extent, been based until now.[40]

Active pluralism as the basic approach

In assistance relationships it is crucial to use a structural approach, which also takes account of the cultural elements that form an essential part of the strength, pride and identity of the client partner. Implementing social work on the basis of an understanding of the living environment of the client families means that modern social workers must be able to deal with difference and plurality. Moreover, the religion or life philosophy of the families must be regarded as an integral part of their environment. The growing diversity of life philosophies can play a useful role in assistance provision: as an element of the living environment, as a network and as a source of strength that can be tapped into by the social workers. However, religion can also be an obstructive factor for the trajectories that social workers and their clients sometimes wish to follow.

Religion is indisputably an important element in the living environment and culture of many ethnic-cultural families. A community of faith can often be a powerful network for social contacts, self-confidence and solidarity. But religious beliefs can also isolate people and groups from the rest of society. As a counterbalance to the increasing secularization of the past 50 years, a number of new religions have sprung to life in recent decades and for a part of the migrant community are playing an ever more important role. Although the growth of Islam is most prominent in this respect, the influence of the many smaller communities of faith should not be underestimated. In many migrant communities the impact of religion is still far greater than is now the case in the majority of the host communities in Europe.

The renewed interest in religion and the rise of Islam are sensitive issues in the West, and often provoke resistance. Nevertheless, different philosophies of life are an inherent part of a pluralistic society. In our Western liberal democracies, the separation of church and state is inextricably linked with the principle of religious freedom as a fundamental legal and human right.

These different philosophies of life frequently cut across the old pillar structures of society, such as the division between Catholic and pluralistic welfare provision or between private and public enterprise. Nowadays, social and economic providers of every kind are increasingly faced with a growing diversity of philosophical backgrounds and worldviews amongst their clients and partners. And they are all faced with the far from simple task of finding the best way to deal with this complex situation within the framework of their organizational structure and its social mission. For some people in need of social assistance the recognition of their beliefs is so fundamental that it is an essential precondition of their recognition as an individual. Narrow-minded attempts to achieve neutrality in assistance relationships fail to recognize the role that religion and faith play in other ethnic-cultural communities. A forced neutrality of this kind only serves to strengthen the polarized 'us' and 'them' thinking that is so detrimental to inter-community understanding. Respect for the living environment of the 'other' implies active recognition of the role of their philosophical life choices, which may or may not be attached to the importance of religious symbols.

This means that active pluralism should be our basic approach towards a superdiverse society and towards the social assistance it provides to its most vulnerable members.[41] People belong to different cultures and have different philosophical and political convictions. Active pluralism is an open and discerning attitude based on the assumption that you can never be wholly neutral. Within this framework, active pluralism not only recognizes the validity of people's differences, but also argues for an open dialogue between their different philosophical viewpoints. This involves more than simply recognizing the right of existence of the philosophical differences. It also requires people to show a genuine interest, whenever this is relevant to their interactions with the 'other'; for example, in their role as a teacher or social worker. Such people are able to see the role of faith and beliefs as a force for positive change, but also realize that in some cases they can serve as an obstruction. When this happens, they must make the obstruction discussable, in a dialogue based on an attitude of mutual respect and recognition. With active pluralism the emphasis is placed more on the process of negotiation than on the result.

As superdiversity continues to grow in the 21st century, so the role of active pluralism will gradually change. The old debate about pluralism was focused on the need for philosophical neutrality in the face of the dominant position of the Catholic pillar in society (and in social work). The old distinction between Catholic and liberal (or pluralist) is now only marginally relevant, mainly in ethical matters such euthanasia. It has very little relevance in matters relating to ethnic-cultural diversity. Today, everyone is searching for a new way forward.

As a result, philosophical diversity is now increasing – albeit gradually – amongst the providers of social assistance in almost every care organization of note. For many of them, pluralism was also a form of neutrality. But this hard-won neutrality is no longer an option in our superdiverse world with its need for 'made-to-measure' assistance, if we wish to take account of the living environment of the beneficiaries of that assistance. When dealing with superdiversity, active pluralism is the best approach.

Chapter 10

How to deal with superdiversity?

'It is specific to living in cities that every social project must be framed in a new intercultural dialogue, in which heterogeneity and difference are the starting points.'
Eric Corijn, 2009. *Het verknopen van verschillen. Cultuurparticipatie in de ongrijpbare stedelijkheid* (Connecting differences. Cultural participation in a confusing urban context), p. 62.

Migration has changed and is still changing our society. In just over half a century, the countries in Western Europe have evolved from relatively homogenous white societies, with relatively few 'foreigners', into superdiverse immigration societies. As a result, many of our fellow countrymen now have a migration background somewhere in their family history. Certainly in the major cities, the 21st century will be a century of continuing superdiversification, with the transition to an ever growing number of majority-minority cities, where the majority of the inhabitants have their roots in migration. Dealing with diversity will be one of the main characteristics of urban life in the years ahead. This is gradually also becoming the reality for our medium-large cities, and even in many smaller municipalities the level of diversity is slowly increasing.

Superdiversity means that there is a growing diversity in diversity. Labour migration started in the second half of the 20th century from a limited number of countries of origin. However, the past two decades have seen the development of migration streams from all around the world, although the original countries of origin of the first generation of migrant labourers still feature prominently in the chain migration of today. The increasing diversity in diversity is not only reflected in the number of different countries of origin, but also in an ever greater diversity in terms of different generations, migration motives, legal statuses, length of stay, religious and linguistic background, social-economic position, etc. Superdiversity also offers us insights into the wider processes of diversification, which, in addition to migration, are also affected by the increasing individualization of society and the development of new lifestyles and personal identities.

The transition to superdiversity has radically altered society as we know it, but this transition is still a sensitive issue for some people. Reality is changing faster than our ability to find new ways of dealing with it. In cities like Brussels, a clear majority culture with a dominant position is gradually becoming a thing of the past. It is being replaced by a new urban culture of living in diversity.

Even so, the manner in which our policy-makers have responded to this new social reality all too often reflects either a partial denial of the existence of superdiversity or a desire to impose unsustainable and polarizing assimilation thinking. This leads to protracted rearguard actions against the new phenomenon, ranging from 'our own people first' mentality to proposals to impose an immigration tax, ban headscarves or even stop support for migrant self-help organizations. Instead of focusing on the potential added value of superdiversity within the framework of an offensive approach, which includes the avoidance of pitfalls and the gradual elimination of problems, the reaction of many majority communities in Europe is defensive. The basic message sent out by these communities is a message based on traditional 'us' and 'them' thinking, which increases rather than reduces polarization. Instead of working together to give new shape and form to the cities of the future, we are locked in a seemingly endless discussion about the margins within which people are free to retain and express their own identity: how visible should Muslims be in our streetscape; where can headscarves be worn and where not; do the self-help organizations work within the frames of reference set by the dominant community?

Of course, for many people the transition towards superdiversity is a process of adjustment, for which society as a whole is not yet ready. But like every process of adjustment, it is pointless to cling desperately to past. Instead, it is better to come to terms with the present and prepare for the future. Those who look backwards rather than forwards are the first to claim that integration has failed and that multiculturalism is dead. Frequently, these cultural pessimists disguise themselves as so-called 'Enlightenment' thinkers, who warn us against the decline and fall of Western civilization in terms that reflect their own dogmatic feeling of superiority.

Living at a turning point

In the 21st century, we are living in a society with a range of ethnic-cultural diversity that has never before been seen. In the decades ahead, this process will intensify still further, not only as a result of refugees coming to Europe, but simply as a result of the present demographic composition of our towns and cities. But instead of seeing the transition to superdiversity as a turning point and seizing it as an opportunity to generate a dynamic that will involve everyone who has come to live with us in this corner of the world, we are allowing a large part of the superdiverse potential to slip through our fingers. This is the paradox of a superdiverse society. The way in which we respond to the presence and interaction of different cultures threatens to intensify rather than diminish 'us-and-them' thinking, a problem that is exacerbated by unacceptably high levels of poverty and inequality in migrant communities. The realities of the situation are much more complex than can be encompassed in simplistic thinking of this kind, but a process of polarization on both sides means that the 'us-and-them' model nevertheless continues to gain ground in many places.

It should be self-evident that the transition to superdiversity will involve a number of problems and a degree of conflict. Transition processes are never trouble-free and always provoke resistance. As far as superdiversity is concerned, this process is characterized by daily discussions and confrontations; by racism and discrimination; by the everyday difficulties of living and interacting together; by unacceptable abuses such as human trafficking, economic exploitation and social fraud. The feelings of uncertainty and insecurity that this generates are real, not only among the migrants but also among the host community. This makes the idea of a retreat into the safety and familiarity of your own ethnic-cultural group an appealing one.

Yet notwithstanding all these ups and downs, superdiversity will continue to grow and will become the next new phase in the development of Europe's cities and European society as a whole. This will continue to provoke hostile reactions, but it is no longer possible to return to the homogenous nation states of the 19th and 20th centuries. Throughout Europe there are now millions of Europeans with their roots in migration. They are now an integral part of European society, even if they are not always accepted as such by everyone.

Meanwhile, more and more children from the second and third generations are moving on to higher education, even though their parents never had the chance to study. Yet at the same time, more and more children from migrant families are also leaving school without a diploma, which seriously limits their opportunities in the labour market. That being said, an increasing number of people with a different ethnic background are building successful careers for themselves, with upward social mobility and the development of a 'migrant' middle class as a result. But this is counterbalanced by levels of poverty and unemployment in some migrant communities that have never been higher. It is possible to find examples of this kind of 'ambivalence' in almost every social domain, and it is precisely this ambivalence which indicates that we are standing at a turning point.

In the heat of the polarizing debate between the supporters and the opponents of increasing diversity, we sometimes lack the common sense to realize that superdiversity in itself is neither good nor bad. The quality of our society and of life within that society is dependent on our collective behaviour as a society and on the individual behaviour of every citizen who is a member of that society. It is our responsibility – irrespective of our origins and no matter how long we have lived here – to make sure that we are successful in this task.

From division and polarization...

This is also the conclusion we can draw from the scenarios developed by Maurice Crul, Jens Schneider and Frans Lelie, inspired by the work of Dominique Moïsi.[1] If we continue to live in the past, with our comforting feeling of 'us-and-them' superiority and a persistent desire to secure assimilation rather than true integration, everybody will lose out in the end. This is the road that leads to further growing social inequality and social dualization, which in turn will lead directly to 'a future scenario – or is it a dystopia – of fear and humiliation'. The key word in this scenario is 'polarization', which ultimately develops into reciprocal polarization.

We should be under no illusions: the seeds for this scenario are already present in our society. If the cities continue to become increasingly unequal, so that coloured poverty also increases; if the precariat[2] continues to grow, so that more and more people are forced to wait at the bottom of the social ladder; if the opportunities for upward social mobility amongst people with a migration background remain limited at their current low levels, then superdiversity does indeed have the potential to turn into a ticking social time-bomb, which will one day explode in all our faces. Cities that intensify the process of dualization and widen the gulf between the rich and the poor, with increasing polarization between the white middle class and the migrant communities as a result, will ultimately become unlivable for everyone.

It is now high time to take the warning signals seriously: the number of young people from migrant backgrounds leaving school without qualifications; the unacceptably high figures for youth unemployment among migrant communities in the cities; the appalling levels of poverty, whether coloured or not. In the 21st century, we are faced with two clear choices: the cities must either belong to all the people who live there, or else they will become uninhabitable places of conflict. If we wish to avoid this latter option, the time has come to stop using origin, language or religion as an excuse for the further polarization of society or as a reason for placing the blame for social-economic exclusion on the shoulders of those who suffer from it the most.

... towards hope and solidarity

Fortunately, our present-day society also contains the seeds for a different kind of scenario, 'a scenario of hope and empowerment'. For an increasing number of city-dwellers, superdiversity is a social reality that they now experience on a daily basis. It has simply become a part of their lives. This everyday superdiversity is often so ordinary, so routine, so commonplace, that the ethnic-cultural differences of the participants are hardly noticed.[3] In the real world of the cities, there is a growing number of people living in positions between 'us' and 'them'. We all combine multiple identities: we are fathers, mothers, sons, daughters, colleagues, neighbours, students, etc. Some of us have roots in migration, others do not. It is just one more additional factor, and not necessarily the most important one. We still share the same residential districts, we still use the same streets, squares and parks, sometimes together, sometimes apart, in reflection of the social layering that is specific to every city. Our children attend the same schools, students follow the same lessons, employees work in the same factories or on the same building sites. Our society, even in its present form, contains powerful normalization processes, certainly amongst the young people who are growing up today and who are therefore gradually discovering this superdiverse world as their 'normal' world.

Even so, much more still needs to be done. Social inequality, poverty, radicalization, racism and other societal problems will not disappear simply because we now regard superdiversity as normal. This will only be possible if we make a real effort at different policy levels to eliminate all structural forms of disadvantage. The discrimination against people with a migration background in education, the labour market and the housing market is wholly unacceptable, but can only be tackled through a structural approach involving massive investment and a process of dialogue with the people living in the superdiverse districts that are worst affected. Further polarization of the situation is the last thing we need. Instead, we must place our trust in greater solidarity as a lever for social improvement, based on redistribution and mutual recognition. In turn, this means actively encouraging integration and participation from an emancipatory perspective, which requires us to adopt active pluralism as our basic attitude for dealing with differences.

What are the chances of success for this 'scenario of hope and empowerment'? For more than half a century people from all around the world have found European society sufficiently attractive (for whatever reason) to leave their homelands, so that they can come and live here. For more than half a century these people have been contributing to our society, enjoying our civil liberties and making use of the provisions of our welfare state. The majority of these new arrivals have made a place for themselves and their families, sometimes in close contact with relatives and friends in their home country (or other European countries), but sometimes not. In the course of time, many of these migrant families succeed in improving their social and economic position, allowing them to move into the middle class. Similarly, the children of the second and third generation are increasingly making their way into higher education and into good jobs in the labour market. It is particularly fascinating when intellectuals and artists with their roots in migration make use of the values of the Enlightenment to enter into an open dialogue about the strengths and weaknesses of our society and about the ways that we can build a better future together, based on the provision of the same fundamental rights for everyone. Opening up real perspectives for upward social mobility is a precondition for meaningful solidarity, but effective measures to tackle societal problems and to improve living conditions in superdiverse districts are equally essential.

The potential for success is available, but we need policies at all levels to create the conditions that will allow us to access the huge range of talents that exist within superdiversity in the most effective way, rather than seeing those talents lost in the second and third generations of migration families, both at school and in the labour market. If we can make living in superdiversity an emancipatory process for more and more people, then our cities will finally be able to fulfil their role as emancipation machines. This will not only benefit people in the cities; it will benefit us all.

The way we deal with superdiversity in the decades ahead will determine to a large extent the future of our cities and of society as a whole. We have a choice and we also have a responsibility to ensure the success of the scenario of hope and empowerment. To make this possible, we must be prepared to adjust our thinking about the social images and certainties of the past.[4]

We must also mobilize people and resources, not only at the different policy levels, but also at local level. Everyone in every community needs to play their part, because it is in the cumulative effect of its many different dynamics that the real power of superdiversity is to be found. The future of our cities does not lie in further polarization; it lies instead in the goodwill and common sense of all people to participate in a process of recognition and redistribution that will one day allow us to mobilise the superdiversity of all our citizens.

Coda

How do you describe contemporary superdiversity? How do you link theory and practice in a book about diversity? How can you use research to better understand our rapidly changing society? And in what ways does this changing society compel us to rethink our frames of reference? These questions have occupied my mind increasingly in recent years. This book is the result of a search process to find useable frameworks that can inspire people in practice to deal with the changes and challenges that the transition to superdiversity inevitably entails.

In the book, I try to link my own sociological knowledge built up over the last two decades with observations and experiences from working in the field. More than 20 years ago, I was given the opportunity as a young sociologist to help set up (under the leadership of Jan Vranken) *The Poverty and Social Exclusion Yearbook* in Flanders. At that time, there was hardly any research material relating to poverty amongst people of a different ethnic origin. What I have learnt above all else during my 20 years of investigating in poverty is the importance of a having a structural perspective, not only for inequality, but also for diversity.

While I was writing my doctoral thesis during the 1990s, I developed a strong interest in the work of the German sociologist Ulrich Beck. Based on his theory of a global risk society and his more recent analyses of diversity, he developed a sociological vision that allows us to view crucial societal change processes more clearly. It is characteristic of Beck's work that he frames research and experiences gained at the micro-level in a broader and more structural macro-context. In fact, in their most recent book Beck and Beck-Gernsheim describe their work as the development of a 'diagnostic theory': strongly inductive and therefore, precisely for that reason, relevant in times of rapid and fundamental social change.[1]

My interest in diversity grew from a number of practical experiences in different settings. During the almost 18 years that I served as a member of the city council in Antwerp, I saw at first hand the way in which the city and its inhabitants were changing, and changing so quickly that policy was unable to keep up. I was the alderman responsible for the civil registry at a moment in time, around the turn of the century, when decades of population decline in the city came to an end and was replaced by a strong upward trend. In the year 2000, I was also responsible for organizing the collective regularization campaign in Antwerp. The stories I heard then, both from people living in the city without papers and from people in the organizations trying to help them, made clear to me just how much of modern city life is played out behind the scenes, hidden from our everyday view.

Another crucial experience was the period from 2007 until the end of 2012, when I was a board member of the Antwerp Public Centre for Social Welfare. For six years, I was confronted almost daily with the pitiable living conditions experienced by people at the bottom of the social ladder, who came to us for help or social assistance. Week after week and case after case, I witnessed the increase in diversity in the city and the corresponding growth in coloured poverty. I heard hundreds of people tell their stories at allocation hearings and read thousands of social reports to assess the proposals made by our social workers to help those in greatest need. I saw many of these newcomers eventually find a place in the city, often thanks to the good guidance they received and the efforts made on their behalf. But I also saw that others were not given the same opportunities or failed to take them. I regularly met people whose survival strategies flirted with the limits of legality and sometimes even went beyond those limits. In cases of individual fraud, people lost their benefit entitlements; in cases of organized fraud, the relevant files were passed on to the police and the courts. These experiences as a councillor of the Public Centre for Social Welfare in a superdiverse city, together with the countless conversations with social workers and the scores of meetings with organizations working in the poorest districts, helped to sharpen my vision as a sociologist with a field knowledge that I could never have obtained as a researcher.

The Knowledge Centre of the Higher Institute for Family Sciences in Brussels, where I have been lecturing on 'Sociology and Society' for more than a decade, kindly provided me with the facilities and resources to carry out a detailed study of the relevant professional literature, the results of which form a crucial part of the book. Together with my colleagues Sophie Withaeckx (Higher Institute of Family Sciences) and Mieke Schrooten (Social Work at Odisee), I conducted between 2013 and 2015 a project-based research study into transmigration and its effect on social work in urban centres.[2]

Another important lever for the book was the opportunity I was given to take up an appointment as lecturer in 'Diversity, Poverty and the City' in the 'Social Work' department at the Karel de Grote University College in Antwerp. In the years ahead, it is intended that this training course will place greater emphasis on the social realities in the city and on the impact of migration and diversity on society in general and on social work in particular. As is so often the case, this will also involve a sometimes difficult search for the best way to achieve greater interculturalization.

Finally, in recent years I have given dozens of lectures, taken part in numerous debates and held countless conversations with people working in the social field. The ideas for this book gradually took further shape in the course of these many fruitful discussions. Equally crucial for me was the feedback I received from people with a migration background. The comments made by my students of different ethnic origin were also invaluable. This meant that the writing of the book involved much more than just a survey of the relevant literature, but was also a search for a new way of looking at and describing the very diverse experiences of people with a migration background. In this respect, however, there is still much work to be done, not only in practical terms on the ground, but also in terms of the interculturalization of our training programmes and higher education facilities.

It should, I hope, be clear that in addition to a thorough survey of the literature, supplemented by relevant research, this book has also been enriched by many different experiences and conversations with people working in social practice. I am grateful to them all for their contributions. In particular, I would like to thank the Knowledge Centre of the Higher Institute for Family Sciences (Odisee) for allowing me the necessary time to write the book and also my colleagues at the Karel de Grote University College for our informative discussions about diversity in the city. Similarly, the editorial team at *Alert* has given me plenty of space in recent years to publish articles in their magazine about my quest of the true meaning of superdiversity.

My sincere thanks also go to Katrijn Vanderweyden, Hayat Amyay, Veerle Matthijs, Steven Debbaut, David De Vaal, Tanja Nuelant, Imade Annouri and Ikrame Kastit for their valuable feedback during the final phases of the writing. Following the publication of the first Dutch edition of the book in 2013, I received useful comments from Maurice Crul, Meryem Kanmaz, Jan Blommaert, Bea Van Robaeys, Jozef De Witte and Nadia Fadil. The congresses, study days and papers of IRIS, the Institute for Research into Superdiversity at the University of Birmingham, were likewise a constant source of inspiration. At Acco, publishers Nancy Derboven and Sophie Vanluchene not only gave me the opportunity to put my thoughts and findings into print, but also provided the necessary support and advice to ensure that finished book met the highest professional standards.

Finally, a special word of thanks for Kristel Driessens. I have lost count of the number of conversations we have had about superdiversity in recent years, but her shrewd insights unquestionably helped to define my search for the best way to translate the rapid changes in urban reality into a new and empowering paradigm for the 21st century. Our thoughts and ideas often complemented each other, so that it is fair to speak of a joint project that transcended the strict boundaries which normally exist between work and private life. I owe her a huge debt of gratitude.

In conclusion, I hope that this book will inspire everyone in the years ahead to enter into a new dialogue that will give shape and form in a positive manner to the superdiverse society in which we now all live – not least here, in my native city of Antwerp.

Notes

On superdiversity

1. Jenny Phillimore (FRSA FAcSS) is Professor of Migration and Superdiversity, and Director of the Institute for Research into Superdiversity (IRiS, University of Birmingham).
2. Steven Vertovec (2007), p. 1025.
3. Tony Judt (2010).
4. Martha Van der Bly (2005).
5. Finex Ndhlovu (2016).
6. OECD (2015).
7. Finex Ndhlovu (2016).
8. Melanie Lowe et al. (2015); Yolande Pottie-Sherman & Daniel Hiebert (2015).
9. Fran Meissner & Steven Vertovec (2015).
10. Johanna Avato, Johannes Koettl & Rachel Sabates-Wheeler (2010).
11. Fran Meissner & Steven Vertovec (2014), p. 541.
12. Andreas Wimmer & Nina Glick Schiller (2002).
13. Steven Vertovec (2015).
14. Susanne Wessendorf (2013b); Eric Laurier & Chris Philo (2006); Sarah Neal, Katy Bennett, Hannah Jones, Allan Cochrane & Giles Mohan (2015).
15. Suzie Hall (2013a & b).
16. Jan Blommaert (2013).
17. Susanne Wessendorf (2014).
18. Tariq Ramadan (2011).
19. Maurice Crul (2015).
20. Tom Vickers, Gary Craig & Karl Atkin (2013).

21. Floya Anthias (2013).
22. Derek Mc Ghee (2008).
23. Jenny Phillimore (2015a&b)

Introduction

1. Patrick Deboosere (2012).
2. Also see Ulrich Beck (2004), p. 110.
3. Tom Naegels (2013), pp. 118-122.

Chapter 1 From migrant labour to superdiversity

1. Ash Amin (2012), p. 1.
2. For the Netherlands see: *Een nuchtere balans van vijfhonderd jaar immigratie*. Lucassen and Lucassen (2011).
3. Based on the Belgian Centre for Equal Opportunities and Combatting Racism (2011, 2012 and 2013). Regional Integration Centre, Foyer Brussels (2014).
4. Triq Salama, *Reis in vrede* (Go in peace). Canvas, Tuesday13 and 20 December 2011, directed for TV by David Verhaeghe.
5. Belgian Centre for Equal Opportunities and Combatting Racism (2013), pp. 10 and 20-22.
6. For the Netherlands, also see Gijsberts, Mérove and Lubbers (2013).
7. Belgian Centre for Equal Opportunities and Combatting Racism (2013), pp. 10 and 20-21.
8. Belgian Centre for Equal Opportunities and Combatting Racism (2013), pp. 28-29.
9. The term 'arrival cities' was first coined by Doug Saunders (2010).

Chapter 2   The superdiversity of the 21st century

1. Veerle Beel, 'I get on my bike and see the whole world. Regional nurses for Child and Family note wide-ranging diversity amongst young families'. In: De Standaard, 25 June 2013, pp. 4-5.
2. Steven Vertovec (2005 & 2007a). For a view of London today, see Ben Kochan (2014).
3. Steven Vertovec (2007). Jan Blommaert (2011a and 2011b).
4. Fran Meisnner and Steven Vertovec (2014).
5. Han Entzinger (2012), p. 13. Paul Scheffer (2012), p. 35.
6. William Frey (2015).
7. Maurice Crul, Jens Schneider and Frans Lelie (2013), pp. 12-13.
8. Philip Kasinitz, John Mollenkopf, Mary Waters and Jennifer Holdway (2009).
9. Maurice Crul, Jens Schneider and Frans Lelie (2013), p. 14. These thoughts are formulated more sharply by the political activist Dyab Abou Jahjah: 'We "allochtonen", of all ethnic and philosophical backgrounds, bear the responsibility of shaking awake our "autoctoon" fellow citizens and seeking to find a better integration in the new reality: the superdiverse society.' Dyab Abou Jahjah (2014), p. 122.
10. Jan Blommaert (2011b), p. 26. See also Steven Vertovec (2007).
11. Belgian Centre for Equal Opportunities and Combatting Racism (2013), pp. 10 and 22-25.
12. Steven Vertovec (2007). Jan Blommaert (2011a and 2011b, 2013).
13. See Sami Zemni (2009) and certainly Bilal Benyaich (2013), who in his book *Islam en radicalisme bij Marokkanen in Brussel* offers sharp insights into the very wide diversity of tendencies within the Islamic community in Brussels.
14. See Jan Blommaert (2013), pp. 90-106. Also see Ico Maly, Jan Blommaert and Joachim BenYakoub (2014), pp. 44-51.
15. Jan Blommaert (2011b). Steven Vertovec (2011), p. 9.
16. Mieke Schrooten, Sophie Withaeckx, Dirk Geldof and Margot Lavent (2015).
17. Also see Steven Vertovec (2012).
18. Steven Vertovec (2011), p. 11; Fran Meisnner (2014).
19. Fran Meisnner and Steven Vertovec (2014).
20. Fran Meisnner (2014); Fran Meisnner and Steven Vertovec (2014).
21. Susanne Wessendorf (2010, 2014), Ico Maly, Jan Blommaert and Joachim Ben Yakoub (2014).

22. Jan Blommaert (2014).
23. Maurice Crul, Jens Schneider and Frans Lelie (2013); Dirk Geldof (2015b).
24. Paolo Boccagni (2014), Jenny Phillimore (2015).
25. Bilal Benyaich (2015)
26. Thomas Faist (2010), p. 300.
27. Jacques Derrida (1998), pp. 33-67.
28. Mark Elchardus and Jessy Siongers (eds.) (2009), p. 11.

Chapter 3 Migration from top to bottom

1. Bea Van Robaeys, Jan Vranken, e.a. (2007). Corluy and Verbist (2010) estimate the risk of poverty for inhabitants with a nationality from outside the European Union at 48% in 2005. In this respect, Belgium scores worse than many other EU member states.
2. An Van Haarlem, Jill Coene and Patrick Lusyne (2011), pp. 186-187.
3. Ignace Glorieux, Ilse Laurijssen and Yolis Van Dorsselaer (2009), pp. 96-98. Also see Yunsy Krols, Bea Van Robaeys and JanVranken (2008), pp. 50-62. Faiza Djait (2014). Bilal Benyaich (2014), pp. 219-306.
4. Nils Duquet, e.a.(2006). Nico Hirtt, Ides Nicaise and Dirk De Zutter (2007). Maurice Crul e.a. (2013), pp. 38-53.
5. Also see Thomas Faist (2010).
6. An Van Haarlem and Jill Coene (2012), pp. 436-439. Marjoke Vander Burg and Jill Coene (2014), pp. 367-371.
7. Monica De Coninck (2011).
8. Patrick Janssens (2011).
9. Dirk Geldof (2012b).
10. Koen Mendonck and Anita Cautaers (2012). Dirk Geldof (2011b and 2013).
11. Mieke Schrooten, Sophie Withaeckx, Dirk Geldof and Margot Lavent (2015). Also see Danielle Dierickx, Anneline Geerts and Sylvie Van Dam (2013); Sylvie Van Dam, Peter Raeymaeckers and Danielle Dierickx (2015).
12. Motief (2012), pp. 9-10 and 64-65. Also see Bart Rogé (2010), p. 63.
13. The Flemish Network of Associations Against Poverty started in 2012 with the project 'Armoede Gekleurd' (Coloured Poverty). See Bart Ketelslegers (2013 and 2015). Ludo Horemans (undated and 2013). Bart Rogé (2010).

14. VRIND (2009), p. 25.
15. Leo Lucassen and Jan Lucassen (2011), p. 42.
16. Ilke Adam and Corinne Torrekens (2015).
17. Leo Lucassen and Jan Lucassen (2011), p. 228.
18. Dirk Geldof (2015 b).
19. Maurice Crul, Jens Schneider and Frans Lelie (2013), pp. 38-52.
20. Maurice Crul, Jens Schneider and Frans Lelie (2013), p. 52.
21. Maurice Crul, Jens Schneider and Frans Lelie (2013), p. 54.
22. Doug Saunders (2010).
23. Doug Saunders (2011).
24. Han Entzinger (2012), p. 25.
25. Leo Platvoet and Maarten Van Poelgeest (2005). Based on Dirk Geldof (2007).
26. Stijn Oosterlynck, Elise Schillebeeckx and Nick Schuermans (2012). Stijn Oosterlynck and Elise Schillebeeckx (2012). Also see Maarten Loopmans (2008).
27. VROM Council (2006). Stijn Oosterlynck and Elise Schillebeeckx (2012).
28. See Jenny Phillimore (2013); G.Walters (2015); Dirk Geldof (2015 a).

Chapter 4 The need for a more cosmopolitan vision

1. This chapter is a reworking of the chapter on migration risks in Dirk Geldof (2011). *Onzekerheid. Overleven in de risicomaatschappij*. Leuven: Acco, pp. 109-129.
2. Robert Putnam (2000 and 2007).
3. Ulrich Beck(2008). For more detail, see Beck (2005 and 2010). Also see Dirk Geldof (2015c).
4. Ulrich Beck (2004), p. 25.
5. A double identity is developing amongst Belgian Moroccans, with a clear religious component. See Saaf, Abdallah, Sidi Hida, Bouchra, Aghbal and Ahmed (2009). Research in Limburg has shown that a majority of the migrants feel that they are both Muslim and Turk or Moroccan. See Maarten Van Craen e.a. (2007), p. 145 and pp. 172-174.
6. Also see Noel Clyck (2010). Tariq Ramadan (2008), pp. 46-47.
7. See Saskia Sassen (2001).

8. Jean-Louis Genard (2013), pp. 114-116.
9. This delineation of who is regarded as 'autochtoon' for research purposes only goes back for a maximum of one generation. A number of children of the third generation, and certainly of the fourth generation, will therefore no longer be counted in the future as 'allochtoon'. For Antwerp, see www.antwerpen.buurtmonitor.be
10. Bilal Benyaich (2013), p. 29.
11. Teju Cole (2011), p. 251-252.

Chapter 5 Transnational lives and families

1. Thomas Faist (2010), p. 313; also see Susanne Wessendorf (2013a).
2. Ulrich Beck and Elisabeth Beck-Gernsheim (2011).
3. The migration experiences of Dutch and Flemish emigrants to Canada after the Second World War were integrated by Erik Vlaminck into his novel *Brandlucht* (2011).
4. Ulrich Beck (2004), p. 110.
5. Eric Corijn (2013a), p. 207.
6. The definition is by Linda Basch, Nina Glick Schiller and Christina Blanc Szanton, quoted in Nathalie Perrin and Marco Matiniello (2011), p. 25.
7. Thomas Faist (2010), pp. 299-310. See also the research by Mieke Schrooten (2012) into the exchanges between Brazilian emigrants in Brussels and their family and friends in Brazil via the social network site 'Orkut'.
8. See, for example, Joris Michielsen, Eva Notteboom and Ina Lodewijckx (2012), pp. 10-13.
9. Integration Survey 2008. See Kris Vancluysen and Maarten Van Craen (2011). See also Nathalie Perrin and Marco Matiniello (2011).
10. Kris Vancluysen and Maarten Van Craen (2011), pp. 214-215.
11. Kris Vancluysen and Maarten Van Craen (2011), pp. 214-215. Joris Michielsen, Eva Notteboom and Ina Lodewijckx (2012), pp. 41-43. Godfried Engbersen e.a. (2003), p. 46.
12. Stuart Hall (2003).
13. Nathalie Perrin and Marco Matiniello (2011), p. 77.
14. Thomas Faist (2010), pp. 310-315.
15. For the Netherlands, see, for example, Godfried Engbersen e.a. (2003).

16. Integration Survey 2008. See Kris Vancluysen and Maarten Van Craen (2011), p. 220.
17. Nathalie Perrin and Marco Matiniello (2011), pp. 75-80.
18. Marta Erdal and Ceri Oeppen (2013); Susanne Wessendorf (2013).
19. For a more detailed overview of transmigration in Belgium, more specifically in Brussels and Antwerp, and its impact on social assistance, see Mieke Schrooten, Sophie Withaeckx, Dirk Geldof and Margot Lavent (2015). Also see Mieke Schrooten, Dirk Geldof and Sophie Withaeckx (2015); Sophie Withaeckx, Mieke Schrooten and Dirk Geldof (2015).
20. Nina Glick Schiller, Linda Basch and Cristina Szanton Blanc (1995), p. 48. Thomas Faist e.a. (2013).
21. Nina Glick Schiller, Linda Basch and Cristina Szanton Blanc (1995), p. 48.
22. Cynthia Hunter, Susannah Lepley and Samuel Nickels (2010), p. 223.
23. J. Schapendonk and G. Steel (2014); Alain Tarrius (2015).
24. B. Mohan and J. Clark Prickett (2010).
25. Ulrich Beck and Elisabeth Beck-Gernsheim (2011, 2013). Dirk Geldof (2012c).
26. Ulrich Beck and Elisabeth Beck-Gernsheim (2011), p. 8.
27. Ulrich Beck and Elisabeth Beck-Gernsheim (2011), p. 23.
28. Ulrich Beck and Elisabeth Beck-Gernsheim (2011), p. 47.
29. Ulrich Beck and Elisabeth Beck-Gernsheim (2011), p. 108 ff.
30. The field of tension created by efforts to prevent marriages of convenience is well covered in Petra Heyse and Marie-Claire Foblets (2011).
31. Ulrich Beck and Elisabeth Beck-Gernsheim (2011), p. 125.
32. Meg Wilkes Karraker (2013), pp. 174-184.
33. Ulrich Beck and Elisabeth Beck-Gernsheim (2011), pp. 168-185.
34. Elisabeth Beck-Gernsheim (2004), p. 17.
35. Ulrich Beck and Elisabeth Beck-Gernsheim (2011), p. 187.
36. Ulrich Beck and Elisabeth Beck-Gernsheim (1990 and 2011), p. 224 ff.
37. 'A good 20% of all the children born in 2008 had a mother of non-Belgian origin. It is also noticeable that about 20% of the children in the Flemish Region do not spreak Dutch as their mother tongue. Resarch suggests that young children who speak a language other than Dutch at home will face a greater challenge to perform well at school or in the job market later on.' Jo Vandeurzen (2009), p. 46 and (2014).
38. Meg Wilkes Karraker (2013), pp. 197-198.

Chapter 6   The hidden city

1. Edwin Pelfrene and Edith Lodewijckx (2014).
2. See Aleidis Devillé (2008). Also see Van Meeteren, Van San and Engbersen (2008). Timmerman, Lodewyckx and Bocklandt (eds.) (2008). DeClerck and Devillé (2011), pp. 191-210.
3. Elisabeth Beck-Gernsheim (2004). Ico Maly and Jan Blommaert (2012), p. 102.
4. See Vincent Corluy and Ive Marx (2011).
5. For more details, the tables and the maps, see Dirk Geldof (2012a).
6. On the basis of the law of 22 December1999, a regularization campaign was launched in Belgium on 10 January 2000, which focused on people who had been involved in an asylum procedure for more than four years without a final decision and on undocumented migrants for whom there were relevant medical or humanitarian factors. For the collective regularization of 2009, asylum seekers and undocumented migrants had the opportunity between 15 September and 15 December 2009 to submit an application (or add to an existing application) requesting the implementation of the new regularization criteria, based on the concept of sustainable local anchoring. The applicants needed to have been in Belgium continually since 31 March 2007 and needed to show that they met the requirement for sustainable local anchoring. This was possible, for example, by producing a contract (or firm offer) of employment for at least one year in a job that paid a wage equivalent to or higher than the statutory minimum wage. In addition to these exceptional (so-called 'collective') regularization campaigns in 2000 and 2009, there is also a permanent possibility to regularize individual cases on the basis of article 9 bis (humanitarian reasons) and 9 ter (medical reasons) of the Immigration Law.
7. For this demographic change, also see Patrick Deboosere (2012).
8. Vincent Corluy e.a. (2008).
9. Vincent Corluy e.a. (2008).
10. As alderman, I had an analysis of the 2000 regularization campaign carried out by the Databank for Social Planning of the City of Antwerp. The analysis of the 2009 campaign was complied by the City Observation and Study Service, once again using details of all the applications submitted in Antwerp. The link to the databank of the City Observation and Study Service makes it possible to analyze the characteristics of particular districts. See Dirk Geldof (2001 and 2012a).

11. Study Service of the Flemish Goverment (2011).
12. Vincent Corluy e.a. (2008).
13. Vincent Corluy e.a. (2008), pp. 81-90.
14. Van Meeteren, Van San and Engbersen (2008), pp. 109-137.
15. Kaizen and Nonneman (2007).
16. Doug Saunders (2010).
17. Ico Maly, Jan Blommaert and Joachim BenYakoub (2014), p. 85.
18. Eric Corijn (2013a), p. 207.
19. Ash Amin (2012, 2014).
20. Herbert Gans (1972).

Chapter 7 They should just learn how to integrate...

1. The quote comes from Oscar Handlin, *The Uprooted* (1952), quoted in Paul Scheffer (2007), pp. 15-17.
2. This matrix is used by different authors with different sources. Godfried Engbersen e.a. refer to the four categories as a two dimensional model of identification, following Verkuyten and the Americans social psychologist Hutnik. See Engbersen e.a. (2003), pp. 49-51.

    Patrick Loobuyck (2002) refers the matrix as the model of the four adaptive forms and refers back to Berry, Poortinga, Segal and Dasen (1992). *Cross-cultural psychology: research and applications.* Cambridge: Cambridge University Press.
3. See, for example, Georg Glasze (2006).
4. Loïc Wacquant (2012).
5. Pieter-Paul Verhaeghe, Koen Vander Bracht and Bart Vande Putte (2012), pp. 22-23 and 68-73.
6. See, for example, the extreme-right Flemish Bloc M.P., Filip Dewinter: "*Mr. Minister, assimilation means that people must adjust, that they must become as Flemish as the Flemings. At the moment, this is not happening.*" (Flemish Parliament, 28 May 2006).
7. Charlotte Williams and Mekada Graham (2014). Also see Stephen Castles (2010), p. 1571. Integration and assimilation are sometimes also confused in the economic literature; see, for example, Paul Collier (2013).

8. Patrick Loobuyck (2002).
9. François Levrau (2011b), p. 29.
10. Rainer Bauböck (2002).
11. Wasif Shadid (2008), p. 143.
12. Practice versions of the British test can be filled in online via http://www.ukcitizenshiptest.co.uk/
13. The Dutch Canon can be consulted via http://www.entoen.nu/
14. Wasif Shadid (2008), pp. 19-30.
15. Sihame El Kaouakibi (2013), p. 92.
16. Paul Scheffer (2007) and (2012), p. 59.
17. Willem Schinkel (2008), p. 15.
18. Willem Schinkel (2008), p. 33.
19. Willem Schinkel (2008), p. 39.
20. Willem Schinkel (2008), pp. 59-69.
21. Willem Schinkel (2008), p. 158.
22. Council for Social Development (2011), p. 43.
23. Jan Blommaert (2011c); also see Ico Maly, Jan Blommaert and Joachim Ben Yakoub (2014), pp. 192-194.
24. Belgian Centre for Equal Opportunities and Combatting Racism (2013), pp. 10 and 20-29.
25. Verkuyten, cited in Godfried Engbersen e.a. (2003), pp. 49-50.
26. Han Entzinger (2012), p. 31. Maurice Crul e.a. (2013), p. 14.
27. Ico Maly (2012), p. 39.
28. Parekh (2000), cited in Rainer Bauböck (2002).
29. Richard Sennet (2010), p. 50. Also see Rainer Bauböck (2002).
30. Jean-Claude Kaufmann (2014), p. 49.
31. http://nl.wikipedia.org/wiki/Prudens_van_Duyse
32. Rudy Janssens (2013). The Language Barometer can be consulted via www.briobrussel.be
33. Rudy Janssens (2013).
34. Figures collected within the framework of the Equal Opportunities Decree for the school year 2011-2012. www.antwerpen.buurtmonitor.be
35. Steven Vertovec (2007).
36. For communication reasons, most PCSWs now insist on a proven language knowledge of at least level 1.2.

37. Kris Van den Brande, e.a. (2011). Also see Griet Ramaut, Sven Sierens and Katrien Bultynck (2013); Orhan Agirdag (2014).
38. Based on www.kruispuntmi.be, History of Flemish integration policy.
39. Flemish Parliament (2013). Draft of the decree realting to Flemish integration and citizenship policy. The text was approved by the plenary sitting. Document 1867 (2012-2013) – No.11. Submitted on 29 May 2013. http://docs.vlaamsparlement.be/docs/stukken/2012-2013/g1867-11.pdf. Also see Gerlinde Doyen (2014).
40. Also see Ash Amin (2012), p. 113.
41. Jozef De Witte (2014), p. 68.
42. Maurice Crul, Jens Schneider and Frans Lelie (2013), pp. 11 and 68.

Chapter 8   Multiculturalism 2.0

1. Rainer Bauböck (2008), p. 2.
2. François Levrau (2011b), pp. 17-23.
3. Rainer Bauböck (2002).
4. Paul Scheffer (2000).
5. Paul Scheffer (2000 and 2002). BobVanden Broeck and Marie-Claire Foblets (eds.) (2002).
6. Also see Baukje Prins and Sawitri Saharso (2010).
7. Steven Vertovec and Susanne Wessendorf (2010), p. 6. François Levrau (2001b), pp. 23-25.
8. Steven Vertovec and Susanne Wessendorf (2010), pp. 6-12.
9. Angela Merkel, in a speech to a party congress on 16/10/2010 in Potsdam.
10. Thilo Sarrazin (2010). Less well known is *'Manifest der Vielen. Deutschlander findet sich neu'*, in which thirty or so young 'allochtoon' intellectuals and artists react to the situation and give their view of the new Germany. See Hilal Sezgin (2011).
11. David Cameron, Munich Security Conference, 5 February 2011.
12. Nicolas Sarkozy, 10 February 2011.
13. Leo Lucassen and Jan Lucassen (2011), pp. 11-19.
14. David Pinto (2007), pp. 106-107.
15. Baukje Prins and Sawitri Saharso (2010).

16. Alessandro Silj (2010), pp. 1 and 10.
17. Rainer Bauböck (2008).
18. Steven Vertovec and Susanne Wessendorf (2010), p. 6.
19. Steven Vertovec and Susanne Wessendorf (2010), pp. 18-28.
20. Ulrich Beck (2007). Dirk Geldof (2011d).
21. Will Kymlicka (2010), pp. 33-40.
22. Kristel Driessens and Michel Tirions (2013), p. 38.
23. Will Kymlicka (2010), pp. 40-47. François Levrau (2011b), p. 22.
24. David Ley (2005).
25. Bas Heijne (2007), pp. 35-36. Also see David Ley (2005).
26. Han Entzinger (2012), p. 32.
27. Ulrich Beck and Elisabeth Beck-Gernsheim (2011), p. 94 ff.
28. Tariq Ramadan (2008), pp. 66-67 and 81.
29. Patrick Loobuyck (2002).
30. Also see Bilal Benyaich (2013).
31. Paul Scheffer (2007), p. 407.
32. Based on Maurice Crul, Jens Schneider and Frans Lelie (2013), p. 69 ff. Also see Dominique Moïsi (2009).
33. Also see Vander Zee e.a. (2012).
34. Maurice Crul, Jens Schneider and Frans Lelie (2013), pp. 23-26.
35. Maurice Crul, Jens Schneider and Frans Lelie (2013), p. 69 ff.

Chapter 9 Dancing around culture

1. See Lena Dominelli (2002 and 2008); Tamara Davis (2009). Models for intercultural communication can be found in, amongst others, Edwin Hoffman (2002), David Pinto (2007) or Shadid. Diversity-sensitive work is a term cited by Bea Van Robaeys and Kristel Driessens (2011). Also see Van Robaeys (2014); Sara Willems and Jos Mertens (2013). Arguments for appropriate visions for dealing with culture can be found, amongst others, in Devillé and Basstanie (2013).
2. Nancy Fraser (2000). Nancy Fraser and Axel Honneth (2003). Charles Taylor (1992, 1994).
3. Richard Wilkinson and Kate Pickett (2009). Dirk Geldof (2011c).

4. See Rainer Bauböck (2008).
5. Charles Taylor (1994). Marc Vanden Bossche (2010), p. 74.
6. See François Levrou (2011), pp. 20-27.
7. Ulrich Beck (2005).
8. See François Levrou (2011a), p. 37 and (2011b).
9. King Boudewijn Foundation (1994).
10. Gerd Baumann (1997 and 1999). Also see Rainer Bauböck (2008); Bea Van Robaeys (2014).
11. Thomas Faist (2010), pp. 318-319.
12. Lena Dominelli (2002).
13. Samuel Huntington (1997).
14. Rik Pinxten (2011), p. 144. Also see Rainer Bauböck (2008); Bea Van Robaeys (2014).
15. Mark Elchardus (2012), p. 340.
16. Ico Maly and Jan Blommaert (2012), p. 108.
17. Jan Blommaert (2011a), pp. 43 and 86.
18. Bleri Lleshi (2010), pp. 174-175.
19. Renée Frissen and Sadik Harchaoui (2011), p. 22 ff.
20. Willem Schinkel (2008), pp. 70-107.
21. Sami Zemni (2009), pp. 16-22.
22. Tariq Ramadan (2008), pp. 10 and 81-83.
23. Yamila Idrissi (2010).
24. Bea Van Robaeys and Kristel Driessens (2011), pp. 80-93 and 116-121.
25. Also see Mark Elchardus and Ignace Glorieux (eds.) (2012), p. 370.
26. Philip Kasinitz, John Mollenkopf, Mary Waters and Jennifer Holdway (2009), pp. 18-19 and 241-273.
27. Birsen Taspinar (2013).
28. See the study 'Families under pressure. Domestic violence in Moroccan and Turkish families' by Ibrahim Yerden (2008).
29. Ilse Derluyn e.a. (2011).
30. Antoine Gailly, Redouane Ben Driss e.a. (2011).
31. Aleidis Devillé and Jurgen Basstanie (2013). Eric Corijn (2013) (1996), pp. 163-166.
32. Crossley, cited in Noel Clyck (2010), pp. 20-23.

33. Stijn Oosterlynck (2012), pp. 94-97.
34. Mark Elchardus and Jessy Siongers (2009), pp. 255-277.
35. Stijn Oosterlynck (2012), pp. 96-97.
36. www.letsgourban.be
37. Paolo Boccagni (2015), p. 618.
38. Bea Van Robaeys and Kristel Driessens (2011); Bea Van Robaeys (2014), p. 34.
39. Michel Tirions (2011); Fatma Arikoglu, Sarah Scheepers and Ama Koranteng Kumi (2015).
40. Paolo Boccagni (2014).
41. Birsen Taspinar and Elke Vandeperre (2012 and 2013).

Chapter 10   How to deal with superdiversity?

1. See Chapter 8. Maurice Crul, Jens Schneider and Frans Lelie (2013). Dominique Moïsi (2009).
2. Guy Standing (2011).
3. See Steven Vertovec (2012) and Susanne Wessendorf (2010 and 2014).
4. Steven Vertovec speaks of 'a gradual transformation of the social imaginary'. Steven Vertovec (2012), pp. 305-306.

Coda

1. Ulrich Beck and Elisabeth Beck-Gernsheim (2011), pp. 15-16. Also see Dirk Geldof (2015c).
2. This research resulted in a separate book: *Transmigratie. Hulp verlenen in een wereld van superdiversiteit*. See Mieke Schrooten, Sophie Withaeckx, Dirk Geldof and Margot Lavent (2015). See also Mieke Schrooten, Dirk Geldof & Sophie Withaeckx (2015).

References

Abou Jahjah, D. (2014). *De stad is van ons. Manifest van de nieuwe meerderheid.* Kalmthout: Pelckmans.
Adam, I., & Torrekens, C. (2015). *Marokkaanse en Turkse Belgen: een (zelf) portret van onze medeburgers.* Brussel: Koning Boudewijnstichting.
Agirdag, O. (2014). Onderwijsongelijkheid tussen anderstalige en Nederlandstalige leerlingen en de effectiviteit van eentalig versus meertalig onderwijs. In B. Benyaich, B. (Red.). *Klokslag 12. Tijd voor een ander migratie- en integratiebeleid* (pp. 173-192). Brussel: Itinera Institute.
Amin, A. (2012). *Land of strangers.* Cambridge: Polity Press.
Amin, A. (2014). *De migrantenstad.* Diegem, http://www.solidariteitdiversiteit.be/uploads/docs/bib/diegem_amin.pdf
Anthias, F. (2013). Intersectional What? Social Divisions, Intersectionality and Levels of Analysis. *Ethnicities*, 13 (1): 3–19.
Arikoglu, F., Scheepers, S., & Koranteng Kumi, A. (2015). *Intersectioneel denken. Handleiding voor professionelen die intersectionaliteit of kruispuntdenken in de eigen organisatie willen toepassen.* Brussel: Ella.
Avato, J., Koettl, J., & Sabates-Wheeler, R. (2010). Social security regimes, global estimates, and good practices: the status of social protection for international migrants. *World Development*, 38(4), 455-466.
Bauböck, R. (2002). Farewell to multiculturalism? Sharing values and identities in societies of immigration. *Journal of International Migration and Integration*, 3:1, 1-16.
Bauböck, R. (2008). Beyond culturalism and statism. Liberal responses to diversity. *Eurosphere working paper*, no. 6, 2-34.
Bauböck, R., & Faist, T. (Ed.) (2010). *Diaspora and transnationalism: concepts, theories and methods.* IMISCOE Research, Amsterdam University Press.
Bauman, Z. (2011). *Collateral damage. Social inequalities in a global age.* Cambridge: Polity Press.

Baumann, G. (1997). Dominant and demotic discourses of culture. In P. Werbner & T. Modood (Ed.), *Debating cultural hybridity: multicultural identities and the politics of racism* (pp. 209-225). London: Zed-Books.

Baumann, G. (1999). The values and the valid. What is it Prof. Taylor should 'recognize'? In G. Baumann (Ed.), *The multicultural riddle. Rethinking national, ethnic and religious identities* (pp. 107-120). New York: Routledge.

Baumann, G., & Vertovec, S. (Eds.) (2011). *Multiculturalism. Critical concepts in sociology. Volume I. Conceiving multiculturalism: from roots to rights*. London/New York: Routledge.

Baumann, G., & Vertovec, S. (Eds.) (2011). *Multiculturalism. Critical concepts in sociology. Volume IV. Crises and transformations: challenges and futures*. London/New York: Routledge.

Beck, U. (2004). *Der kosmopolitische Blick, oder: Krieg ist Frieden*. Frankfurt am Main: Suhrkamp.

Beck, U. (2005). Inequality and recognition: pan-European social conflicts and their political dynamic. In A. Giddens & P. Diamond (Eds), *The new egalitarianism* (pp. 120-142). Cambridge: Polity Press.

Beck, U. (2007). *Weltrisikogesellschaft: auf der Suche nach verlorenen Sicherheit*. Frankfurt am Main: Suhrkamp.

Beck, U. (2008). *Die Neuvermessung der Ungleichkeit unter den Menschen: Soziologische Aufklärung im 21. Jahrhundert*. Frankfurt am Main: Suhrkamp.

Beck, U. (2010). *Große Armut, großer Reichtum. Zur Transnationalisierung sozialer Ungleichkeit*. Frankfurt am Main: Suhrkamp.

Beck, U., & Beck-Gernsheim, E. (1990). *Das ganz normale Chaos der Liebe*. Frankfurt am Main: Suhrkamp.

Beck, U., & Beck-Gernsheim, E. (2011). *Fernliebe. Lebensformen im globalen Zeitalter*. Berlin: Suhrkamp.

Beck-Gernsheim, E. (2004). *Wir und die Anderen. Vom Blick der Deutschen auf Migranten und Minderheiten*. Frankfurt am Main: Suhrkamp.

Benyaich, B. (2014). Welkom in het tijdperk van super-diversity. Boekessay. *Sampol*, 3, 83-88.

Benyaich, B. (2015). *# Radicalisme # Extremisme # Terrorisme*. Leuven: Uitgeverij Van Halewyck.

Benyaich, B. (Red.) (2014). *Klokslag 12. Tijd voor een ander migratie- en integratiebeleid*. Brussel: Itinera Institute.

Benyaich, B., m.m.v. Zibar, O. (2013). *Islam en radicalisme in Brussel*. Kessel-Lo: Uitgeverij Van Halewijck.

Blommaert, J. (2011a). *De heruitvinding van de samenleving*. Berchem: Epo.

Blommaert, J. (2011b). Superdiversiteit. *Samenleving en politiek*, 9, 24-35.

Blommaert, J. (2011c). Superdiversiteit maakt integratiebeleid irrelevant. In *Sociale vraagstukken*, geplaatst op 27/10/2011 op www.socialevraagstukken.nl/site/2011/10/27/superdiversiteit-maakt-integratiebeleid-irrelevant/#more-4516

Blommaert, J. (2013). *Ethnography, superdiversity and linguistic landscapes. Chronicles of complexity*. Bristol: Multilingual Matters.

Bloomfield, J., & Bianchini, F. (2004). Examples of best practice. Intercultural initiatives at city level. In J. Bloomfield & F. Bianchini (Eds.), *Planning for an intercultural city* (pp. 71-102). Stroud: Comedia.

Boccagni, P. (2015). (Super)diversity and the migration-social work nexus: a new lens on the field of access and inclusion? *Ethnic and racial studies*, 38:4, 608-620.

Bracke, S., & Fadil, N. (2009). Tussen dogma en realiteit. Secularisme, multiculturalisme en nationalisme in Vlaanderen. In K. Arnaut e.a. *Een leeuw in een kooi. De grenzen van het multiculturele Vlaanderen* (pp. 93-110). Antwerpen: Meulenhoff/Manteau.

Calvino, I. (2003). *De onzichtbare steden*. Amsterdam/Antwerpen: Uitgeverij Atlas.

Castel, R. (2007). *La discrimination négative. Citoyens ou indigènes*. Paris: Editions du Seuil & La République des Idées.

Castles, S. (2010). Understanding global migration: a social transformation perspective. *Journal of Ethnic and Migration Studies*, 36:10, 1565-1586.

Centrum voor gelijkheid van kansen en racismebestrijding (2012). *Jaarverslag migratie 2011*. Brussel: CGKR.

Centrum voor gelijkheid van kansen en racismebestrijding (2013). *Jaarverslag migratie 2012*. Brussel: CGKR.

Centrum voor gelijkheid van kansen en racismebestrijding (2014). *Jaarverslag migratie 2013*. Brussel: CGKR.

Centrum voor Gelijkheid van Kansen en voor Racismebestrijding (2011). *Migraties en migrantenpopulaties in België. Statistisch en demografisch verslag 2010*. Brussel: CGKR.

Clyck, N. (2010). Identiteit socioantropologisch beschouwd. In B. Lleshi & M. Van den Bossche (Eds.), *Identiteit en interculturaliteit. Identiteitsconstructie bij jongeren in Brussel* (pp. 15-39). Brussel: VUBPress.

Coene, J., & Raeymakers, P. (2011). Getekend op verschillende domeinen: deprivatie bij personen van buitenlandse herkomst. In D. Dierckx, e.a. (Red.), *Armoede en sociale uitsluiting. Jaarboek 2011* (pp. 199-213). Leuven/Den Haag, Acco.

Cole, T. (2011). *Open city*. London, Faber & Faber.

Collier, P. (2013). *Exodus. Hoe migratie onze wereld verandert.* Houten/Antwerpen: Uitgeverij Unieboek/Het Spectrum.

Corijn, E. (2009). Het verknopen van verschillen. Cultuurparticipatie in de ongrijpbare stedelijkheid. In M. Bultynck (Red.), *360° participatie* (pp. 52-69). Brussel: Demos.

Corijn, E. (2013) (1996). Cultuurbeleid, wijkontwikkeling en burgerschap. In S. Vermeulen (Red.), *Kan de stad de wereld redden? Teksten van Eric Corijn* (pp. 162-175). Brussel: VUBPRESS.

Corijn, E. (2013). *Waarheen met Brussel? Toekomstperspectieven voor de Belgische en Europese hoofdstad.* Brussel: VUBPRESS.

Corijn, E., & Vloeberghs, E. (2009). *Brussel!* Brussel: VUBPRESS.

Corluy, V. et al. (2008). *Before and after: de sociale en economische positie van personen die geregulariseerd werden in uitvoering van de Wet van 22/12/1999. Onderzoek op initiatief van het Centrum voor Gelijkheid van Kansen en voor Racismebestrijding in opdracht van de minister van maatschappelijke integratie, gelijke kansen en grootstedenbeleid en m.m.v. de minister van binnenlandse zaken.* http://www.diversiteit.be/?action=publicatie_detail&id=47&thema=4

Corluy, V., & Marx, I. (2011). Dringende medische hulp voor mensen zonder wettig verblijf. In C. Timmerman, e.a. (Red.), *MInteGRATIE. Over nieuwe vormen van migratie en integratie* (pp. 157-184). Brussel: University Press Antwerp.

Corluy, V., & Verbist, G. (2010). *Inkomen en diversiteit: onderzoek naar de inkomenspositie van migranten in België.* Antwerpen: UA/Centrum voor Sociaal Beleid Herman Deleeck.

Crul, M. (2015). Super-Diversity vs. Assimilation: How Complex Diversity in Majority–minority Cities Challenges the Assumptions of Assimilation. *Journal of Ethnic and Migration Studies* 0 (0): 1–15. doi:10.1080/1369183X.2015.1061425.

Crul, M., Schneider, J., & Lelie, F. (2013). *Superdiversity. A new perspective on integration.* Amsterdam: VU University Press.

Dalrymple, T. (2004). *Leven aan de onderkant. Het systeem dat de onderklasse in stand houdt.* Houtem: Spectrum, DK.

Danso, R. (2009). Emancipating and empowering de-valued skilled immigrants: what hope does anti-oppressive social work offer? *British Journal of Social Work*, vol. 39, no. 3, 539-555.

Davis, T. (2009). Diversity Practice in Social Work: Examining Theory in Practice. *Journal of Ethnic And Cultural Diversity in Social Work*, 18:1-2, 40-69

De Clerck H., & Devillé, A. (2011). Irreguliere migratie. Hoe België voorbij gaat aan deze migratierealiteit. In C. Timmerman, e.a. (Red.), *MInteGRATIE. Over nieuwe vormen van migratie en integratie* (pp. 191-210). Brussel: University Press Antwerp.

De Coninck, M. (2011). Welke migratie voor welke integratie? *Samenleving en politiek,* 18, 1, 20-28.

De Witte, J. (2014). Is het integratiebeleid mislukt? In B. Benyaich (Red.), *Klokslag 12. Tijd voor een ander migratie- en integratiebeleid* (pp. 51-68). Brussel: Itinera Institute.

Deboosere, P. (2012). De stad van aankomst: de stedeling als migrant. In D. Holemans (Red.), *Mensen maken de stad. Bouwstenen voor een sociaal-ecologische toekomst* (pp. 48-67). Berchem: Epo.

Derluyn, I., e.a. (2011). *Naar een interculturele gezondheidszorg: aanbevelingen van de ETHEALTH-groep voor een gelijkwaardige gezondheid en gezondheidszorg voor migranten en etnische minderheden.* Location: Publisher.

Derrida, J. (1998). *Over gastvrijheid.* Amsterdam: Boom.

Devillé, A. (2006). De onzichtbare rechteloze klasse. De leef- en belevingswereld van mensen zonder wettig verblijf in Vlaanderen en Brussel. *Tijdschrift voor Sociologie,* 27, 2, 131-156.

Devillé, A. (2008). *Schuilen in de schaduw. Mensen zonder wettig verblijf in de Belgische samenleving. Een kwalitatieve 'multi-method' benadering.* Mechelen: Kluwer.

Devillé, A., & Basstanie, J. (2013). *Van etikettering tot hulpverlening – Hulpverlening aan immigranten in de 21ste eeuw.* www.kifkif.be/actua/van-etikettering-tot-hulpverlening-hulpverlening-aan-immigranten-in-de-21ste-eeuw

Dierckx, D., Coene, J., & Raemaeckers, P. (2014). *Armoede en sociale uitsluiting. Jaarboek 2014.* Leuven/Den Haag: Acco.

Dierckx, D., e.a. (2011). *Armoede en sociale uitsluiting. Jaarboek 2011.* Leuven: Acco

Dierickx, D., Geerts, A., & Van Dam, S. (2013). *De teloorgang van de thouiza? Een verkenning van de oplossingsstrategieën van personen van buitenlandse herkomst in armoede. Onderzoeksrapport.* Antwerpen: Oases.

Djait, F. (2014). Integratie op de Vlaamse arbeidsmarkt. In E. Pelfrene & C. Van Peer (Red.), *Internationale migraties en migranten in Vlaanderen* (pp. 85-96). Brussel: Studiedienst van de Vlaamse Regering.

Dominelli, L. (2002). *Anti-oppressive social work theory and practice.* London: Palgrave.

Dominelli, L. (2008). *Anti-Racist Social Work.* Basingstoke: Palgrave.

Dominelli, L. (2012). *Green social work. From environmental crises to environmental justice.* Cambridge: Polity Press.

Dominelli, L., Lorenz, K., & Soydan, H. (2001). *Beyond Racial Divides. Ethnicities in Social Work Practice.* Ashgate: Aldershot.

Doyen, G. (2014). Inburgering in Vlaanderen en Brussel. In E. Pelfrene & C. Van Peer (Red.) *Internationale migraties en migranten in Vlaanderen.* (pp. 137-155). Brussel: Studiedienst van de Vlaamse Regering.

Driessens, K., & Tirions, M. (2013). Mensenrechten en multicultureel sociaal werk. Lessen uit India. *Alert*, 39, 3, 35-43.

Duquet, N., e.a. (2006). *Wit krijt schrijft beter. Schoolloopbanen van allochtone jongeren in beeld.* Antwerpen/Apeldoorn: Garant.

Düvell, F. (2008). Irregular immigration in Europe: patterns, causes and consequences. In C. Timmerman, I. Lodewyckx & Y. Bocklandt (Red.), *Grenzeloze solidariteit? Over migratie en mensen zonder papieren* (pp. 17-30). Leuven/Voorburg: Acco.

Duyvendak, J.W. (2006). *De staat en de straat. Beleid, wetenschap en de multiculturele samenleving.* Amsterdam: Boom-Onderwijs.

Duyvendak, J.W. (2011). *The politics of home. Belonging and nostalgia in Western Europe and the United States.* London: Palgrave MacMillan.

El Kaouakibi, S. (2013). *# Believe. Waarom iedereen zegt maar niemand echt gelooft dat jongeren de toekomst zijn.* Leuven: LannooCampus.

Elchardus, M. (2012). Van de losgezongen elite naar de gefrustreerde achterban en terug: twintig jaar TOR-onderzoek over onderwijsverschillen. In M. Elchardus & I. Glorieux (Eds.), *Voorspelbaar uniek. Dieper graven in de symbolische samenleving* (pp. 325-352). Leuven: LannooCampus.

Elchardus, M., & Glorieux, I. (Eds.) (2012). *Voorspelbaar uniek. Dieper graven in de symbolische samenleving.* Leuven: LannooCampus.

Engbersen, G., e.a. (2003). *Over landsgrenzen. Transnationale betrokkenheid en integratie.* Rotterdam: RISBO Contractresearch/Erasmus Universiteit.

Engbersen, G., Van San, M., & Leerkes, A. (2006). A room with a view. Irregular migrants in the legal capital of the world. *Ethnography*, 7, 2, 209-242.

Entzinger, H. (2012). Amsterdam – Rotterdam: allebei divers, maar ook verschillend. In *De staat van integratie. Rotterdam Amsterdam* (pp. 11-33). Rotterdam: Gemeente Rotterdam.

Erdal, M., & Opeppen, C. (2013). Migrant balancing acts: understanding the interactions between integration and transnationalism. *Journal of Ethnic and Migration Studies*, 39(6), 867-884.

Fadil, N., & Kanmaz, M. (2009). Identiteitspolitiek en burgerschap in Vlaanderen. Een meervoudige kritiek. In K. Arnaut e.a., *Een leeuw in een kooi. De grenzen van het multiculturele Vlaanderen* (pp. 111-127). Antwerpen: Meulenhoff/Manteau.

Faist, T. (2008). Diversity-a new mode of incorporation? *Ethnic and Racial Studies*, 32:1, 171-190

Faist, T. (2010). Cultural diversity and social inequalities. *Social research*, 77, 1, 297-324.

Faist, T. (2010b). Diaspora and transnationalism: What kind of dance partners? In R. Bauböck & T. Faist, *Diaspora and transnationalism. Concepts, theories and methods*. Amsterdam: Amsterdam University Press.

Faist, T., Fauser, M., & Reisenauer, E. (2013). *Transnational migration*. Cambridge: Polity Press.

Flynn, D. (2008). Protecting the rights of undocumented migrants: a perspective from civil society. In C. Timmerman, I. Lodewyckx & Y. Bocklandt (Red.), Grenzeloze solidariteit. Over migratie en mensen zonder papieren (pp. 323-328). Leuven/Voorburg: Acco.

Foblets, M.-C., & Vanheule, D. (2011). Circulaire migratie: ambivalenties van een nieuwe aanpak. In M. More & C. Ryngaert (Red.), *Migratie. Winnaars en verliezers* (pp. 67-81). Leuven/Den Haag: Acco.

Fraser, N. (2000). Rethinking recognition. *New Left Review*, 3, May-June.

Fraser, N., & Honneth, A. (2003). *Redistribution or recognition? A political-philosophical exchange*. London/New York: Verso.

Frey, W. (2015). *Diversity explosion. How new racial demographics are remaking America*. Washington: Brookings Institute Press.

Frissen, R., & Harchaoui, S. (2011). Randstad 2040 en zijn bewoners. Van sociaal-culturele naar sociaaleconomische frames. In R. Frissen & S. Harchaoui (Red.), *Integratie & de metropool. Perspectieven voor 2040* (pp. 9-28). Amsterdam: Van Gennep.

Gailly, A., Redouane, B.D., e.a. (2011). *Migranten in tijd en ruimte. Culturen van ouder worden*. Antwerpen: Garant.

Galbraith, J.K. (1992). *The culture of contentment*. London, Sinclair-Stevenson Ltd.

Gans, H. (1972). The positive functions of poverty. *American Journal of Sociology*, 78, 2, 275-289.

Geldof, D. (2001). De regularisatieprocedure in Antwerpen. Een voorlopige stand van zaken en profiel van de aanvragers. In D. Cuypers, B. Hubeau & M.-C. Foblets (Eds.), *Migratie- en Migrantenrecht. Deel VI: recente ontwikkelingen* (pp. 327-344). Brugge: Die Keure.

Geldof, D. (2006). De stad is een kosmos. *Alert*, 32, 3, 66-79.

Geldof, D. (2007). Maak van steden kosmopolitische emancipatiemachines. *Ruimte & Planning*, 1, 40-48.

Geldof, D. (2011a). New challenges for urban social work and urban social work research. *European Journal of Social Work*, 14, 1, 27-39.

Geldof, D. (2011b). Nood aan interculturalisering. Steden verkleuren sneller dan sociaal werk. *Alert*, 37, 2, 8-18.

Geldof, D. (2011c). Geluk, gelijkheid, duurzaamheid. Denkkaders voor structureel sociaal werk. *Alert*, 37, 4, 17-24.

Geldof, D. (2011d) (3de herziene uitgave). *Onzekerheid. Over leven in de risicomaatschappij*. Leuven/Voorburg: Acco.

Geldof, D. (2012a). Stadsbewoners zonder papieren. Een verkennende analyse van de regularisatieaanvragen in Antwerpen in 2000 en 2009. *Ruimte en Maatschappij*, 3, 3, 1-24.

Geldof, D. (2012b). Voor wie hoort wat? Over wederkerigheid, sociaal beleid en diversiteit. *Oikos*, 61, 42-56.

Geldof, D. (2012c). Gezinnen over grenzen. *Alert*, 38, 3, 62-71.

Geldof, D. (2013). Superdiversiteit als onverwerkte realiteit. Een uitdaging voor sociaal werk. *Alert*, 39, 3, 12-24.

Geldof, D. (2015a). Veranderende woonbehoeften in een context van superdiversiteit. In D. Luyten, K. Emmery, I. Pasteels & D. Geldof (Red.), *De sleutel past niet meer op elke deur. Dynamische gezinnen en flexibel wonen* (pp. 77-95). Antwerpen: Garant.

Geldof, D. (2015b). Nood aan een nieuwe democratiseringsgolf. De transitie naar superdiversiteit als uitdaging voor hoger onderwijs. *Tijdschrift voor Onderwijsrecht en Onderwijsbeleid*, 2014-2015, nr. 4, pp. 67-77.

Geldof, D. (2015c). Van risicomaatschappij tot reflexiviteit, van individualisering tot kosmopolitisering. Een terugblik op het oeuvre van Ulrich Beck (1944-2015). In *Sociologos*, vol. 36, nr. 2, pp. 156-171.

Geldof, D. (2016). Superdiversity and the city. In Williams, C. (ed.) *Social Work and the city*. Palgrave (forthcoming)

Geldof, D., & Driessens, K. (2011). Armoede in de 21ste eeuw. *Welzijnsgids (Noden, Armoede)*, Kluwer, 82, 23-47.

Genard, J.-L. (2013). Voor een ambitieuze verbeelding. In E. Corijn, (Red.), *Waarheen met Brussel? Toekomstperspectieven voor de Belgische en Europese hoofdstad* (pp. 111-141). Brussel: VUBPRESS.

Gijsberts, M., & Lubbers, M. (2013). *Nieuw in Nederland. Het leven van recent gemigreerde Bulgaren en Polen*. Den Haag: Sociaal en Cultureel Planbureau.

Glasze, G. (2006). Segregation and seclusion: the case of compounds for western expatriates in Saudi Arabia. *GeoJournal*, 66, 83-88.

Glick Schiller, N., Basch, L., & Blanc-Szanton, C. (1995). From immigrant to transmigrant: Theorizing transnational migration. *Anthropological Quarterly*, 68, 1, 46-63.

Glorieux, I., Laurijssen, I., & Van Dorsselaer, Y. (2009). *Zwart op wit. De intrede van allochtonen op de arbeidsmarkt*. Antwerpen/Apeldoorn: Garant.

Graham, J., Bradshaw, C., & Trew, J. (2009). Addressing Cultural Barriers with Muslim Clients: An Agency Perspective. *Administration in Social Work*, 33:4, 387-406.

Hall, S. (2003). Political belonging in a World of multiple identities. In S. Vertovec & R. Cohen (Eds.), *Conceiving cosmopolitanism* (pp. 25-32). New York: Oxford University Press.

Hall, S. (2013a). The Politics of Belonging. *Identities*, 20 (1): 46–53.

Hall, S. (2013b). Super-Diverse Street: A 'trans-Ethnography' across Migrant Localities. *Ethnic and Racial Studies*, 38 (1): 22–37.

Heijne, B. (2007). *Onredelijkheid*. Amsterdam: De Bezige Bij.

Heyse, P., & Foblets, M.-C. (2011). Een analyse van het spanningsveld binnen het Belgische gezinsherenigingsbeleid. In C. Timmerman, e.a. (Red.), *MInteGRATIE. Over nieuwe vormen van migratie en integratie* (pp. 163-190). Brussel: University Press Antwerp.

Heyse, P., e.a. (2007). *Liefde kent geen grenzen: een kwantitatieve en kwalitatieve analyse van huwelijksmigratie vanuit Marokko, Turkije, Oost-Europa en Zuid-Oost-Azië. Rapport in opdracht van het Centrum voor Gelijkheid van Kansen en Racismebestrijding*. Oases/CEMIS/HIVA.

Hirtt, N., Nicaise, I., & De Zutter, D. (2007). *De school van de ongelijkheid*. Berchem: Epo.

Hoffman, E. (2013). *Interculturele gespreksvoering. Theorie en praktijk van het TOPOI-model*. Houten: Bohn Stafleu Van Loghum.

Hoffman, E., Geldof, D., & Koning, M. (2014). Superdiversiteit op de frontlijn. Diversiteitsbewuste communicatie is een noodzaak. *Alert*, 40, 4, 6-13.

Holemans, D. (Red.) (2012). *Mensen maken de stad. Bouwstenen voor een sociaalecologische toekomst*. Berchem: Epo.

Horemans, L. (2013). Migratie en armoede: armoede bij etnisch-culturele minderheden in een bredere context. *Terzake*, nr. 2, 26-30.

Horemans, L. zd. *Arm in arm. Aandacht voor allochtone armoede*. Antwerpen: Samenlevingsopbouw.

Humphris, R. (2015). *Intersectionality and superdiversity: What's the difference?* IRiS Key Concepts Roundtable Series – 30 April 2015. http://superdiversity.net/2015/05/28/intersectionality-and-superdiversity-whats-the-difference/

Hunter, C., Lepley, S., & Nickels, S. (2010). New practice frontiers: Current and future social work with transmigrants. In N. Negi & R. Furman (Eds), *Transnational social work practice*. New York: Columbia University Press.
Huntington, S. (1997). *Botsende beschavingen. Cultuur en conflict in de 21ste eeuw*. Antwerpen/Baarn: Anthos/Icarus.
Idrissi, Y. (2010). Het islamdebat voorbij. *Samenleving en politiek*, 17, 2, 4-10.
Janssens, P. (2011). *Voor wat hoort wat. Naar een nieuw sociaal contract*. Antwerpen, De Bezige Bij.
Janssens, R. (2013). Meertaligheid als cement van de stedelijke samenleving. Een analyse van de Brusselse taalsituatie op basis van Taalbarometer 3. Brussel, VUBPRESS.
Juchtmans, G., & Wets, J. (2010). Focus op: maatschappelijk werk en etnisch-culturele minderheden in Leuven. OCMW-Leuven/Hiva.
Judt, T. (2011). *Ill Fares the Land: A Treatise on Our Present Discontents*. Penguin UK.
Kaizen, J., & Nonneman, W. (2007). Irregular Migration in Belgium and Organized Crime: An Overview. *International Migration*, 45, 2, 121-146.
Kara, S., & Drossau, O. (2011). *Transnationalismus & Migration*. Berlin: Heinrich-Böll-Stiftung.
Karraker, M.W. (2013). *Global families*. Los Angeles/London: Sage.
Kasinitz, P. , Mollenkopf, J. Waters, M. & Holdway, J. (2009). Inheriting the city. The children of immigrants come of age. New York: Russell Sage Foundation.
Kaufmann, J., (2014). *Identités, la bombe à retardement*. Paris: Editions textuel.
Kesteloot, C., & Meert, H. (1999). Informal spaces: the socio-economic functions and spatial location of urban, informal economic activities. *International Journal of Urban and regional Research*, 23, 2, 233-252.
Ketelslegers, B. (2013). Armoede Gekleurd wil meer inclusieve en gekleurde beleidsadviezen. *Terzake*, 2, 46-49.
Ketelslegers, B. (2015). *Kleur in het armoededebat. Voor een sterkere stem van mensen in armoede met een migratieachtergrond*. Brussel: Netwerk tegen armoede.
Kochan, B. (Ed.) (2014). *Migration and London's growth*. London: LSE.
Koning Boudewijnstichting (1994). Algemeen Verslag over de Armoede, Rapport in opdracht van de Minister van Sociale Integratie gerealiseerd door de Koning Boudewijnstichting in samenwerking met de Beweging ATD Vierde Wereld België en de Vereniging van Belgische Steden en Gemeenten (Afdeling Maatschappelijk Werk), Brussel.

Krols, Y., Van Robaeys, B., & Vranken, J. (2008). *Gelijke kansen voor morgen. Een verkenning van armoede bij Turkse en Marokkaanse vrouwen in Vlaanderen*. Leuven/Voorburg: Acco.

Kymlicka, W. (2005). Multiculturele staten en interculturele burgers. In B. Van Leeuwen & R. Tinneveldt (Red.), *De multiculturele samenleving in conflict. Interculturele spanningen, multiculturalisme en burgerschap* (pp. 55-77). Leuven/Voorburg: Acco.

Kymlicka, W. (2010). The rise and fall of multiculturalism? New debates on inclusion and accommodation in divers societies. In S. Vertovec & S. Wessendorf (Eds.), *The multiculturalism Backlash. European discourses, policies and practices* (pp. 32-49). London & New York: Routledge.

Kymlicka, W. (2012). *Multiculturalism: success, failure, and the future*. Washington DC: Migration Policy Institute.

Lagrange, H. (2010). *Le déni des cultures*. Paris: Editions du Seuil.

Lamrabet, R. (2007). *Vrouwland*. Antwerpen: Meulenhof/Manteau.

Lamrabet, R. (2008). *Een kind van god*. Antwerpen: Meulenhoff/Manteau.

Laurier, E. & Philo, C. (2006). Possible Geographies: A Passing Encounter in a Café. *Area*, 38 (4): 353-63.

Levrau, F. (2010). *De politiek van de erkenning. Een politiek-filosofische literatuurstudie*. Steunpunt Gelijkekansenbeleid – Consortium Universiteit Antwerpen en Universiteit Hasselt.

Levrau, F. (2011a). *Politieke, culturele en redistributieve rechtvaardigheid. Over de politiek-filosofische dimensies van erkenning in een multiculturele samenleving*. Steunpunt Gelijkekansenbeleid – Consortium Universiteit Antwerpen en Universiteit Hasselt.

Levrau, F. (2011b). Het multiculturalisme is dood, lang leve het multiculturalisme?! Pleidooi voor conceptuele helderheid en een herwaardering van de erkenning van verschil. In J. Ackaert & T. Van Regenmortel (Red.), *Gelijk oversteken. Een staalkaart van onderzoeksbevindingen rond integratie* (pp. 17-40). Brugge: Vanden Broele.

Ley, D. (2005). Post-multiculturalism. *Research on immigration and integration in the Metropolis. Working Paper Series*, 05-18, 1-28.

Lleshi, B. (2010). De facetten van identiteit: tussen theorie en praktijk. In B. Lleshi & Van den Bossche, M. (Eds.), *Identiteit en interculturaliteit. Identiteitsconstructie bij jongeren in Brussel* (pp. 171-199). Brussel: VUBPress.

Lleshi, B., & Van den Bossche, M. (Eds.) (2010). *Identiteit en interculturaliteit. Identiteitsconstructie bij jongeren in Brussel*. Brussel: VUBPress.

Loobuyck, P. (2002). Multicultureel burgerschap. Voorbij integratie, assimilatie, segregatie en marginalisatie. *Ons Erfdeel*, 45, 3, 399-411.

Loopmans, M. (2008). Relevance, gentrification & development of a new hegemony on urban policies in Antwerp. *Urban Studies*, 45, 12, 2499-2519.
Lowe, M., et al. (2015). Planning Healthy, Liveable and Sustainable Cities: How Can Indicators Inform Policy? *Urban Policy and Research*, 33 (2): 131-144.
Lucassen, L., & Lucassen, J. (2011). *Winnaars en verliezers. Een nuchtere balans van vijfhonderd jaar immigratie*. Amsterdam: Uitgeverij Bert Bakker.
Maly, I. (2012). De stilte in het debat. Over macht, Antiverlichting en superdiversiteit. *Vlaams Marxistisch Tijdschrift*, 46, 1, 35-40.
Maly, I., & Blommaert, J. (2012). 'Realisme' als ideologie. Over superdiversiteit, precariteit en de nood aan Verlichting. F. Coussée & L. Bradt (Red.), *Jeugdwerk en sociale uitsluiting. Handvatten voor een emanciperend jeugdbeleid* (pp. 99-111). Leuven/Den Haag: Acco.
Maly, I., Blommaert, J., & Ben Yakoub, J. (2014). *Superdiversiteit en democratie*. Berchem: Epo.
McGhee, D. (2008). A Past Built on Difference, a Future Which Is Shared – a Critical Examination of the Recommendation Made by the Commission on Integration and Community Cohesion. *People, Place and Policy Online*, June, 48–64.
Meissner, F. (2014). Migration in migration-related diversity? The nexus between superdiversity and migration studies. *Ethnic and Racial Studies*, 38(4), 556-567.
Meissner, F., & Vertovec, S. (2014). Comparing superdiversity. *Ethnic and Racial Studies*, 38(4), 541-555
Mendonck, K., & Cautaers, A. (2012). *CAW in beeld. Cijfers 2011*. Onderzoeksdossier Steunpunt Algemeen Welzijnswerk.
Michielsen, J., Notteboom, E., & Lodewijckx, I. (2012). *Diaspora en ontwikkelingssamenwerking. Een onderzoek naar de rol van de diaspora uit Congo, Ghana en Marokko bij ontwikkelingssamenwerking en de samenwerking met de stad Antwerpen*. Cemis.
Mohan, B., & Clark Prickett, J. (2010). Macro social work practice with transmigrants. In N. Negi, & Furman, R. (Eds), *Transnational social work practice* (pp. 191-204). New York: Colombia University Press.
Moïsi, D. (2009). *De geopolitiek van de emotie. Hoe culturen van angst, vernedering en hoop de wereld veranderen*. Amsterdam: Nieuw Amsterdam Uitgevers.
Motief (2012). *Buren zoals we ze (niet) kennen. Moslims en niet-moslims onderaan de ladder*. Antwerpen: Motief.
Musterd, S., & Ostendorf, W. (2005). Social exclusion, segregation and neighbourhood effects. In Y. Kazepov (Red.), *Cities of Europe. Chang-*

ing contexts, local arrangements and the challenge to urban cohesion (pp. 170-189). Malden/Oxford: Blackwell.

Naegels, T. (2013). *Alles of niets. Vlaanderen op zoek naar zichzelf.* Antwerpen: De Bezige Bij.

Ndhlovu, F. (2016). A Decolonial Critique of Diaspora Identity Theories and the Notion of Superdiversity. *Diaspora Studies*, 9 (1): 28–40. doi:10.1080/09739572.2015.1088612.

Neal, S., Bennett, K., Jones, H., Cochrane, A. & Mohan, G. (2015). Multiculture and Public Parks: Researching Super-Diversity and Attachment in Public Green Space. *Population Space and Place*, 21 (5): 463–75. doi:10.1002/psp.1910.

Nijs, R. (2011). Van lijn tot cirkel: de menselijke kosten van circulaire migratie. In M. More & C. Ryngaert (Red.), *Migratie. Winnaars en verliezers* (pp. 83-95). Leuven/Den Haag: Acco.

Noppe, J., & Lodewijckx, E. (2012). *Personen van vreemde herkomst in Vlaanderen.* Studiedienst van de Vlaamse Regering, SVR-Webartikel 2012/3: http://www4.vlaanderen.be/dar/svr/Pages/2012-03-26-webartikel2012-3-vreemde-herkomst.aspx

Nussbaum, M. (2012). *The New Religious Intolerance. Overcoming the Politics of Fear in an Anxious Age.* Harvard University Press.

OECD. 2015. *International Migration Outlook 2015.* OECD Publishing.

Oosterlynck, S. (2012). De cultuur van armoede: terug van weggeweest? In F. Coussée & L. Bradt (Red.), *Jeugdwerk en sociale uitsluiting. Handvatten voor een emanciperend jeugdbeleid* (pp. 87-97). Leuven/Den Haag: Acco.

Oosterlynck, S., & Schillebeeckx, E. (2012). Stad en sociale ongelijkheid: naar een sociale stijgings-perspectief? D. Holemans (Red.), *Mensen maken de stad. Bouwstenen voor een sociaalecologische toekomst* (pp. 128-144). Berchem: Epo.

Oosterlynck, S., & Schuermans, N. (2013). Superdiversiteit. Solidariteit herdenken. *Alert*, 39, 4, 13-19.

Oosterlynck, S., Loopmans, M., Schuermans, N., Vandenabeele, J., & Zemni, S. (2014). *Putting flesh to the bone: Looking for solidarity in diversity, here and now.* DieGem working paper D 1.2.

Oosterlynck, S., Schillebeeckx, E., & Schuermans, N. (2012). Voorbij de sociale mix. In D. Holemans (Red.), *Mensen maken de stad. Bouwstenen voor een sociaalecologische toekomst* (pp. 117-127). Berchem: Epo.

Pelfrene, E., & Lodewijckx, E. (2014). De bevolking ingeschreven in het wachtregister van asielzoekers. In E. Pelfrene, & C. Van Peer (Red.) *Inter-*

nationale migraties en migranten in Vlaanderen (pp. 123-135). Brussel: Studiedienst van de Vlaamse Regering.

Pelfrene, E., & Van Peer, C. (Red.) (2014). *Internationale migraties en migranten in Vlaanderen.* Brussel: Studiedienst van de Vlaamse Regering.

Perrin, N., & Martiniello, M. (2011). *Transnationale activiteiten van migranten in België. Factor van integratie of van terugtrekking in de eigen groep?* Brussel: Koning Boudewijnstichting.

Phillimore, J. (2013). Housing, home and neighbourhood renewal in the era of superdiversity: some lessons from the West Midlands. *Housing Studies,* 28(5): 682-700.

Phillimore, J. (2015a). Delivering maternity services in an era of superdiversity: the challenges of novelty and newness. *Journal of Ethnic and Racial Studies,* 38(4): 568-582.

Phillimore, J. (2015b) Migrant maternity in an era of superdiversity: new migrants' access to, and experience of, antenatal care in the West Midlands, UK. *Social Science & Medicine,* Available online 25 November 2015, http://dx.doi.org/10.1016/j.socscimed.2015.11.030.

Pinto, D. (2007). *Interculturele communicatie. Een stap verder.* Houten: Bohn Stafleu van Loghum.

Pinxten, R. (2011). *Het plezier van het zoeken. Filosofie tegen de angst.* Antwerpen/Utrecht: Houtekiet.

Platvoet, L., & Van Poelgeest, M. (2005). *Amsterdam als emancipatiemachine.* Bussum: Toth.

Pottie-Sherman, Y. & Hiebert, D. (2015). Authenticity with a Bang: Exploring Suburban Culture and Migration through the New Phenomenon of the Richmond Night Market. *Urban Studies,* 52 (3): 538–54.

Prins, B., & Saharso, S. (2010). From toleration to repression. The Dutch backlash against multiculturalism. In S. Vertovec & S. Wessendorf (Eds.), *The multiculturalism Backlash. European discourses, policies and practices* (pp. 72-91). London & New York: Routledge.

Putman, R. (2000). *Bowling Alone: The Collapse and Revival of American Community.* New York: Simon & Schuster.

Putman, R. (2007). E Pluribus Unum: Diversity and Community in the Twenty-first Century – The 2006 Johan Skytte Prize. *Scandinavian Political Studies,* 30, (2).

Raad voor Maatschappelijke Ontwikkeling (2011). *Migratiepolitiek voor een open samenleving.* Den Haag: RMO.

Ramadan, T. (2008). *Een jihad van vertrouwen.* Amsterdam: Van Gennep.

Ramadan, T. (2011). *On Super-Diversity*. Rotterdam/Berlin, Witte de With/Sternberg Press.

Ramaut, G., Sierens, S., & Bultynck, K. (2013). *Evaluatieonderzoek van het project 'Thuistaal in onderwijs' (2009-2012). Eindrapport*. Een onderzoek in opdracht van het Departement Onderwijs en Opvoeding van de Stad Gent.

Ramdas, A. (2011). *Badal*. Amsterdam: De Bezige Bij.

Regionaal Integratiecentrum Foyer Brussel (2014). *'On est là.' De eerste generatie Marokkaanse en Turkse migranten in Brussel (1964-1974)*. Antwerpen: Garant.

Rogé, B. (2010). De groeimarge in het armoedebeleid: gekleurde armoede. *Momenten*, 7, 59-67.

Roseeuw, I. (2011). *Kleurrijke maatzorg. Aan de slag met interculturalisering*. Berchem: vzw De Touter.

Saaf, A., Sidi Hida, B., & Aghbal, A. (2009). *Belgische Marokkanen. Een dubbele identiteit in ontwikkeling*. Brussel: Koning Boudewijnstichting.

Said, E. (1999). *Out of place. A memoir*. New York, Alfred A. Knopf.

Sarrazin, T. (2010). *Deutschland schafft sich ab. Wie wir unser Land aufs Spiel setzen*. München: DVA.

Sassen, S. (2001). *The global city. New York, London, Tokyo* (second edition). Princeton/Oxford: Princeton University Press.

Sassen, S. (2012). Urban capabilities: an essay on our challenges and differences. *Journal of International Affairs*, 65, 2, 85-95.

Saunders, D., 2011. *Arrival City: How the Largest Migration in History is Reshaping Our World*. London: William Heinemann.

Saunders, D. (2011). *De trek naar 't stad. 2060 Antwerpen*. Nawoord: Hoop en Vrees in de Stad van Buitenstaanders. Bijlage bij 'De trek naar de stad'. Stad Antwerpen.

Schapendonk, J., & Steel, G. (2014) Following migrant trajectories: The im/mobility of Sub-Saharan Afraicans en route to the European Union. *Annals of the Association of American Geographers*, 104, 2, 262-270.

Scheffer, P. (2000). Het multiculturele drama, NRC, 29 januari 2000. http://retro.nrc.nl/W2/Lab/Multicultureel/scheffer.html

Scheffer, P. (2002). Het multiculturele drama. B. Van den Broeck & M.-C. Foblets (Red.). *Het failliet van de integratie? Het multiculturalismedebat in Vlaanderen* (pp. 71-82). Leuven: Acco.

Scheffer, P. (2007). *Het land van aankomst*. Amsterdam: De Bezige Bij.

Scheffer, P. (2012). De hoofdstad en de havenstad: een verhaal van twee immigratiesteden. In *De staat van integratie. Rotterdam Amsterdam* (pp. 35-59). Gemeente Rotterdam: Rotterdam.

Schinkel, W. (2008). *De gedroomde samenleving*. Kampen: Klement.

Schrooten, M. (2012). Moving ethnography online: researching Brazilian migrants' online togetherness. *Ethnic and Racial Studies*, 35, 10, 1794-1809.

Schrooten, M., Geldof, D., & Withaeckx, S. (2015). Transmigration and urban social work: towards a research agenda. *European Journal of Social Work*, DOI:10.1080/13691457.2014.1001725

Schrooten, M., Withaeckx, S., Geldof, D., & Lavent, M. (2015). *Transmigratie. Hulp verlenen in een wereld van superdiversiteit*. Leuven/Den Haag: Acco.

Sennet, R. (2010). *De mens als werk in uitvoering*. Amsterdam: uitgeverij Boom/Internationale Spinozalens.

Severiens, S. (2014). *Professionele capaciteit in de superdiverse school*. Rede uitgesproken bij de aanvaarding van het ambt van bijzonder hoogleraar 'Onderwijskunde, in het bijzonder het ontwerpen van onderwijs voor kwetsbare jongeren' aan de Universiteit van Amsterdam op donderdag 20 maart 2014. Amsterdam, Vossiuspers UvA.

Sezgin, H.(Hrsg.) (2011). *Manifest der Vielen. Deutschland erfindet sich neu*. Berlin: Blumenbar Verlag.

Shadid, W. (2008). *De multiculturele samenleving in crisis. Essays over het integratiebeleid in Nederland*. Heerhugowaard: Gigabook.

Silj, A. (Ed.) (2010). *European multiculturalism revisited*. London/New York: Zed Books.

Soenen, R. (2006). *Het kleine ontmoeten. Over het sociale karakter van de stad*. Antwerpen: Garant.

Standing, G. (2011). *The precariat. The new dangerous class*. London/New York: Bloomsbury Academic.

Studiedienst van de Vlaamse Regering (2011). *SVR-projecties van de bevolking en de huishoudens voor Vlaamse steden en gemeenten, 2009-2030. Eerste resultaten*. Brussel.

Sunderhaus, S. (2006). *Regularization Programs for Undocumented Migrants*. Köln/New York (http://ccis.ucsd.edu/wp-content/uploads/2012/07/wrkg142.pdf)

Tarrius, A. (2015). *Etrangers de passage. Poor to poor, peer to peer*. La Tour d'Aiges: Editions de l'aube.

Taspinar, B. (2013). *Moeders van de stilte. Drie vrouwen in een ander land*. Antwerpen: De Bezige Bij.

Taspinar, B., & Vandeperre, E. (2012). *Levensbeschouwing en hulpverlening. Visietekst studiedag Levensbeschouwing in de hulpverlening.* Motief.

Taspinar, B., & Vandeperre, E. (2013). Levensbeschouwing en etnisch-culturele diversiteit. De impact op de hulpverlening. *Alert,* 36, 3, 25-31.

Taylor, C. (1994). The politics of recognition. In A. Gutmann (Ed.), *Multiculturalism. Examining the politics of recognition* (pp. 25-74). Princeton: Princeton University Press.

Taylor, C., et al. (1992). *Multiculturalism and the politics of recognition.* Princeton: Princeton University Press.

Timmerman, C., Lodewyckx, I., & Bocklandt, Y. (Red.) (2008). *Grenzeloze solidariteit? Over migratie en mensen zonder papieren.* Leuven/Voorburg: Acco.

Tirions, M. (2011). Kruispuntdenken. Diversiteit in sociaal werk. *Alert,* 37, 2, 19-28.

TOR-groep (2012). Tussen de oren en aangepraat. In M. Elchardus & I. Glorieux (Eds.), *Voorspelbaar uniek. Dieper graven in de symbolische samenleving* (pp. 354-375). Leuven: LannooCampus.

Van Besien, W. (2013). Pleidooi voor culturele vrijheid. *Samenleving en Politiek,* 20, 5, 4-12.

Van Craen, M., Vancluysen, K., & Ackaert, J. (2007). *Voorbij wij en zij? De sociaal-culturele afstand tussen autochtonen en allochtonen tegen de meetlat.* Brugge: Vanden Broele.

Van Dam, S., Raeymaeckers, P., & Dierickx, D. (2015). Hulpverlening aan personen van buitenlandse herkomst in de periferie: netwerken en drempels tot samenwerking. In K. Driessens e.a. (Eds.), *Een caleidoscoop van sociaalwerkonderzoek. Een sociaalwetenschappelijke benadering*(pp. 35-50). Leuven/Den Haag: Acco.

Van den Bossche, M. (2010). Identiteit: het dialogisch model van Charles Taylor. In B. Lleshi & M. Van den Bossche (Eds.), *Identiteit en interculturaliteit. Identiteitsconstructie bij jongeren in Brussel* (pp. 65-98). Brussel: VUBPress.

Van den Brande, K., e.a. (2011). *Vorderingen van leerlingen in het leren van Nederlands. Beleidssamenvatting en aanbevelingen.* Leuven: Centrum voor onderwijseffectiviteit & -evaluatie, Centrum voor Taal en Onderwijs KU Leuven.

Van den Broeck, B., & Foblets, M.-C. (red.) (2002). *Het failliet van de integratie? Het multiculturalismedebat in Vlaanderen.* Leuven: Acco.

Van der Bly, S. (2005), Globalization: a triumph of ambiguity. *Current Sociology,* 53(6), 875-893.

Van der Burg, M., & Coene, J. (2014). Armoede en uitsluiting ontcijferd. In D. Dierckx, J. Coene & P. Raemaeckers, *Armoede en sociale uitsluiting. Jaarboek 2014* (pp. 357-415).Leuven/Den Haag: Acco.

Van der Zee, K., e.a. (2012). *Superdiversiteit en sociaal vertrouwen. Eindrapportage project 'Recht doen aan superdiversiteit'*. Groningen: Instituut voor integratie en sociale weerbaarheid (ISW).

Van Haarlem, A., & Coene, J. (2012). Armoede en sociale uitsluiting ontcijferd. In D. Dierckx, e.a. (Red.), *Armoede en sociale uitsluiting. Jaarboek 2012* (pp. 429-485). Leuven/Den Haag: Acco.

Van Haarlem, A., Coene, J., & Lusyne, P. (2011). De superdiversiteit van armoede en sociale uitsluiting. In D. Dierckx, e.a. (Red.), *Armoede en sociale uitsluiting. Jaarboek 2011* (pp. 177-198). Leuven/Den Haag: Acco.

Van Meeteren, M., Van San, M., & Engbersen, G. (2008). *Zonder papieren. Over de positie van irreguliere migranten en de rol van het vreemdelingenbeleid in België*. Leuven/Voorburg: Acco.

Van Puymbroeck, N. (2014). *Migratie en de Metropool 1964-2013*. Leuven/Den Haag: Acco.

Van Robaeys, B., & Driessens, K. (2011). *Gekleurde armoede en hulpverlening. Sociaal werkers en cliënten aan het woord*. Leuven: Lannoo Campus.

Van Robaeys, B., e.a. (2007). *De kleur van de armoede. Armoede bij personen van buitenlandse herkomst*. Leuven/Voorburg: Acco.

Van Robaeys, B., m.m.v. Geerts, L., & Balli, S. (2014). *Verbinden vanuit diversiteit. Krachtgericht werken in een context van armoede en culturele diversiteit*. Leuven: Lannoocampus

Van Robaeys, B., & Driessens, K. (2011). Naar een divers-sensitieve en empowerende hulpverlening. In D. Dierckx, e.a. (Red.), *Armoede en sociale uitsluiting. Jaarboek 2011* (pp. 345-361). Leuven/Den Haag: Acco.

Van Rooy, W. (2008). *De malaise van de multiculturaliteit*. Leuven/Voorburg: Acco.

Vancluysen, K., & Van Craen, M. (2011). Transnationale activiteiten en sociaalculturele integratie: verenigbaar of niet? In J. Ackaert & T. Van Regenmortel (Red.), *Gelijk oversteken. Een staalkaart van onderzoeksbevindingen rond integratie* (pp. 203-225). Brugge: Vanden Broele.

Vandeurzen, J. (2009). *Welzijn, Volksgezondheid en Gezin. Beleidsnota 2009-2014, ingediend door de Vlaamse minister van Welzijn, Volksgezondheid en Gezin*. Brussel.

Vandeurzen, J. (2014). *Welzijn, Volksgezondheid en Gezin. Beleidsnota 2014-2019, ingediend door de Vlaamse minister van Welzijn, Volksgezondheid en Gezin*. Brussel.

Verhaeghe, P.-P., Van der Bracht, K., & Van de Putte, B. (2012). *Migrant zkt toekomst. Gent op een keerpunt tussen oude en nieuwe migratie*. Antwerpen/Apeldoorn: Garant.

Vermeersch, E. (2011). *De multiculturele samenleving*. Antwerpen: Luster.

Vermeulen, S., e.a. (Red.). *Kan de stad de wereld redden? Teksten van Eric Corijn*. Brussel: VUBPRESS.

Vertovec, S. (2004). Cheap Calls: The Social Glue of Migrant Transnationalism. *Global Networks*, 4 (2): 219-224.

Vertovec, S. (2005). *Opinion: Super-diversity revealed*. BBC News, September 20. http://news.bbc.co.uk/2/hi/uk_news/4266102.stm

Vertovec, S. (2007). Super-diversity and its implications. *Ethnic and Racial Studies*, 30, 6, 1024-1054.

Vertovec, S. (2007b). *New complexities of cohesion in Britain. Super-diversity, transnationalism and civil integration*. West Yorkshire: Commission on Integration and Cohesion.

Vertovec, S. (2011). *Migration and new diversities in global cities: comparatively conceiving, observing and visualizing diversification in urban public spaces*. MMG Working Paper 11-08. Göttingen: Max Planck Institute for the study of religious and ethnic diversity.

Vertovec, S. (2012). 'Diversity' and the Social Imaginary. *European Journal of Sociology*, 53 (3): 287-312.

Vertovec, S. (ed.) (2015). *Diversities Old and New: Migration and Socio-spatial Pattern in New York, Singapore and Johannesburg*. Basingstoke: Palgrave.

Vertovec, S., & Wessendorf, S. (Eds.) (2010). *The multiculturalism Backlash. European discourses, policies and practices*. London & New York: Routledge.

Vickers, T., Craig, G. & Atkin, K. (2013). Addressing Ethnicity in Social Care Research. *Social Policy & Administration*, 47 (3): 310-326.

Vlaminck, E. (2011). *Brandlucht*. Amsterdam: Wereldbibliotheek.

Vranken, J., e.a. (2010). *Armoede en sociale uitsluiting. Jaarboek 2010*. Leuven: Acco.

VRIND (2009). *Vlaamse Regionale Indicatoren*. Brussel: Studiedienst van de Vlaamse Regering.

VROM-raad (2006). *Stad en stijging: sociale stijging als leidraad voor stedelijke vernieuwing*. Den Haag: VROM-raad, Advies 054.

Wacquant, L. (2010). *Straf de armen. Het nieuwe beleid van de sociale onzekerheid*. Berchem: Epo.

Wacquant, L. (2012). *Paria's van de stad. Nieuwe marginaliteit in tijden van neoliberalisme*. Berchem: Epo.

Walters, G. (2015). *The challenges of superdiversity for social housing*. Birmingham: IRIS Working Paper Series, 5.

Wessendorf, S. (2010). *Commonplace diversity: social interactions in a super-diverse context*. Göttingen: MMG Working Paper 10-11.

Wessendorf, S. (2013a). *Second-generation transnationalism and roots migration. Cross-border lives*. Aldershot Ashgate.

Wessendorf, S. (2013b). Commonplace Diversity and the 'ethos of Mixing': Perceptions of Difference in a London Neighbourhood. *Identities*, 20 (4): 407-22.

Wessendorf S. (2014). *Commonplace diversity. Social relations in a super-diverse context*. Basingstoke: Palgrave Macmillan.

Wilkinson, R., & Pickett, K. (2009). *The Spirit Level. Why more equal societies almost always do better*. London:Allen Lane/Penguin books.

Willems, S., & Mertens, J. (Ed.) (2013). *Professioneel omgaan met diversiteit*. Mechelen: Kluwer.

Williams, C., & Graham, M. (2014). A world on the move: migration, mobilities and social work. *British Journal of Social Work*, 44, Supplement 1, i1-i17.

Wimmer, A., & Glick Schiller, N. (2002). Methodological nationalism and beyond: nation-state building, migration and the social sciences. *Global networks*, 2(4), 301-334.

Withaeckx, S., Schrooten, M., & Geldof, D. (2015). Living across borders: The everyday experiences of Moroccan and Brazilian transmigrants in Belgium. Crossings: *Journal of Migration & Culture* 6 (1): 23-40.

Yerden, I. (2008). *Families onder druk. Huiselijk geweld in Marokkaanse en Turkse gezinnen*. Amsterdam: Van Gennep.

Zemni, S. (2009). *Het islamdebat*. Berchem: Epo.

Zemni, S. (2010). *Belgische Marokkanen: een stap verder. Analyse en vergelijking van het onderzoek om de Marokkaanse gemeenschappen in België beter te leren kennen*. Brussel: Koning Boudewijnstichting.

Printed by BoD"in Norderstedt, Germany